POCKET
ENCYCLOPEDIA

ORGANIC
GARDENING

POCKET
ENCYCLOPEDIA

ORGANIC
GARDENING

Contributing editor
Geoff Hamilton

DORLING KINDERSLEY
LONDON · NEW YORK · STUTTGART

A Dorling Kindersley Book

First published in Great Britain in 1991
by Dorling Kindersley Limited,
9 Henrietta Street, London WC2E 8PS

Designed and edited by Swallow Books,
260 Pentonville Road, London N1 9JY

A CIP catalogue record for this book is available
from the British Library

ISBN 0–86318–668–8

Typeset by Bournetype, Bournemouth
Reproduced by Colourscan, Singapore
Printed in Singapore by Kyodo Printing (Co) Pte Ltd.

CONTENTS

Introduction 6

INTRODUCTION

Organic gardening is an emotive subject. Some people think that it is the sole remaining way to save the planet; others that organic gardening is the refuge of bearded loonies in kaftans and sandals who live in grubby communes on brown rice and sunflower seeds. In fact, it is neither. Millions of gardeners the world over are beginning to consider organic gardening methods and evaluate them rationally. Even long-sceptical scientists are having second thoughts as the public demands more chemical-free food and a safer environment.

The organic way

There is nothing mystical or magical about organic gardening. It is simply a way of working with nature rather than against it, of recycling natural materials to maintain soil fertility, and of encouraging natural methods of pest and disease control rather than relying on chemicals to do the job.

These basic cultivation principles closely follow those found in nature, the complex workings of which have sustained life successfully over millions of years. These principles will not have a detrimental effect on yield or quality, but are much more likely to increase both, at the same time providing an alternative habitat for wildlife, and producing fruit and vegetables that are safe, flavoursome, and chemical-free.

The chemical gardener

The chemical gardener uses soil simply to anchor plant roots, and to hold artificial fertilizers to provide plant nutrients, an approach with excellent short-term results, but disastrous long-term consequences. Because organic matter is not replaced, the soil organisms die; without

The well-kept organic garden
The organic gardener aims at a beautiful, interesting and productive garden, a habitat for wildlife in which nature is in balance.

them, soil structure breaks down and the soil becomes hard, airless, and unproductive. "Force-feeding" plants results in soft, sappy growth, prone to attack by pests and diseases. Chemical pesticides often have short-term success, but, in killing the pest, also kill its natural predators: the problem worsens, and ever stronger and more poisonous pesticides then have to be used.

The organic gardener

The organic gardener has a more constructive approach, aware of the fine balance in nature that allows all species to co-exist. Growing a wide diversity of plants attracts a miniature eco-system of pests and predators so no single species can build up to an unacceptable level.

The soil teems with millions of micro-organisms, which release from organic matter the nutrients required for healthy plant growth. So, instead of feeding the plants, the soil is fed with natural materials; the plants draw on that reservoir of nutrients as and when required, becoming stronger and more resilient.

Improving on nature

However, the natural methods of sustaining plant growth shown in the illustration were never intended to support the kinds of demands we now make on our gardens. The technique itself is perfect, but has to be intensified by feeding soil with added compost and manure, improving its texture by digging to allow air and water to enter, protecting germinating seeds by giving them optimum conditions and spacings, giving plants adequate water in very dry weather, and controlling pests and diseases.

Worms
These help aerate the soil, and pull plant remains into the upper layers. They also leave "worm casts", a valuable fertilizer.

Soil feeds the plants

Fungi and algae
Help release nutrients from soil so that plants can use them.

The natural cycle
This diagram helps to illustrate how every element of nature – animals, insects, plants, and soil – all work together to create a natural cycle of events in the garden.

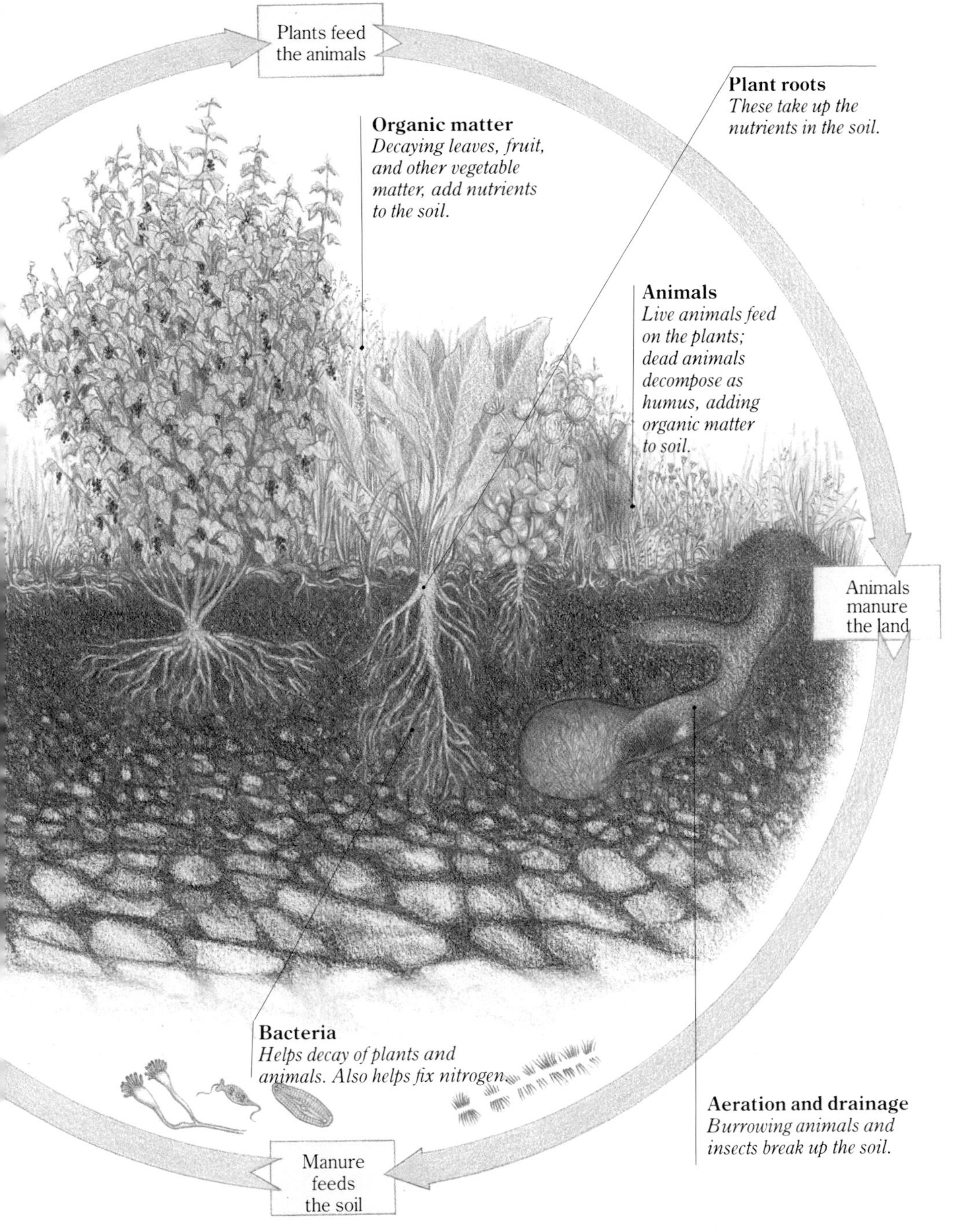

Plants feed
the animals

Plant roots
*These take up the
nutrients in the soil.*

Organic matter
*Decaying leaves, fruit,
and other vegetable
matter, add nutrients
to the soil.*

Animals
*Live animals feed
on the plants;
dead animals
decompose as
humus, adding
organic matter
to soil.*

Animals
manure
the land

Bacteria
*Helps decay of plants and
animals. Also helps fix nitrogen.*

Aeration and drainage
*Burrowing animals and
insects break up the soil.*

Manure
feeds
the soil

Chapter One

What You Can Grow

The essence of an organic garden is a wide diversity of plants to attract a balanced community of wildlife that will include pests and predators. Such a garden must always be treated as a complete entity. While the fruit and vegetable gardens produce the edible crops as well as material for the compost heap, the ornamental section and herbs attract useful wildlife such as predators, and insects to pollinate the fruit garden.
The "cottage garden" style (*see page 56*) is ideal for such a garden. Here, each border contains a mixture of permanent plants such as trees, shrubs, perennials, bulbs, bedding plants, even vegetables.
The result will inevitably be informal, but there is no reason why it should be neglected or untidy, and every reason why not. Pests and diseases go hand-in-hand with slovenly gardening; a neat and tidy garden will be more productive.
Pages 12–47 offer a wide choice of plants for you to grow, but there are many others you can try – and indeed should aim to do so – especially vegetables, so you do not miss out on something better.

Growing vegetables in a mixed border
In a very small garden, you can combine flowers, fruit and vegetables in a mixed border. Here, crops such as lettuces, tomatoes, and ruby chard grow with a variety of flowers and a small apple tree.

Winter plants

E ven in winter the garden can be interesting. Some bulbs and tubers flower at this time of year and many shrubs have interesting leaves, flowers, or catkins. Even without leaves, shrubs with coloured or twisted stems are attractive, and glowing berries brighten dull days. The tracery of deciduous trees like birches complements the warmer-looking evergreens.

Daphne mezereum
Mezereon
Small shrub with fragrant flowers in pink, purple or white. Prefers sun or partial shade. Height and spread 1.2m (4ft).

Salix sachalinensis "Sekka"
Willow
One of the many attractive shrub willows with winter appeal: chestnut-brown shoots covered in furry buds. Prefers sun. Height 4.5–6m (15–20ft), spread 10m (30ft).

Helleborus corsicus
Hellebore
Sprawling perennial that looks untidy unless staked. Prefers partial shade and deep, well-drained soil.

Cyclamen coum
Cyclamen
Attractive hardy bulb. Dislikes exposed situations and prefers shade.

Hamamelis mollis "Goldcrest"
Chinese witch hazel
Shrub with scented flowers. Prefers sun or partial shade. Height 2.5–3m (8–10ft), spread 4m (12ft).

Rhododendron "Praecox"
Rhododendron
Striking shrub in many colours and sizes. Prefers partial shade. Acid soil. Height 1–1.5m (3–5ft), spread 1.2–1.8m (4–6ft).

Iris reticulata
Iris
Well-known early-flowering bulb. Prefers sun. Well-drained, alkaline soil.

Hepatica nobilis
Hepatica
Perennial in shades of blue, red, white, or purple. Prefers sun or partial shade.

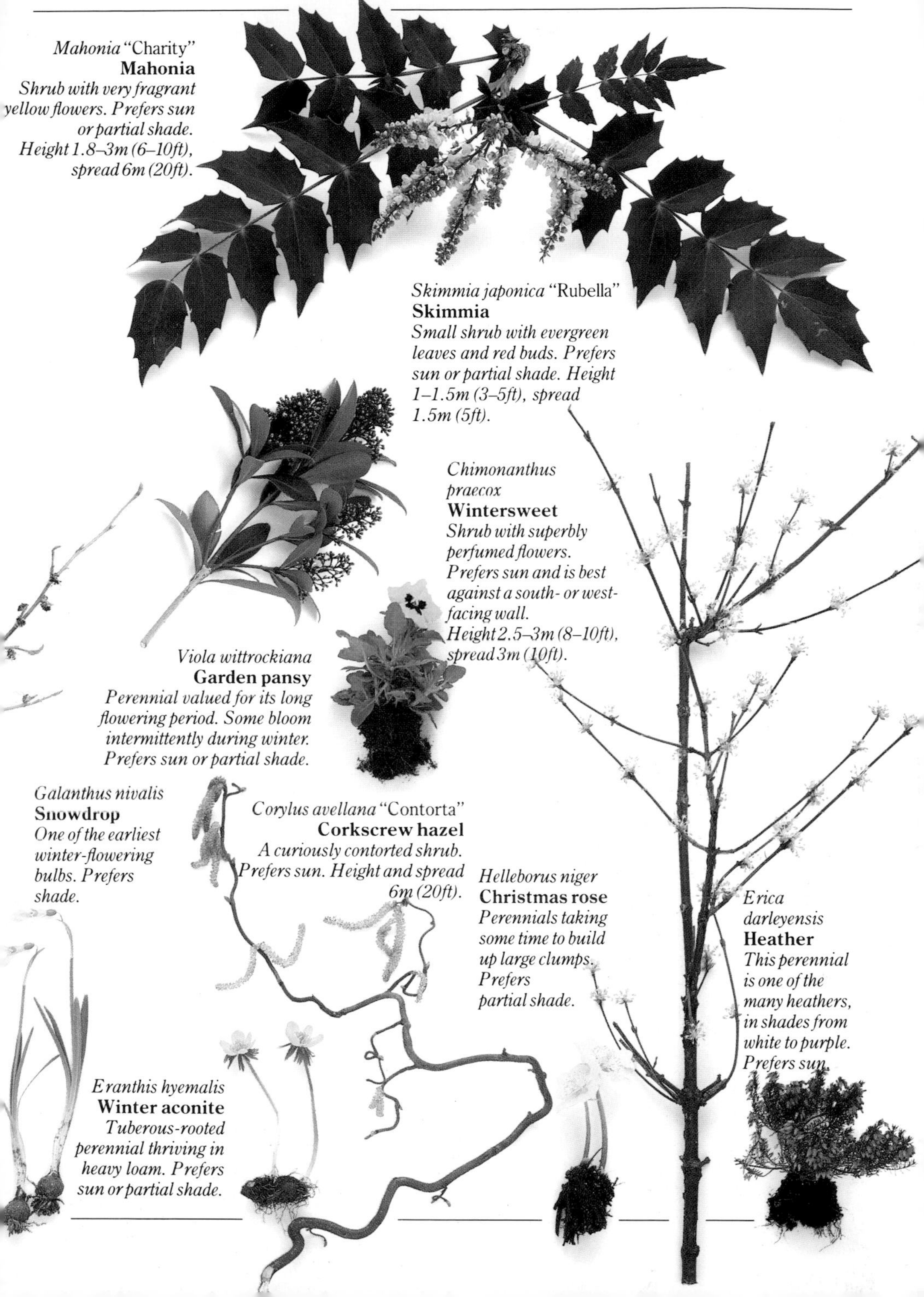

Mahonia "Charity"
Mahonia
Shrub with very fragrant
yellow flowers. Prefers sun
or partial shade.
Height 1.8–3m (6–10ft),
spread 6m (20ft).

Skimmia japonica "Rubella"
Skimmia
Small shrub with evergreen
leaves and red buds. Prefers
sun or partial shade. Height
1–1.5m (3–5ft), spread
1.5m (5ft).

Chimonanthus
praecox
Wintersweet
Shrub with superbly
perfumed flowers.
Prefers sun and is best
against a south- or west-
facing wall.
Height 2.5–3m (8–10ft),
spread 3m (10ft).

Viola wittrockiana
Garden pansy
Perennial valued for its long
flowering period. Some bloom
intermittently during winter.
Prefers sun or partial shade.

Galanthus nivalis
Snowdrop
One of the earliest
winter-flowering
bulbs. Prefers
shade.

Corylus avellana "Contorta"
Corkscrew hazel
A curiously contorted shrub.
Prefers sun. Height and spread
6m (20ft).

Helleborus niger
Christmas rose
Perennials taking
some time to build
up large clumps.
Prefers
partial shade.

Erica
darleyensis
Heather
This perennial
is one of the
many heathers,
in shades from
white to purple.
Prefers sun.

Eranthis hyemalis
Winter aconite
Tuberous-rooted
perennial thriving in
heavy loam. Prefers
sun or partial shade.

Early spring plants

These plants are at their best in early spring. Some, such as the almond and the camellia, have spectacular blooms at this time of the year; others, for example, photinia, have particularly attractive new growth. Combined in the same border, these plants make a very impressive early spring display, underplanted by colourful bulbs.

Fritillaria imperialis
Crown Imperial
Majestic bulb flowering freely on most soils. Available in red and yellow. Prefers sun or partial shade. Height 1m (3ft).

Lonicera japonica "Aureo-reticulata"
Honeysuckle
Rampant evergreen climber, its bright green leaves having conspicuous golden veining. Prefers partial shade. Height 10m (30ft).

Prunus triloba
Flowering almond
Spectacular, pink-blossomed shrub. Prefers sun. Alkaline soil. Height and spread 4m (12ft).

Hyacinthus hybrid
Hyacinth
Intensely fragrant bulb in a range of colours. Grows in most soils but likes sun.

Aubrieta deltoidea
Aubrieta
Easy-to-grow small perennial for border edges, walls or rock gardens. Shades of purple and pink. Prefers sun. Alkaline soil.

Photinia fraseri
Red robin
*Evergreen shrub grown
for its brilliant-red young
shoots. Prefers sun or
partial shade. Height
1.8–3m (6–10ft), spread
1.5–1.8m (5–6ft).*

Camellia japonica
Camellia
*Exotic-looking but hardy shrub in a
range of colours. Prefers partial
shade. Acid soil. Height 1.8m (6ft),
spread 3.5m (11ft).*

Narcissus sp.
Daffodil (left) **Narcissus** (right)
*Popular bulbs in shades of
yellow and white. Prefer
partial shade. Any fertile soil.*

Primula hybrid
Primrose
*Small perennial
available in many
colours, a hybrid of the
wild* Primula vulgaris.
*Prefers sun or
partial shade.*

Clematis macropetala
Clematis
*Climber for a trellis or
over shrubs. Prefers
sun or partial shade.
Alkaline soil.
Height 3m (10ft).*

Mid spring plants

As the season begins to warm up, the variety of ornamental plants in flower in the garden changes. By mid spring many of the tulips, in all their different shapes, are ablaze with colour. Shrubs like forsythia will be covered in golden-yellow flowers and fresh green leaves begin to appear. The colourful barberry is welcome at this time of year too.

Ribes sanguineum
Flowering currant
Shrub with bunches of tiny red or pink flowers. Inedible berries. Prefers sun or partial shade. Height 2.4m (8ft), spread 1.5m (5ft).

Vinca minor
Periwinkle
Rapidly spreading perennial used extensively for ground cover but can become invasive. Prefers sun, but will grow in shade. Height 30cm (12in), spread unlimited.

Pieris formosa "Forest Flame"
Pieris
The foliage of this evergreen shrub is red when young, turning pink, through yellow to deep green as it matures. Partial shade. Acid soil. Height and spread 3m (10ft).

Spiraea bumalda "Goldflame"
Spiraea
Small shrub grown for its spring foliage. Red flowers in summer. Prefers sun. Height and spread 1.5cm (5ft).

Anemone blanda
Windflower
A colourful bulb for the spring rock garden. Prefers sun or partial shade.

Arabis ferdinandi-coburgii
Rock cress
Small perennial forming mats of green leaves. Prefers sun or partial shade. Best on well-drained soils.

Forsythia intermedia
"Lynwood"
Forsythia
*A popular shrub
covered in bright
yellow flowers which
appear before the
leaves. Prefers sun
or partial shade.
Height and spread
2.4m (8ft).*

Berberis thunbergii
"Atropurpurea Nana"
Barberry
*Colourful shrub bearing
deep-red foliage. Prefers sun
or partial shade. Height 1m
(3ft), spread 60cm (2ft).*

Tulipa sp.
Tulip
*The many species and
hybrids of tulip bulb
extends the flowering
period for several weeks.
Many colours of flowers,
and attractively marked
foliage on some plants.
Prefers sun or partial
shade.*

Cheiranthus cheiri
Wallflower
*Very popular bedding
biennial easily grown from
seed. Sweetly-scented
flowers in yellow, red, or
orange. Prefers sun.
Alkaline soil*

Primula denticulata
Drumstick primrose
*A small perennial with
flowers in blue, white,
crimson, or lilac.
Prefers sun or
partial shade.*

Late spring plants

As the season progresses, a whole new range of plants comes into flower, including the spectacular magnolias and flowering cherries, followed by the breathtaking display of camellias, rhododendrons and azaleas. Fresh, young, green leaves appear on the trees; some even have colourful foliage – for example, the maple's pale orange leaves.

Spiraea sp.
Spiraea
Useful, informal hedging shrubs. Prefers sun. Height and spread 2.4m (8ft).

Rhododendron "Elizabeth"
Rhododendron
A magnificent shrub needing a raised bed if soil is alkaline. Prefers partial shade. Height and spread 1.2m (4ft).

Berberis stenophylla
Barberry
An evergreen shrub covered with small yellow flowers in spring. Prefers sun or partial shade. Well-drained soil. Height and spread 3m (10ft).

Prunus cerasifera "Nigra"
Cherry plum
Small tree which flowers profusely. Black-purple leaves. Prefers sun. Alkaline soil. Height and spread 10m (30ft).

Muscari armeniacum
Grape hyacinth
A bulb making an ideal border edging. Untidy leaves. Prefers sun. Well-drained soil.

Myosotis alpestris
Forget-me-not
A good biennial for edging. Easily spread by shaking a seeded plant over the border. Prefers partial shade.

Symphyandra wanneri
Symphyandra
*An uncommon perennial closely related to the bellflowers (*Campanula *sp.). Prefers sun.*

Tulipa tarda
Tulip
Delicate bulbs with pointed petals best grown in light soil. Prefers sun.

Gentiana verna
Gentian
Small perennial that does well in limy soil. Prefers partial shade.

Prunus "Kanzan"
Flowering cherry
Do not plant too deeply as these trees are shallow-rooting. Prefers sun. Alkaline soil. Height and spread 15m (50ft).

Magnolia soulangiana
Magnolia
Plant these magnificent shrubs in a sheltered spot as frost can blemish their exotic flowers. Prefers sun. Height and spread 6m (20ft).

Prunus tenella "Fire Hill"
Dwarf Russian almond
Shrub covered with flowers. Prefers sun. Alkaline soil. Height and spread 1.8m (6ft).

Acer pseudoplatanus "Brilliantissimum"
Maple
A vivid tree which should not be planted on a windy site (to prevent damage to its pale orange foliage). Prefers sun. Height and spread 10m (30ft).

Aquilegia vulgaris
Columbine
Spurred petals distinguish the flowers of this perennial. Prefers sun or partial shade.

Primula veris
Cowslip
A native wild flower, this charming small perennial is easily grown in gardens. Prefers sun or partial shade. Alkaline soil.

Lobularia "Maritima"
Alyssum
A very popular annual for rock gardens or walls. Clusters of small white or purple flowers. Prefers sun.

Euphorbia polychroma
Euphorbia
Perennial that makes an attractive, dome-shaped bush. Prefers sun.

Early summer plants

Summer is the most abundant time of the year in the ornamental garden. The range of colours, shapes and fragrances of both flowers and foliage available in this season is immense. The profusion of perennials and biennials begins now, often lasting until autumn. Actual flowering times may vary with location and the position of the plant in your garden.

Rosemarinus officinalis
Rosemary
Attractive shrub grown as a herb. Well-drained soil and sun. Height and spread 1.8m (6ft).

Cytisus praecox
Warminster broom
A shrub whose green stems are covered with a mass of creamy-yellow flowers. Prefers sun. Height and spread 1.8m (6ft).

Potentilla fruticosa
Cinquefoil
Compact shrub with butter-yellow flowers. Prefers sun. Height and spread 1.5m (5ft).

Fuchsia "Peggy King"
Fuchsia
The many hybrids of this perennial make a striking display all summer. Prefers sun. Height and spread 45cm (18in).

Astrantia major "Rubra"
Masterwort
Perennial bearing flowers with an interesting and attractive shape. Spreads by underground runners. Prefers sun or partial shade.

Nepeta faassenii
Catmint
A small perennial, excellent for ground cover. Prefers sun or partial shade.

Potentilla "Gibson's scarlet"
Potentilla
An easy perennial to grow, excellent for attracting hover-flies. Prefers sun.

Polygonatum hybridum
Solomon's seal
Prefers sun or partial shade, though the roots of this perennial should always be shaded.

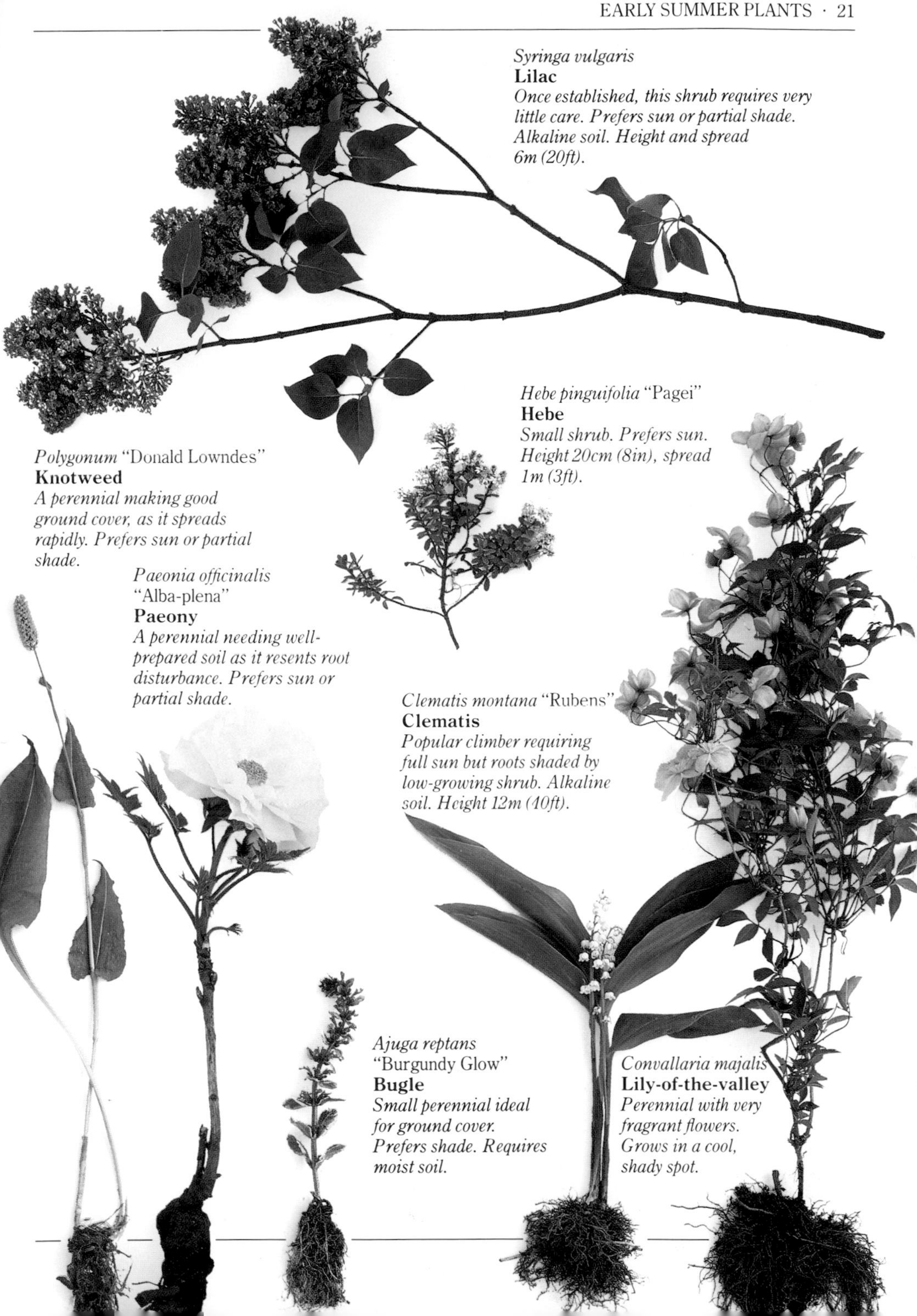

Syringa vulgaris
Lilac
*Once established, this shrub requires very
little care. Prefers sun or partial shade.
Alkaline soil. Height and spread
6m (20ft).*

Hebe pinguifolia "Pagei"
Hebe
*Small shrub. Prefers sun.
Height 20cm (8in), spread
1m (3ft).*

Polygonum "Donald Lowndes"
Knotweed
*A perennial making good
ground cover, as it spreads
rapidly. Prefers sun or partial
shade.*

Paeonia officinalis
"Alba-plena"
Paeony
*A perennial needing well-
prepared soil as it resents root
disturbance. Prefers sun or
partial shade.*

Clematis montana "Rubens"
Clematis
*Popular climber requiring
full sun but roots shaded by
low-growing shrub. Alkaline
soil. Height 12m (40ft).*

Ajuga reptans
"Burgundy Glow"
Bugle
*Small perennial ideal
for ground cover.
Prefers shade. Requires
moist soil.*

Convallaria majalis
Lily-of-the-valley
*Perennial with very
fragrant flowers.
Grows in a cool,
shady spot.*

Mid summer plants

The borders will be a blaze of colour at this time of year as the brilliant annuals start to flower, adding sparkle to the green of a garden now in full leaf. Here is just a selection of the large variety of plants which will not only look attractive in the borders but will also encourage the diversity of wildlife necessary in the organic garden.

Kolkwitzia amabilis
Beauty bush
A shrub easily increased by hardwood cuttings. Prefers sun.

Lupinus
"New Generation"
Lupin
A perennial with many varieties, some with two-colour flowers. Prefers sun.

Dianthus allwoodii
Pink
The modern varieties of this perennial have a long flowering period, but need propagating every three years to maintain flower numbers. Prefers sun.

Papaver alpinum
Alpine poppy
Perennial for rock gardens, paving slabs, and good drainage areas. Prefers sun.

Philadelphus
"Virginal"
Mock orange
Double-flowering variety of this shrub, with a strong fragrance. Prefers sun or partial shade. Well-drained soil. Height and spread 3m (10ft).

Iris "Xiphium" hybrids
Dutch iris
Bulbs with elegant-looking flowers in many colours. Prefers sun.

Tagetes patula
"Royal Crested"
French marigold
Annuals whose brightly-coloured, open flowers attract hover-flies. Prefers sun.

Potentilla fruticosa
Potentilla
Small, compact shrub flowering throughout the summer. Prefers sun. Height and spread 1.5m (5ft).

Delphinium "Dreaming Spires"
Delphinium
The tall flower spikes of this perennial need supporting with canes. Prefers sun. Height 1.8m (6ft).

Digitalis purpurea
Foxglove
Normally grown as a biennial, but in peaty soils this perennial can be left in year after year. Prefers partial shade.

Hosta "Thomas Hogg"
Plantain lily
Grown on rich, damp soil, this perennial will quickly form large, dense clumps of foliage. Prefers partial shade.

Lychnis flos-jovis
Campion
Easy to raise from seed, these perennials will grow in almost any soil. Prefers sun.

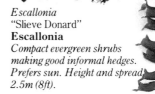

Escallonia "Slieve Donard"
Escallonia
Compact evergreen shrubs making good informal hedges. Prefers sun. Height and spread 2.5m (8ft).

Dahlia "Coltness"
Dahlia
Annual dahlias for bedding, raised from seed. The flowers attract hover-flies. Prefers sun.

Late summer plants

As summer draws to a close, the "cottage garden" borders will continue to attract, and provide food for, insects and birds. This is one of the best seasons for flowers with many of the perennials still in bloom, and also for fruits. Any wildlife activity in your garden is likely to increase at this time of year as creatures gather food for the winter.

Buddleia davidii
"Royal Red"
Butterfly bush
The flowers of this shrub attract butterflies and other insects. Prefers sun. Height and spread 6m (20ft).

Phygelius aequalis
Phygelius
Not truly hardy, this shrub should be grown against a wall for protection. Prefers sun. Height and spread 1.5m (5ft).

Coreopsis verticillata
"Grandiflora"
Tickseed
A perennial easy to raise from seed sown outside. Several cultivars are available, with flowers of different shades of yellow and varying sizes of head and height. Prefers sun.

Gentiana septemfida
Gentian
There are several varieties of gentian, with flowers ranging from white, through bright blues, to mauve. This is one of the easiest to cultivate. Can be raised from seed. Prefers sun.

Campanula rotundifolia
Harebell
A graceful perennial which can be naturalized in large clumps. Prefers sun or partial shade.

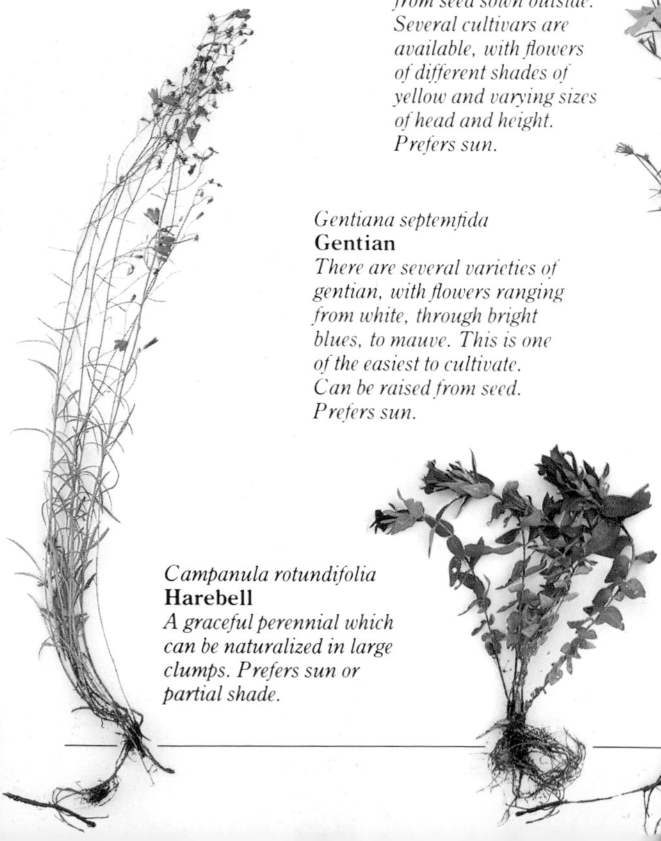

Phlox paniculata "Eva Cullum"
Phlox
A tall perennial responding well to mulching with organic matter. Prefers sun or partial shade.

Passiflora caerulea
Passion flower
Very vigorous climber which should be grown on a warm, south-facing wall. Prefers sun or partial shade. Height 10m (30ft).

Agapanthus "Bressingham Blue"
African lily
In temperate areas this perennial should be grown in a sheltered, sunny position. Height 1m (3ft).

Lythrum salicaria "Robert"
Purple loosestrife
Perennial ideal for growing in a damp area as it needs moist soil. Prefers partial shade.

Anaphalis triplinervis
Pearl everlasting
Unlike other grey-leaved plants, this perennial will not tolerate drought. Prefers sun or partial shade.

Gladiolus "Peter Pears"
Gladiolus
Brightly-coloured flowers borne on tall spikes which arise from underground corms. Prefers sun.

Autumn plants

The borders are now an interesting mixture of flower and foliage colour. Autumn-flowering bulbs add colour to the rock garden and borders. Many plants, like the species roses and the cotoneasters, produce colourful hips and berries to brighten borders and attract wildlife stocking up for the winter. Many plants have spectacular autumn leaves.

Caryopteris clandonensis "Heavenly Blue"
Caryopteris
Erect, compact shrub with aromatic, grey-green leaves. Prefers sun. Height and spread 1m (3ft).

Aster sp.
Michaelmas daisy
Easy-to-grow perennial if soil is kept moist during flowering. Some varieties prone to mildew. Prefers sun.

Rosa moyesii "Geranium"
Rose
Shrub with geranium-red flowers in summer and bright orange hips in autumn. Prefers sun. Height 3m (10ft), spread 2.5m (8ft).

Oxalis deppei
Good-luck plant
Low-growing bulbs forming dense mats. Leaves and flowers close at night. Prefers sun. Acid soil.

Sternbergia clusiana
Sternbergia
Bulbs that can be planted in drifts and left undisturbed for many years. Prefers sun.

Hosta fortunei "Aureo-marginata"
Plantain lily
The large, ribbed leaves of this perennial are edged in pale yellow. Good ground cover plants, can be left undisturbed for many years. Prefers sun or partial shade.

Cotinus coggygria "Flame"
Smoke tree
*The purple foliage of this shrub
turns bright orange-red in autumn.
Prefers sun. Height and spread
6m (20ft).*

Hydrangea "Sybille"
Hydrangea
*A shrub needing a
sheltered position for
protection against
frost. Prefers partial
shade. Height
1.5–1.8m (5–6ft),
spread 1.8–2.5m
(6–8ft).*

Vitis vinifera "Purpurea"
Tienturier grape
*Climber with claret-red leaves
gradually deepening to dark
purple. Prefers sun or partial
shade. Height 6m (20ft).*

*Thalictrum
dipterocarpum*
Meadow rue
*Perennial that should be
staked in an exposed site
as it can reach 1.8m
(6ft) high. Prefers sun
or partial shade.*

Cotoneaster conspicuous
"Decorus"
Cotoneaster
*Easy-to-grow perennial with
berries that are excellent
food for birds. This variety
is useful for covering banks
and the ground generally.
Prefers sun. Spread 1m (3ft).*

Sedum spectabile "Brilliant"
Ice plant
*Perennial with flat heads of tiny
pink or red flowers attracting
many butterflies. Prefers sun.*

Crocus scharojanii
Crocus
*Plant these bulbs beneath
trees or near shrubs where
digging is less likely to
disturb them. Prefers sun.
Acid soil.*

*Colchicum
byzantinum*
Autumn crocus
*Bulbs that can be
naturalized in grass
or border. Prefers sun
or partial shade.*

Herbs

Herbs are easy to grow, decorative and useful plants. They can be made into pot-pourri and used fresh, dried or frozen to add flavour to food. Plant them in the borders, in a special herb garden or in any odd corner. This is a basic collection, but there are many more. For cultivation details, see pages 122–25.

Anthriscus cerefolium
Chervil
Fast-growing annual with spicy, aniseed flavour. Prefers shade. Height 60cm (2ft).

Borago officinalis
Borage
Easy-to-grow annual, with decorative flowers attractive to bees. Prefers sun. Height 75cm (2ft 6in).

Melissa officinalis
Balm
Robust and aromatic perennial attractive to bees. Lemon flavour. Prefers sun or partial shade. Height 90cm (3ft).

Allium schoenoprasum
Chives
Fast-growing perennial, with decorative lilac flowers. Prefers shade. Height 20cm (8in).

Mentha spicata
Spearmint
Fast-growing perennial excellent for cooking. Prefers semi-shade. Height 90cm (3ft).

Anethum graveolens
Dill
Fast-growing annual, with feathery leaves and delicate yellow flowers. Prefers sun. Height 75cm (2ft 6in) in warm conditions.

Satureia montana
Winter savory
Erect, evergreen shrub attractive to bees. Prefers sun. Height 30cm (12in), spread 20cm (8in).

Ocimum basilicum
Sweet basil
Perennial grown as annual in temperate areas where frost might kill it. Prefers sun. Height 60cm (2ft).

Laurus nobilis
Bay
Frost-tender tree, with leaves much used in the kitchen. Prefers semi-shade. Height 6m (20ft), spread 10m (30ft).

Artemisia dracunculus
French tarragon
*Aromatic perennial with a
subtle flavour. Prefers
sun. Height 60–90cm
(2–3ft). For Russian
variety, see page 123.*

Thymus citriodorus
Lemon thyme
*Evergreen shrub
attractive to bees and one
of the most popular
kitchen varieties. Prefers
sun. Height 20cm (8in).*

Levisticum officinale
Lovage
*Very tall perennial with
bold, strongly-flavoured
foliage and attractive seed
heads. Prefers sun or
partial shade. Height
2.5m (8ft).*

Salvia officinalis
Sage
*Hardy shrub with
decorative blue flowers
and aromatic foliage.
Sometimes variegated.
Prefers sun. Height
60cm (2ft).*

Origanum onites
Pot marjoram
*Hardy perennial used
widely in the kitchen.
Prefers sun. Height
35cm (15in). For other
varieties, see page 123.*

Rosmarinus officinalis
Rosemary
*Aromatic evergreen with
blue flowers attractive to
insects. Prefers sun.
Height and spread
1.8m (6ft).*

Foeniculum vulgare
Fennel
*Fast-growing perennial
with impressive foliage
and decorative yellow
flowers. Prefers sun.
Height 1.5m (5ft).*

Juniperus communis
Juniper
*Tall conifer with aromatic
grey foliage and blue-
black berries. Prefers sun.
Height 3m (10ft).*

Salad vegetables

Growing salad vegetables is particularly beneficial, as their quality and flavour depends upon freshness. They take up comparatively little space and most can be grown all year round, given protection against frost. Salad vegetables are fast-growing and not usually troubled by pests and diseases. For cultivation details, see pages 134–35.

Brassica hirta and *Lepidum sativum*
Mustard and cress
Quick and easy-to-grow seedlings eaten fresh all year. Can be germinated indoors on moist kitchen paper.

Nasturtium officinale
Watercress
Grows wild in fast-flowing streams, so needs shade in gardens, moisture-retentive soil and much watering.

Lactuca sativa
Cut-and-come-again lettuce
New leaves grow to replace those that have been harvested.

Lactuca sativa
Cos lettuce
Particularly crisp and refreshing salad vegetable bearing bright-green leaves with prominent central vein.

Cichorium intybus
Chicory
A "chicon" dug up and blanched in deep, moist bark or compost. Chicons and the unforced green leaves are very useful in winter salads.

Lactuca sativa
Red-leaved lettuce
Distinctive form with crinkle-edged leaves. Like other lettuces, suitable for greenhouses.

Lactuca sativa
Loose-head lettuce
Perhaps the most popular form of lettuce, with especially soft leaves. Often interplanted between slower-growing crops.

Cichorium endivia
Endive
Often cooked, as well as eaten raw. Harvested through autumn and winter.

Shoot vegetables

This diverse group, grown for their succulent stems, provides an assortment of flavours and forms. Several are prized as gourmet delicacies and they certainly demand more careful attention during cultivation than most other crops. Globe artichokes are decorative enough for the flower border. For cultivation details, see pages 136–37.

Cynara scolymus
Globe artichoke
*Grown as an
annual or perennial,
needing a sunny and
sheltered position.*

Apium graveolens
Celery
*Both types – self-blanching and the
more demanding blanched – need
moisture-retentive soil.*

Rheum rhaponticum
Rhubarb
*Eaten as a dessert,
but technically referred
to as a vegetable because we
eat the stem and not the
fruit. Hardy, tolerating a
wide range of conditions.*

*Foeniculum
vulgare dulce*
Florence fennel
*Grown for its aniseed
flavour, needing moist
conditions to prevent it
running to seed.*

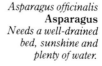

Asparagus officinalis
Asparagus
*Needs a well-drained
bed, sunshine and
plenty of water.*

Bulb vegetables

The edible bulbs of the onion family are in fact compacted layers of swollen leaf bases in which the plant stores food. All onions prefer a rich soil which makes them particularly suited to organic cultivation. These bulbs are among the easiest vegetables to grow and most store well, so you can maintain a constant supply. For cultivation details, see pages 138–39.

Allium sativum
Garlic
Sometimes classified as a herb, this easy-to-grow vegetable needs only a warm, sunny spot. Sown from cloves (individual segments of the bulb), dried and stored for year-round use.

Allium cepa
Onion
One of the most useful kitchen vegetables, storing well. For year-round supply, plant combination of maincrop and Japanese varieties.

Allium porrum
Leek
Hardy, easy-to-grow, and requires little maintenance. A winter vegetable that can be left in the ground until needed except in exceptional cold. May run to seed if planted too early.

Allium ascalonicum
Shallot
Maturing earlier and tasting milder than maincrop onions, but needing similar growing conditions. Easily grown from "sets", usually disease-free and storing well for winter use.

Allium cepa
Salad (or spring) onion
Picked before the mature bulb forms; they have a milder flavour than the larger onions.

Pod and seed vegetables

The vegetables in this group are an excellent source of protein and fibre. The nitrogen-fixing qualities of peas and beans are another good reason for growing them. After picking, save some seeds for next year; the rest of the plants can be dug into the soil or lifted to release their nitrogen on the compost heap. For cultivation details, see pages 140–42.

Pisum sativum
Pea
Eat peas soon after picking, before their sugar changes to starch. Sow early and maincrop varieties for successional harvesting.

Zea mays
Sweetcorn
Has an especially sweet flavour when home-grown. Should be eaten as soon as picked, before the sugar turns to starch. Needs plenty of sun. Grow in blocks to aid wind-pollination.

Pisum sativum
Mangetout
Also known as "snow peas" or "snap peas" and becoming increasingly popular. Cook and eat the whole pod including the tiny peas inside.

Vicia faba
Broad bean
Very rewarding to grow, being high in protein and a good source of green manure (page 79). Pick young. Can be dried and stored for winter use.

Phaseolus lunatus
Lima bean
*Also known as "butter beans".
Highly nutritious and can be
dried for winter use. Need
particularly warm soil conditions;
only grown successfully in warm
climates.*

Abelmoschus (syn. *Hibiscus*) *esculenta*
Okra
*Also known as "gumbo" or "lady's
fingers". In an average temperature of
21°C (70°F) two crops a year can be
harvested of this fast-maturing vegetable.*

Phaseolus vulgaris
French bean
*Available in bush and climbing
varieties, needing warm soil
conditions. Suitable for greenhouses.*

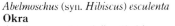

Phaseolus coccineus
Runner bean
*Popular and very prolific. Attractive
flowers and foliage suitable for
ornamental borders or for training up
cane wigwams. Needs carefully
prepared and water-retentive soil.*

Fruiting vegetables

Although technically fruits (the seeds of the plant), these crops are usually classified as vegetables because we eat them as such. They are not frost-hardy, so must be started off or grown under glass, where their brightly coloured forms are extremely decorative. Perennials in their native tropics, they are grown as annuals in temperate climates and need a rich, moist soil and plenty of sunshine. For cultivation details, see pages 143–45.

Lycopersicon sp.
Tomatoes
Very versatile vegetables, usually considered the most important greenhouse crop. Bush and upright types (which require training) are available. The various forms include elongated plum, large beefsteak, cherry and yellow tomatoes.

Salad tomato

Plum tomato

Beefsteak tomato

Yellow tomato

Cherry tomato

Solanum sp.
Aubergine
Aubergines are treated as annuals in temperate climates, and must have a sunny sheltered position if grown outside. Feed weekly at the height of the growing season.

Capsicum sp.
Sweet peppers
Attractive vegetables in an assortment of bright colours. Red peppers are merely green peppers left longer on the plant to ripen, with therefore a slightly spicier taste. Colour is usually not a reliable guide to flavour.

Red pepper

Yellow pepper

Green pepper

Capsicum sp.
Hot peppers
Also called "chilli" peppers, smaller and considerably hotter than sweet peppers. Only small numbers of these heavy-yielding plants are needed for an adequate crop. Can be raised in a greenhouse and then planted outside; needs cloche protection in all but the warmest areas.

Hot peppers

Squash vegetables

These members of the *Cucurbitae* family are half-hardy annuals which can be grown outside in warm conditions. They require well-manured, slightly acid soil and plenty of water.

Marrows and courgettes form small, bushy plants, while cucumbers and melons have a trailing habit, but can be trained up canes. For cultivation details, see pages 146–47.

Cucumis sativus
Cucumber
Needs well-matured soil in greenhouse or outside and can be trained up cane wigwams to save space. Newer "all-female" varieties are best under glass.

Cucurbita pepo
Courgette
May be green, striped or bright yellow, and are simply miniature marrows harvested early for a superior flavour. Pick regularly to encourage continued production. These bush plants take up relatively little space.

Cucurbita pepo
Marrow
Large, fast-maturing vegetables needing soil enriched with as much organic matter as possible. Pick before the fruits get too large. Can be stored in nets for a short time and kept in a frost-free place.

Honeydew melon

Canteloupe melon

Cucumis melo
Melons
New, fast-maturing varieties can be grown under cloches or in the open in warm areas. Need plenty of water. Support the maturing fruits with nets.

Cucurbita maxima and *C. moschata*
Pumpkins
Taking a long time to mature, these true pumpkins are best grown in warm areas, but many related squashes do well in cooler climates. All can be stored in nets for winter use. Use in both sweet and savoury dishes.

Root vegetables

M ost root vegetables are biennials; they store food in the swollen roots for use in the second year of the growth cycle when the plants would normally flower and produce seed.

Therefore, by harvesting them at the end of the first year, we benefit from this reserve of nourishment. Many root vegetables can also be stored. For cultivation details, see pages 148–51.

Tragopogon porrifolius and
Scorzonera hispanica
Salsify and Scorzonera
Good sources of iron and not difficult to grow, both vegetables produce long, tapering roots.

Solanum tuberosum
Potato
Always grow a few early varieties for their delicious flavour.

Ipomoea batatas
Sweet potato
Only suitable for cultivation in warm climates.

Daucus carota sativus
Carrot
Rich in vitamins and dietary fibre.

Helianthus tuberosus
Jerusalem artichoke
Excellent winter alternative to potatoes, these large plants are easy to grow but can become invasive if not carefully controlled.

*Brassica napus
napobrassica*
Swede
*Member of the
Brassica family,
easy to grow and
can be stored all
winter in moist
bark or compost.*

Raphanus sativus
Radish
*Fast-maturing
and very easy.*

Pastinaca sativa and
*Petroselinum crispum
"Tuberosum"*
**Parsnip and
Hamburg parsley**
*These vegetables require
similar growing conditions.*

Brassica rapa rapa
Turnip
*Can be harvested from
spring to autumn and
stored in a frost-free
place for winter use.
Needs plenty of water.*

Beta vulgaris esculenta
Beetroot
*A summer vegetable
which can be stored for
winter use. The delicate
roots will "bleed"
if damaged.*

Apium graveolens
Celeriac
*Actually a swollen
stem that grows
just above ground.*

Leaf vegetables

M any of these vegetables are members of the *Brassica* family, able to store much water in their leaves, making them fleshy and succulent. Being biennials, they also store nutrients during their first year and these are available to us if the crops are harvested before they flower and seed. For cultivation details, see pages 152–55.

Brassica oleracea botrytis
Cauliflower
The central "curds" are eaten, not the leaves. Three main seasonal types allow for year-round harvesting. The most difficult of the brassicas to cultivate successfully.

Brassica oleracea italica
Calabrese (above left) **and Broccoli** (above right)
Calabrese is simply broccoli that matures in summer. Easy to grow, producing green or purple "curds".

Spring cabbage

Brassica oleracea capitata alba
Cabbages
Can be harvested all year if the right spring, summer and winter varieties are sown and transplanted at the correct time. There are conical, round-hearted, savoy and red cabbages – all producing a large weight of edible material for the space occupied.

Savoy cabbage

Red cabbage

White cabbage

Spinacea oleracea
Spinach
Very nutritious and easy to grow, though shade is necessary to prevent it running to seed. Harvest all year round.

Beta vulgaris cycla
Spinach beet
Even easier to grow than spinach and, being biennial, does not run to seed. Two sowings will ensure a succession.

Brassica oleracea gemmifera
Brussels sprouts
Often interplanted between other crops. Sprouts of the new varieties can stay on the plant a long time.

Brassica pekinensis
Chinese cabbage
Also known as "Chinese leaves", a fairly demanding cabbage needing plenty of water and soil retaining plenty of moisture.

Beta vulgaris cycla
Swiss chard
Also known as "seakale beet", with stems that can be eaten as well as its broad leaves.

Brassica oleracea acephala
Kale
New varieties, both smooth- and curly-leaved, are greatly improved and make kale a valuable winter vegetable, rich in vitamins.

Tree fruit

No garden is too small for a fruit tree. With the increased use of special rootstocks, which limit size, trees can be both decorative and productive features. Make use of walls and fences, by training trees as cordons, fans or espaliers. If you have only a very small garden, you can grow fruit trees in tubs on the terrace. For cultivation details, see pages 164–68.

Prunus sp.
Nectarine
Smooth-skinned fruits cultivated in the same way as peaches.

Prunus armeniaca
Apricot
Plenty of sun needed to guarantee a crop. In temperate areas apricots are best grown as fans on a south-facing wall.

Prunus sp.
Cherry
Sweet cherries can be grown as fans against a south-facing wall, acid varieties on a north-facing wall.

Prunus persica
Peach
Needs well-drained soil and a sunny position. Best as a fan on a south-facing wall.

Prunus domestica
Plum
Fan-trained trees are hardy enough for north-facing walls, but fruits earlier if facing south or west.

Ficus carica
Fig
Tolerates any soil so long as well-drained and moisture-retentive.

Olea europaea
Olive
Long-lived tree only suitable for warmer areas. Eventually develops a twisted, gnarled appearance, adding greatly to its decorative value.

Morus sp.
Mulberry
Large, slow-growing trees. Self-fertile, so only one tree need be planted.

Cydonia oblonga
Quince
Relative of pears, needing plenty of sun. In temperate climates grow against a south-facing wall.

Malus domestica
Dessert apples
The most popular fruit of temperate climates, easy to grow in organic gardens. Can be grown on a shape to suit even the smallest garden. Grow a late-flowering variety in a frost pocket. Some varieties are not self-fertile.

Suntan

William

Pyrus communis
Pears
Flowering early, pears should not be planted in a frost pocket but in a sunny, sheltered spot.

Greensleeves　　**Jonared**

Malus domestica
Cooking apples
Usually larger and more acid-tasting than dessert apples. Branches may need support as crops can be heavy.

Bramley

Conference

Citrus fruit

In warmer areas, these sub-tropical fruits grow on evergreen trees which need plenty of warmth and shelter. In temperate climates they can only be grown successfully in the greenhouse or conservatory as they are not frost-hardy. In the right conditions they are not difficult to grow. They grow best in well-drained soils; if your soil is heavy, raise the planting area above the surrounding soil. For cultivation details, see page 169.

Citrus limon
Lemon
Best on slightly heavy, acid soils. If grown outside on badly drained soil, the planting area should be raised at least 45cm (18in).

Citrus aurantiifolia
Lime
Cultivated exactly as its close relative the lemon, but tasting slightly more acid.

Fortunella japonica
Kumquat
Dwarf evergreen trees producing good crops of miniature oranges. Can be grown outside if temperature is above –10°C (15°F).

Citrus paradisi
Grapefruit
Needs a sunny, sheltered spot, as well as acid, well-drained soil.

Citrus sinensis
Orange
Not frost-hardy so best grown in greenhouses in temperate areas.

Soft fruit

Soft fruits grow on bushes, canes or briars and are ideal for the small garden. Because their fruits soon deteriorate after picking, those you grow in your garden will be of superior quality to anything in the shops. Most fruits shown are relatively easy to grow in a range of climates and conditions. For cultivation details, see pages 170–75.

Fragaria × ananassa
Strawberry
One of the simplest and most rewarding soft fruits, preferring soil that is both well-drained and moisture-retentive.

Ribes sativum
Redcurrant
Redcurrants and whitecurrants are easy to grow and very prolific.

Ribes nigrum
Blackcurrant
Produces heavy crops in a sunny position with plenty of minerals.

Rubus idaeus
Raspberry
Easy to grow in temperate climates, especially organically.

Rubus sp.
Blackberry
A briar fruit taking up much room. Newer varieties taste better.

Ribes uva-crispa
Gooseberry
The earliest soft fruits to crop; Unsuitable for very cold areas.

Vaccinium sp.
Blueberry
Decorative shrub responding well to organic culture. Acid soil.

Rubus loganobaccus
Loganberry
A briar fruit growing best in cooler climates. Tie in regularly.

Vitis vinifera
Grapes
Grapes grown outside in temperate regions are usually only suitable for wine-making. Grow dessert grapes in greenhouses.

· Chapter Two ·

Planning Your Organic Garden

A garden is essentially a personal place, and so its final design must be something that you have conceived and put into practice yourself. We all have the innate creative ability to transform that muddy patch of ground outside the back door into a beautiful, productive and, above all, enjoyable place.

When planning your organic garden, first take account of its physical characteristics – soil type, direction it faces, and so on – and plan its boundaries. Second, draw up lists of essential features such as a dustbin screen – and desirable ones like a greenhouse. Then, draw a plan and work out where you want to site things. These principles apply whether you are starting a garden from scratch, taking over an established garden, or simply changing to organic gardening. However, if you have moved to an established garden, it may be advisable to wait a year before activating any plans, so you can discover exactly what the borders contain.

The mature border
This wide, mature border illustrates very well the principle of mixed, "cottage-garden" planting ideal for organic gardens. Herbaceous plants flourish in front of an old wall, giving a delightful impression of unruly abundance.

Physical characteristics

The physical characteristics within your power to change, or improve, include drainage and the quality of your soil and the contour of the land. The techniques for improving them, however, will vary according to the soil type and your situation.

Aspect and climate

It is not possible to do anything about your garden's orientation and you can rarely remove shade, generally caused by the house, walls, or fences. Likewise, you can do nothing about the weather. Altitude, rainfall, and the wind will all dictate certain features such as the amount of protection you need to provide. If frosts are regular, or you live in a frost pocket (a low-lying area where frost accumulates), choose the correct type of hedging and late-flowering or especially hardy plants.

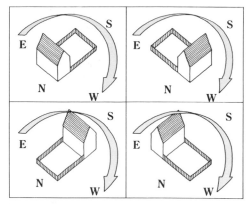

The garden's aspect
The direction your house and garden face will affect the amount of sun the garden receives. The diagrams show the difference between north-, south-, east-, and west-facing gardens: north-facing gardens can be cold and sunless, whereas a south-facing garden receives full sun all day.

Steep slopes

Steep slopes are difficult to maintain. It is much better to terrace the garden to form a series of "plateaux", with the different levels linked by paths, with ramps or steps. Informal wooden steps blend in particularly well with a "cottage garden" design.

It is not good enough simply to level the topsoil because that results in an extra deep layer of topsoil at the front and very little at the back. The only satisfactory way is to dig off all the topsoil from the area and level the subsoil before replacing it.

Wooden steps (above)
The wooden steps were made with railway sleepers. Hammer stakes into the ground behind them and nail them to the sleepers. Stone can also be used to make attractive steps.

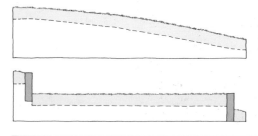

Levelling slopes (left)
Remove all the topsoil from the area, level the subsoil, then replace the topsoil evenly. Build a supporting wall at the front to hold the topsoil.

Soil types

There are five main soil types – clay, silt, sand, chalk, and peat, each made up of a mixture of minerals, the proportions of which are highly variable even within a small area.

It is important to know what kind of soil you are dealing with because the way in which you manage the timing of cultivations, and the plants you can, whether in the ornamental garden or the vegetable garden, will depend to a large extent on the nature of the soil.

The soils illustrated are as near to the pure mineral as possible. However, most soils contain a mixture of minerals. A soil referred to as "clay" indicates its major constituent. Soil mixtures are known as loams: soil with 50 per cent clay and 50 per cent sand is a "medium loam". A soil with a high proportion of sand might be described as a "sandy loam".

Soils may also be heavy or light, acid or alkaline (governing the types of plants you can grow), stony or gravelly (affecting drainage and fertility). See pages 64–65 for cultivation of different soil types.

Clay (right)
Heavy and cold, sticky when moist, compacted and hard when dry. Particles less than 0.002mm. Does not drain easily, difficult to work when wet; can be made very workable and fertile. Usually full of plant foods, supporting a wide variety of plants.

Silt (right)
Neither gritty nor sticky. Particle size: 0.002 to 0.02mm. When wet, packs down, making it cold, heavy and badly drained like clay. Texture can be improved by applying much well-rotted compost or manure. Same range of plants as clay.

Sand (left)
A dry, light soil. Particle size: 0.2 to 2mm. Easy to work and particularly good because it warms up quickly in spring, so can be cultivated earlier than most soils. Free-draining, tending to lose nutrients easily; needs much added organic matter and fertilizer.

Chalk (left)
A pale, very "hungry-looking" soil, often with many stones and flints. Large particles. Free-draining, very quick to lose nutrients and water. Topsoil often rather shallow, unsuitable for deep-rooted plants. Contains much lime: inhospitable to many plants.

Peat (below)
Distinctive dark colour, spongy texture. Rich in organic matter, so needs little extra. Tends to become waterlogged, needing artificial drainage. Needs liming.

Identifying your soil
Rub a little soil between your finger and thumb. Clay feels sticky and will roll into a ball that simply changes shape when pressed. Sand is coarse and gritty, while silt feels silky smooth. Chalk feels dry and crumbly and is greyish-white. Peat is the reverse – black and moist.

Drainage

It is easy to recognize a badly drained site, since the garden, or large parts of it, will be wet under foot and water may lie on the top, particularly in winter. The most common reason for badly drained land is an impervious layer of compacted soil beneath the surface, often caused during the building of a house. Digging to break up the compacted layer usually solves the problem.

Sometimes the impervious layer is caused by constant ploughing to the same depth, so with a new house built on old farmland, dig deeply into the subsoil to investigate any hard layer of soil.

If, however, the problem is simply one of heavy soil, you can generally overcome this simply by using the correct cultivation methods without resorting to complicated drainage systems. Dig deeply, incorporating gravel and organic matter, to raise the areas that will be cultivated. Each piece of land requires slightly different amounts, but one or two bucketfuls each of gravel and organic matter per square metre/yard should be sufficient. Improvement will take some time, but just growing plants helps to improve drainage, as the roots break up and open up the soil.

In the ornamental garden, if you raise the flower borders, your lawn will be at risk of constant dampness. To counter this, put down a 15cm (6in) layer of ash or gravel below the topsoil before sowing or turfing a new lawn.

Installing a drainage system
In a very badly drained garden, you may have to install a drainage system before you do anything else. First, check that you have somewhere to drain the water! It is sometimes suggested that you dig a soakaway in one corner of the garden. This hole is filled with gravel or other drainage material and will, in theory, absorb excess water. In fact, soakaways can only take so much water and, once full, it is back to square one.

The only possible way for a drainage system to be effective is if you are lucky enough to have a drainage ditch near the garden into which water can be drained and subsequently

removed. You can sometimes obtain local authority permission to run your drainage system into the public storm drains, but check *before* you start; it is illegal in some areas. If you have an outlet for the water, a herringbone system of drains is ideal. The distance between the "arms" will vary according to the soil – constantly wet soil needs arms closer together than soil with only a mild problem. On average, 2.5–3m (8–10ft) between arms is ideal.

Fill the arms with twiggy material or, better still, earthenware or perforated plastic pipes, available from agricultural merchants; then cover them with soil. Plastic pipes are no cheaper than earthenware, but much easier to lay – just roll them out into trenches.

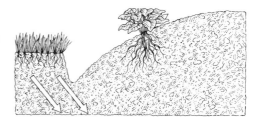

Improving drainage
If your soil is heavy and badly drained, raise the borders above the level of the lawn by digging in organic matter and grit. The borders will drain more freely and excess water on the lawn will drain straight into the subsoil.

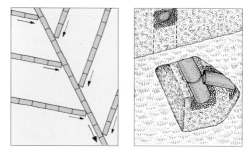

Herringbone pattern drains
Dig a series of trenches, about 45cm (18in) deep, that slope gently towards the outlet. Put a 15cm (6in) layer of stones or twiggy material in the bottom of each, then refill with soil. Better still, lay tile drains (short lengths of pipe) on a bed of gravel to form a continuous run. Cover the pipes with about 10cm (4in) of gravel and then refill the trench with soil. The water seeps in through the spaces left between the pipes and is carried away.

Garden boundaries

Your garden will almost certainly need some sort of wall, fence, or hedge for privacy. There are many different types of man-made fencing available, so choose one to suit your needs and to blend with your house and style of garden.

In addition, if you live in an exposed position, fencing or hedging can help protect your plants from high winds. Winds can be particularly damaging to all plants, especially in winter if they are not protected by a covering of snow. Protected, your fruit and vegetables will produce heavier crops and your ornamental plants will grow and flower better too.

Barriers for wind protection

The most effective windbreaks are those that merely slow the wind down, such as hedges, slatted wooden fences, or barriers made from perforated plastic windbreak material. Solid barriers can be worse than useless as wind protection unless they are extremely high. The wind tends to whip over the top and swirl and eddy over the other side, increasing in speed during the process. With man-made barriers, sink the posts deep into the ground and, if using a plastic windbreak material, fix it to the fence posts with battens.

Hedges

Hedges make very good garden boundaries as they are far less obtrusive than man-made barriers. They also make the best windbreaks. You can choose from either formal hedges or informal ones, those that are allowed to flower (*see page 86*). Hedges do, however, take up a lot of growing room and compete for water and nutrients. Never, for example, choose privet (*Ligustrum ovalifolium*) unless you are prepared to sacrifice at least 1 metre/yard along either side of the length of the hedge. If your garden is small, plan a formal hedge that can be kept compact by clipping. Choose informal hedges only if your garden is large because they need at least 1–2m (3–6ft)

growing room either side. If your garden is on a slope, make sure that your hedge does not act as a barrier, and prevent frost-laden air escaping from the garden.

Trees

Ornamental trees serve many purposes. First, they provide shade, which extends the range of plants you can grow. Second, they form the framework of the garden, along with the hedges and lawns, and can be planted to act as windbreaks, especially in the larger garden. And third, they attract wildlife to feed and breed. Birds use them for perching and nesting and for food. Trees with deeply furrowed or flaking bark provide homes for insects.

Enticing view
A hedge can not only keep out prying bystanders and straying animals, but also frame a vista which entices the eye onwards.

Garden features

While carrying out necessary groundwork on the physical aspects of your garden, think about features you want to include. Working out a plan is not easy because there are so many possibilities. Take time over it and put your ideas on paper first. Your budget may not allow you to complete everything at once, but a plan will give cohesion to the end product.

Allowing for the essentials

Start with a list of the features you simply *must* include – a clothes line, coal bunker, or a gate to stop the children running out into the road. If simply changing over to organic methods, you may already have these, but list them in case you want to alter, improve or abandon them.

A water supply is absolutely essential for maintaining the garden. Ideally, you should have an outside tap and a hose pipe long enough to water every part of the garden. If you want a stand-pipe at the far end of a long garden, lay the necessary pipes early on.

Desirable features

The items you want to include will exceed the space available, so draw up an order of priority. If you have a family, you may need an area where the children can play, but also a leisure area for yourself. After all, gardening is not all hard work!

In an organic garden, you will certainly need an ornamental area for plants to attract birds and insect predators. A greenhouse or cold frame is useful, and allow for the utility area (compost bins, tool shed, and so on).

HARD SURFACES
Decide first on the position of hard surfaces such as terraces and paths: they determine the level and position of many other items. Soften stark areas of concrete or gravel with raised beds or plant-filled tubs.

Terraces
A paved area for sitting out does not necessarily have to be against the house, although this is, in fact, the most convenient place. If the back of your house faces north, this will be a bleak place to sit, but in a hot, sunny climate the shade may be preferable.

Make the area a useful shape. A narrow strip along the back of the house is almost useless, without room for table and chairs. A square or triangular area in one corner is more practical and uses no more slabs.

If you butt paving right up to the house, it must end not less than two courses of bricks below the level of the damp-proof course and airbricks, or damp may creep into the house.

Paving material should blend with your style of garden and house. Soften stark lines with spaces between the slabs for low-growing plants like alpines. Edge paved areas with raised beds to bring colour up to the house. Edging a patio or terrace with a hedge provides both privacy and a windbreak. If planned for, it is easy to build a barbecue into paving.

Paths
Paths tend to cut gardens into pieces, a disaster in a small garden. If a path is essential, make it curved, so that it disappears from view here and there, giving the illusion of hidden nooks and crannies.

Never make a dead straight path in a small, informal garden, or allow a path to run either across a plot or straight down the middle. In large gardens, paths can be an extremely effective way of linking features. They look good when made of gravel or grass.

Sometimes a path is essential. Children generate much washing, so you will need easy access to a clothes line. This path will probably also have to be straight: site it at the edge of the garden, hiding it with a border.

An attractive way of making a path, especially in small gardens, is to set stepping stones in gravel. Space the stones out to slow you down, and enjoy the garden's beauty.

THE LAWN

An area of grass is a highly desirable garden feature: an excellent feeding place for birds, a comfortable playing surface for children, and a superb foil to borders. Planning a lawn will also, in effect, be shaping the flower borders. Traditional "cottage garden" mixed borders (*see page 56*) have no place for formality, so lay out the edges of the grass in long, sweeping curves to produce borders of varying widths. Long, simplified sweeps of grass make the garden look bigger, and are easier to cut.

Wild flowers

If you have room, allow a small patch of grass to grow tall, and sow some wild flowers to help attract insect predators. This "miniature meadow" will soon become a very attractive feature (*see page 89*). Include some bulbs with the wild flowers. Wild flowers also look very attractive in the borders.

An early summer meadow (above)
Specially sown wild flower mixtures quickly give the effect of an ancient hay meadow.

Feast for wildlife (below)
A splash of bright red poppies attracts insects. Later in the season, birds will feast on their seeds.

THE ORNAMENTAL GARDEN

For a moderately sized garden, the "cottage-garden" design offers very many distinct advantages. This style was developed by the old "cottagers" in England as a way of combining a productive garden with ornamental plants and later developed and romanticized by the Victorians in the nineteenth century. It also suits modern architecture and building materials just as well as it did traditional stone cottages with roses around the door.

A cottage garden allows you to grow a mixture of ornamental and vegetable plants in the same beds, so making maximum use of any available space; the informality of the style encourages the use of native plants, which will attract useful insects and pest predators. A side-effect of the close-planting technique adopted in this style of garden is the suppression of weeds and the saving of much tedious labour. Height can be added with climbing plants scrambling over pergolas or up walls, fences, hedges, shrubs, or trees. Choose a variety in flower when the shrub or tree is not, to extend the flowering season.

The alpine garden

Cultivated varieties of wild flowers from the high, mountainous areas of the world are amongst our most beautiful garden flowers. Most have little or no value in attracting wildlife and, therefore, pest predators, but once you have grown a few, you will want to make room for more. The best way to grow them is in a rock garden, a scree garden, in holes in walls or between paving slabs.

THE VEGETABLE PLOT

Fresh, home-grown vegetables are part of the organic gardener's way of life, so allow as much room as possible for the vegetable plot. The idea that vegetable plants are unsightly is nonsense; a well-ordered and productive vegetable plot is a truly heartening sight. There is no reason at all why you should not have an irregular-shaped plot if this blends in better with the rest of the garden.

Plan the plot in a sunny part of the garden and never plant a screening hedge between the vegetables and their source of sun. If space is limited, use deep beds (*see page 132*).

If your garden is too small for even the most restricted vegetable plot, grow a few fresh salads and some of the more ornamental vegetables among the flowers in the borders.

PONDS

An area of water is particularly useful in an organic garden to increase the range of wildlife. A small pond will attract birds and insects, frogs, and many other pest predators. It will also enable you to grow a much wider range of plants in the garden.

Plan the pool with rounded edges, instead of harsh angles, to blend in with a more informal garden. And allow for very shallow water at the edges, or provide a ledge at the side of the pond and a marshy area for marginal or bog-loving plants.

Siting the pond

Ideally, the pond should form a feature in the garden, rather than being tucked away out of view. Choose a site which receives plenty of sunlight for at least part of the day and as far from deciduous trees as possible. If leaves fall into the pond they will turn the water sour as they rot. Trees will also shade the pond.

Any water is dangerous for young children, so make sure the pond can be easily seen from the house but, if there is any risk, it is better not to build one at all until the children are older. Include a bird bath instead.

If you do not have room for a large pond, choose instead to sink tubs filled with water into the soil for growing aquatic plants and attracting wildlife.

THE FRUIT GARDEN

Not so long ago, growing fruit trees in a tiny garden would have been impossible. Now you can grow many types of fruit on special dwarfing rootstocks and, with modern pruning methods, restrict them to the smallest of spaces. You can train trees or soft fruit up walls or fences as either fans or espaliers, or as cordons, parallel to each other at a 45° angle to form a hedge. More compact still are stepovers, trees only 30cm (12in) high, ideal as a low hedge around the vegetable plot. Try to plan a fruit cage into your scheme to protect against birds.

THE UTILITY AREA

Organic gardeners tend to accumulate materials that other people would class as rubbish: pieces of wood, old polystyrene coffee cups for use as pots, and so on. So plenty of room is needed to store these valuable, money-saving materials. A few climbing plants will soon transform a garden shed into a thing of beauty. Without room for a shed, or room in the garage, arrange some kind of cover for tools and equipment. It is possible to buy garden "chests" or "lockers" for this purpose.

You will also need room for compost heaps, a leaf-mould container, perhaps a manure pile, and an area for storing bags of fertilizer (if you do not have a shed, buy them in plastic sacks and keep outside). Set aside a general-purpose utility area for these things and screen it from the rest of the garden behind tall-growing shrubs or hedging plants. If space is limited, erect a trellis (or posts and wires) and plant some fast-growing climbers in front.

THE HERB GARDEN

Locate this in the sunniest part of the garden, as well as reasonably near the kitchen. Also, since most herbs die down completely in the winter, it is important to make the area as interesting as possible.

In traditional herb gardens, the plants are arranged in formal patterns, enclosed by low hedges, usually of box (*Buxus sempervirens*) or lavender (*Lavandula* sp.). Pathways or stepping stones help you harvest each plant easily. Herbs can also be grown very successfully in the flower garden and were one of the main constituents of the "real" old cottage gardens.

THE GREENHOUSE

A greenhouse is an asset to any garden, well worth finding space for. Obviously, it needs as sunny a place as possible, and near to the house, since this makes the installation of electricity or gas for heating cheaper and, above all, makes the trip to attend to it on raw winter nights less daunting. Contrary to popular belief, however, it does not really matter it if faces east–west or north–south.

The cold frame

If you plan to raise your own plants, try to find space near the greenhouse for a cold frame, essential for acclimatizing plants to outside temperatures before planting out, or to grow early vegetables in colder climates. Most cold frames are a wooden, metal, or brick box with a glass lid. It is possible to make your own.

GREENHOUSE SHAPES

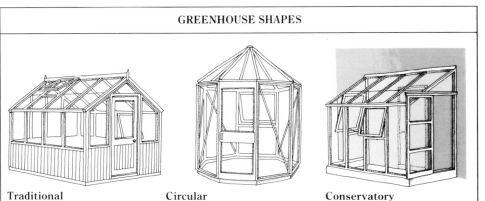

Traditional
The standard rectangular "barn" shape is a very popular and practical design, and enables you to make the best possible use of the available space. The walls may be glass or timbered, as shown here, to staging level.

Circular
Round or lantern-shaped greenhouses usually have six, nine or twelve sides and are one of the most attractive designs. The working space inside is usually fairly limited, but they are very useful for small gardens.

Conservatory
Conservatories, or "lean-to" greenhouses, also serve as an additional room in the house. Their location makes heating and regular plant care convenient, but means that light enters from only three sides, not four.

Drawing a plan

Once you have made your lists and have a good idea of your priorities, make a detailed plan of how you will carry out the work. First measure the boundaries of the garden, draw the area on a piece of paper, then transfer it to some squared paper. If your house and garden are absolutely rectangular, it is easy to measure and transfer this to paper. If not (and a perfectly rectangular plot is rare), you will have to use the system of measurement below known as "triangulation".

Starting work on the garden
Once you have finalized your plan, you can start work. Transferring your ideas from paper to the ground can be tricky, and it is a good idea to set a "datum line" (a line down the middle of the garden from which you can take all your measurements). Then it is relatively easy to work out curves from the drawing and transfer them to the garden itself, marking out each step with canes.

Be prepared to be flexible when you come to dig the garden or cut the lawn edges. If, for example, the curve on a border looks wrong when it comes to cutting it out of the lawn, do not stick slavishly to the plan. There is nothing to stop you making an alteration here and there in order to perfect the final garden layout. Remember, if it looks right, it *is* right.

MEASURING YOUR GARDEN BY TRIANGULATION

You need two fixed points from which to measure everything. The corners of the house are ideal. Since walls are generally at right angles to each other, you can be fairly certain that the house itself will be more or less straight. Start by measuring the house, then measure the distance to each corner of the boundary, first from one corner of the house and then from the other, and make a note of these measurements on your rough plan. Use the same method to determine the position of any features, such as trees, that you do not intend to change.

When you come to draw your master plan, decide on a scale. It is best to work in units of ten – 1cm:1m, for example (or, alternatively, 1in:1ft). Start by transferring your house measurements to the paper. If you use squared paper you will find it easier to obtain accurate angles and lengths. Then, set a pair of compasses to the relevant scale distances for each feature and draw an arc from both points marking the corners of the house. The point where the arcs intersect gives the precise location of the feature.

Draw all these details on the master plan in ink. Then fix a piece of tracing paper over the top of the squared paper to experiment with various designs without spoiling the master plan itself. There will inevitably be plenty of mistakes and mind-changing before the process is completely to your satisfaction.

Two plans opposite will give you an idea of how you can allocate space.

Measuring the existing features (right)
On a rough piece of paper mark down the distance between the corners of the house and the boundary, and the house and existing features such as trees.

Drawing the plan (far right)
Choose a scale and draw the outline of the garden and existing features on to squared paper using compasses.

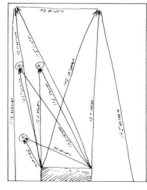

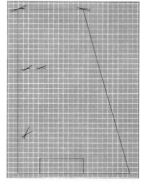

LAYING OUT A GARDEN

Below are ideas for two gardens: one for a large garden and one for a small one. Both demonstrate clearly how many different elements you can incorporate into any sized garden. The small garden is rectangular, the large garden is narrower at one end and slopes away from the house. It is based on the measurements taken for the diagrams opposite.

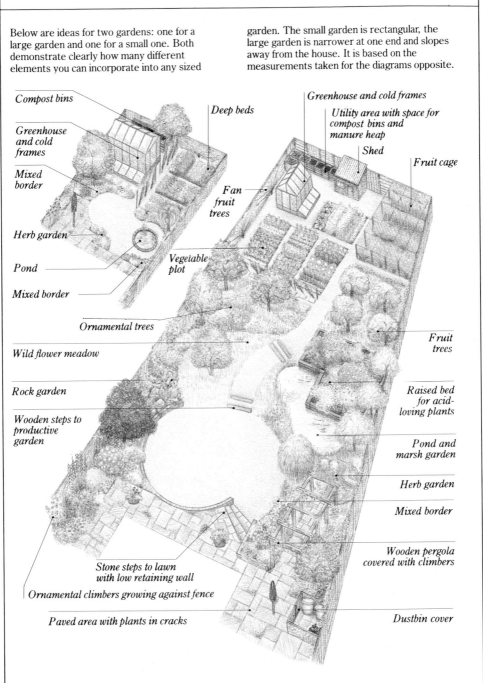

Compost bins

Greenhouse and cold frames

Mixed border

Herb garden

Pond

Mixed border

Deep beds

Fan fruit trees

Vegetable plot

Greenhouse and cold frames

Utility area with space for compost bins and manure heap

Shed

Fruit cage

Ornamental trees

Wild flower meadow

Rock garden

Wooden steps to productive garden

Stone steps to lawn with low retaining wall

Ornamental climbers growing against fence

Paved area with plants in cracks

Fruit trees

Raised bed for acid-loving plants

Pond and marsh garden

Herb garden

Mixed border

Wooden pergola covered with climbers

Dustbin cover

Chapter Three

Soil Improvement

The soil is the basic raw material of the gardener's art. It should never be dismissed as a mere collection of mineral particles used to anchor roots or, worse still, as "dirt". It is much more than that. Certainly, its basic structure consists of rock particles broken down by frost and thaw action, wind, and river flow, to produce the different soil "types" (clay, chalk, and so on). However, a large part of its make-up is organic matter – vegetable and animal remains in various stages of decay – along with air and water, all essential for the support of plant and animal life. All of this provides a home for millions of living organisms, such as soil fungi, algae, bacteria, insects, and worms, which work to provide just the right conditions for healthy plant growth. It is perhaps in the treatment of soil, more than anywhere, that organic gardening differs from other gardening methods. The very first principle of organic gardening is to nurture and encourage this subterranean life so that it can support a much larger plant population than nature ever intended.

Care of the soil

Plants are only as good as the soil in which they grow. Taking time and trouble over digging, then carefully feeding and improving texture with recycled organic matter, will all guarantee good results.

What is soil?

Soil is formed over millions of years by the physical or chemical weathering of rock. Clay soils (*see page 51*) are formed by chemical weathering, where the mineral composition of the rock is changed, usually by the action of weak acids. Other types of soil are the result of physical weathering, which mechanically erodes the soil either within the rock or externally.

In hot climates, the widely fluctuating temperatures of day and night cause rocks to expand and contract regularly, eventually causing the physical disintegration of the rock and the formation of soil particles.

In colder conditions, like those in the last Ice Age, water entered cracks in the rock, froze, and expanded, eventually forcing the rock to split open. The movement of giant glaciers, as well as the action of streams and rivers, helped to form the soil by wearing away fragments of surrounding rock.

The soil in your garden is therefore a very complex structure and its cultivation depends on many different elements. The several different soil types all have advantages and disadvantages. For example, the soil may be acid or alkaline; it may be heavy or light; it may drain well or badly; it may be very stony.

Heavy or light

A heavy soil contains a much higher proportion of clay. The very small particles of this type of soil tend to pack together, preventing the free passage of water. Heavy soil is often very difficult to work initially because it tends to be either very wet and sticky or very dry and hard. Eventually though, when it has been ameliorated by the natural drainage afforded by plant roots and the addition of organic matter, heavy soil becomes an excellent moisture- and nutrient-retaining medium.

Light soils, on the other hand, are easy to dig, and warm up quickly in the spring but allow very free drainage, which has its own problems. Water and nutrients disappear through the topsoil and into the subsoil and eventually the drainage system. Light soils require constant additions of organic matter to form a topsoil that retains moisture and generally need more applications of fertilizer than heavy soils.

Stones

The proportion of stones or gravel in your soil does not influence its texture classification, but may affect its fertility and drainage. Stony soil

---

TESTING YOUR SOIL pH

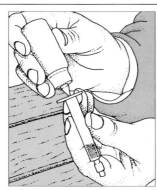

1 *Put a pH filter in the bottom of a syringe and add some soil. Pour some pH testing fluid into the syringe.*

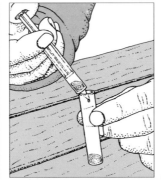

2 *Using the syringe plunger, push the mixture of soil and pH testing fluid through the filter and into a test tube.*

3 *Hold the test tube up against a pH colour chart and match the mixture to one of the colour bands to find your soil pH.*

has the advantages and disadvantages of a soil that drains freely and may need regular applications of bulky organic matter to improve water retention. If you have a heavy topsoil and a very stony subsoil, you have the best of both worlds, with surface moisture and nutrient retention, plus good drainage.

Acidity and alkalinity

Soil may contain lime, which will cause it to be either "acid" or "alkaline", depending on the amount. The lime content will make a considerable difference to the fertility of the soil, and will govern the range of plants you can grow, as it has the ability to make some nutrients unavailable to plants (*see pages 66–67*). There are several different types of kit for testing soil pH, all simple to use and accurate enough for home use (*see opposite*).

Certain plants prefer certain types of soil and, while you can do much to improve the general fertility or drainage qualities of a poor soil, and even make special provisions for "unsuitable plants", it is easier, in ornamental areas, to grow plants that are happy in the existing soil conditions. You may, though, have to take measures to alter the soil pH for your vegetable and fruit areas (*see page 81*).

Soil profile

What you see in your garden is simply the surface of the soil. Soil is made up of three layers: topsoil, subsoil, and the soil parent matter. Topsoil is formed over the years by the addition of organic matter that follows the decomposition of dead plants or animals. It is inhabited by a wide range of living organisms, and it is in this layer that the majority of the feeding roots of plants exist. Topsoils can be improved and deepened by the regular addition of organic matter (*see pages 68–79*).

The second layer is the subsoil, which is low in nutrients, generally contains few or no micro-organisms, and is therefore inhospitable to roots. Thus, when digging deeply, it is advisable to bring to the surface only very small amounts of subsoil; these can be mixed with organic matter and will, eventually, turn into topsoil. Double digging breaks up subsoil,

and improves drainage, without bringing the subsoil to the surface (*see page 182*). The nature of the subsoil has a profound effect on the water-holding capacity of the soil in general. If you have light sand or chalk subsoil, which drains very freely, you will need to increase the bulky organic matter content (*see pages 64–65*), and thus the water-holding capacity, of the topsoil. On the other hand, heavy clay subsoil, which drains poorly, may necessitate an artificial drainage system.

The third layer – the parent material – is the original mineral from which the soil was formed. This layer is normally deep enough not to concern the gardener, but may, on high ground, be comparatively near the surface. If so, try to increase the depth of the topsoil by adding organic matter to the top layer.

If you dig a deep hole in the garden, the varying colours and textures make it easy to identify the different layers. The depth of each layer will vary considerably.

IDENTIFYING SOIL LAYERS

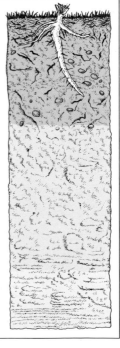

Topsoil
The darkest layer of soil, containing the organic matter, fungi, bacteria, insects, and worms necessary for healthy plant growth. Topsoil depth can range from 5cm (2in) to 2m (6ft); the deeper the better.

Subsoil
Lighter in colour than topsoil because it contains no humus, this layer is largely devoid of plant nutrients. Its structure affects soil drainage.

Parent matter
This consists mostly of unaltered rock. It is the area least affected by any cultivation of the topsoil.

Soil management

The ideal soil has a good crumbly structure, is rich in organic matter, drains enough to prevent topsoil becoming waterlogged in heavy rain, and provides the nutrients for healthy plant growth. Having established the type predominating in your garden (*see pages 50–51*), you can then use one of the following management techniques to get the best from it.

Clay

In the early stages, clay is not nearly as convenient to work as a light soil. When wet, it rapidly becomes a soggy mess of mud and, when dried out, it sets like concrete. However, work and sound management produce good results.

Clay is badly drained, cold, and heavy, because the spaces between the particles are too small to allow free passage of water and air. Improving its structure can take a few years, but then clay will grow far better crops than a light, sandy soil ever could.

Digging

When heavy soil gets wet and dries out again, it expands and contracts, cracking into innumerable small clods. If water then penetrates these, and cracks and freezes, it forces them farther apart, breaking the soil down to a sowable tilth. So dig clay soils in autumn, either when a little rain has softened the hard-baked ground, or when it is drying out after being soaked, but before it is hard again. Leave the surface rough through the winter to expose the maximum amount of soil surface, and work organic material into it.

Drainage

Because clay was broken down chemically, you can also combine the particles chemically by a process known as "flocculation". If sufficient lime is added to the clay, the tiny soil particles will bind together to form much larger crumbs, through which air, water, and plant roots can freely pass. Check your plants' needs and use as much lime as you can without making life intolerable for them (*see page 81*). If your soil is very heavy, dig coarse grit into it – about one to two bucketfuls every square metre/yard. Raising ornamental beds higher than their immediate surroundings will improve drainage quite considerably, helping the soil dry out and warm up. Grow vegetables on deep beds (*see page 132*). Never tread on wet clay or you will destroy years of work. Lay boards first.

Organic matter

Adding plenty of bulky organic matter to a clay soil holds the particles apart so that roots and water can pass through. After a few years of this, clay becomes much easier to work.

Silt

The main problem is also drainage. Minute particles tend to pack together very closely when wet, preventing free passage of water and air. So silt tends to settle as an airless mass. However, if you never walk on it when wet (use boards), and condition as suggested for clay, silt is perfectly manageable.

Digging

Cultivate only when silt is dry enough not to stick to your boots. Aim to dig during autumn to take advantage of water which will help break down the soil to a sowable tilth.

Drainage

To improve drainage, soil particles have to be forced apart physically. Dig in one or two bucketfuls of coarse grit every square metre/yard with organic matter. Raise ornamental beds and grow vegetables on deep beds.

Organic matter

Silt soils benefit greatly from liberal addition of well-rotted compost or manure to hold the particles apart for roots and water to pass through more easily. If possible, keep the soil covered with green manure (*see page 79*).

Sand

A very light soil, sand tends to drain easily and can therefore be cultivated when other soils are lying sodden and quite unworkable. It also warms up quickly, ideal for raising early crops. However, it is also extremely demanding, needing extra organic matter and fertilizers because nutrients and water drain away.

Digging
It is relatively unimportant when you cultivate sand. You need not leave it rough in winter because its large particles make it easy to cultivate to a fine tilth. Dig in spring just before you intend to sow or plant. Never venture on it when it is wet enough to stick to your boots.

Drainage
Sandy soil loses water, both through surface evaporation and free drainage. Spread organic matter ("mulch" – *see page 69*), over the beds between plants as often as you can to lower evaporation rate and improve soil structure.

Organic matter
It is very important to improve sandy soils by adding masses of bulky organic material each year. It will work down into the subsoil very quickly, so dig it into the top few centimetres, or mulch. Try to maintain a cover of vegetation more or less all the time, and certainly in winter when "leaching" of nutrients is at its most rapid. Grow a green-manure crop during winter and dig in during spring.

Chalk

Chalk soils are thin, dry, and "hungry"; water drains through rapidly, taking plant nutrients with it. Organic fertilizers will therefore need to be added (*see pages 80–83*). Secondly, perhaps even worse, chalk is very alkaline and so unsuitable for many plants.

Digging
Generally, there is no need to worry too much about the timing of cultivations. Chalk soils are normally dry enough to work, even in the depths of winter; dig in spring a few weeks before sowing. Topsoil is usually not very deep, so keep your digging shallow and, if possible, add a layer of topsoil.

Drainage
Generally, drainage on chalk soil is *too* good, so retain water and nutrients by adding bulky organic matter which will also help acidity.

Organic matter
On chalk, more than any other type of soil, it is important to try and keep the surface covered. Grow a crop of green manure during winter and dig in during spring. During the growing season, it is even worth sowing a fast-growing green-manure crop between vegetables, just to keep the soil covered. Mulching is also important during the growing season. Use acid materials (grass cuttings, compost, or manure) to counteract alkalinity.

Peat

If you are lucky enough to have peaty soil, grow as intensively as you can, as it is always potentially very fertile. It is liable to be acid and needs generous applications of lime in fruit and vegetable plots (*see page 81*). In the ornamental garden, with the correct plants, liming should not be necessary. When drained, peat soils dry out quite rapidly in hot weather. If they dry out completely, they will shrink and may be difficult to wet again, so water in dry weather.

Digging
The timing of cultivation is not critical: peaty soils are workable all year round. You need not leave peat soils rough during winter.

Drainage
Moorland and fenland peats are often badly drained and tend to become waterlogged, so you may need a drainage system.

Organic matter
It is not normally necessary to add any humus-making materials: peat is largely made up of decomposed matter. However, the soil is likely to be low in nutrients, so may need fertilizers.

Nutrients

All plants need oxygen, carbon, and hydrogen, which they obtain from the air, sunlight, and water. However, just as important for growth is the presence of a range of chemical elements in the soil. These are divided into the major elements (nitrogen, phosphorus, potassium, magnesium, calcium, and sulphur) and trace elements (needed in very small amounts but nonetheless essential). Oxygen, hydrogen, and carbon are needed in very large quantities (*see opposite*). By comparison, the other nutrients are needed in much smaller amounts, but still in specific proportions: too much of one can inactivate another. For example, too much potassium can inactivate magnesium (*see below*).

MAJOR ELEMENTS

Nitrogen (N), phosphorus (P), and potassium (K) are the major elements needed in the largest quantities. These are present in all general fertilizers, some of which also contain magnesium (Mg). Most soils have adequate levels of calcium and sulphur, which can be retained by regular additions of organic matter and by using proper cultivation techniques.

Nitrogen
One of the most important plant foods, a component of chlorophyll – the pigment which gives plants their green colour – and a vital part of the structure of plant protein. It is responsible for growth of shoots and leaves.

Deficiency is not unusual because nitrogen is easily lost by leaching in open soils and can be depleted by digging in unrotted material. With a deficiency, leaves turn yellow, particularly the older ones, and plants are stunted. Too much nitrogen causes plants to grow too quickly, with an abundance of "soft" leaves, often darker green than normal. The softer growth will be liable to an insect and frost attack.
Treating deficiency
Apply a fertilizer high in nitrogen, such as dried blood (see page 82).

Phosphorus
The next most important element after nitrogen, phosphorus is needed in smaller quantities (only about one-tenth of the amount). Phosphorus, or phosphate, is mainly responsible for good root growth, so a deficiency causes slight stunting of the plant. It can be diagnosed by distinct blue, which affects the older leaves first. Sometimes the leaves darken and develop a blue/green tinge. Also, the plant's root system is likely to be underdeveloped.
Treating deficiency
Apply a dressing of bone meal fertilizer (see page 82).

Potassium
Also known as potash, this is required in the same quantities as nitrogen. It affects the size and quality of flowers and fruit, and is essential for the synthesis of protein and carbohydrates. Deficiency results in small, inferior flowers and fruit, and stunted plants. Older leaves have yellowing around the edges, followed by brown scorching. Leaves may also become bluish and eventually bronzed all over. With excess potassium, plants are not able to take up magnesium (*see right*) and could cause an imbalance with other elements.
Treating deficiency
Apply a dressing of rock potash (see page 83).

Magnesium
Another element needed in much larger quantities than many gardeners realize, magnesium should be present in about the same quantities as phosphorus (*see left*). It is also a constituent of chlorophyll, so deficiency causes yellowing, which starts between the veins of the leaves. The deficiency generally affects older ones first. Magnesium deficiency is sometimes caused by plants not being able to take up the magnesium in the soil, perhaps because too much potassium is present, or because soil structure is poor, if there is insufficient organic matter in the soil.
Treating deficiency
Apply a dressing of seaweed meal, liquid seaweed, or liquid animal manure (see page 83).

Calcium
Another element required in relatively large amounts, calcium neutralizes certain acids formed in plants and helps in the manufacture of protein. Deficiency is rare in a well-managed organic garden, but plants sometimes develop an inexplicable inability to

PROPORTIONS OF ELEMENTS REQUIRED FOR HEALTHY PLANT GROWTH

Of the elements required for healthy plant growth, oxygen, carbon, and hydrogen account for 96 per cent (45 per cent oxygen, 45 per cent carbon, and 6 per cent hydrogen). Nutrients described opposite and below, as well as some unspecified trace elements, make up the rest.

Nitrogen *1.5 per cent*
Phosphorus *0.15 per cent*
Potassium *1.5 per cent*
Magnesium *0.2 per cent*
Calcium *0.5 per cent*
Sulphur *0.1 per cent*

Iron *0.01 per cent*
Zinc *0.002 per cent*
Copper *0.0006 per cent*
Manganese *0.005 per cent*
Boron *0.002 per cent*
Molybdenum *0.00001 per cent*

distribute calcium through their systems, though no one really knows why this occurs. The classic example is blossom-end rot in tomatoes, when the tip of the fruit blackens and rots. Lack of calcium also causes tip-burn on lettuce, black heart in celery and browning in the centres of Brussels sprouts. Deficiency is most pronounced in young plant tissue.

Treating deficiency
No specific cure. Use correct cultivation methods, incorporate plenty of compost or manure to build up a balanced nutrient level in the soil.

Sulphur
Sometimes classed as a trace element, although sulphur is needed in fairly large quantities. Sulphur forms part of many plant proteins and is involved in the formation of chlorophyll. Sulphur deficiency causes plant stunting and yellowing of the plant, but the problem is rare since there is generally enough sulphur in organic soils because of the regular applications of compost and manure.

Treating deficiency
As soon as you notice a sulphur deficiency, apply a very light dusting of calcium sulphate (gypsum) over the soil surface.

TRACE ELEMENTS

Needed in very small quantities, but vital to plant growth. The six of major importance are iron, zinc, copper, manganese, boron, and molybdenum. In an organic garden, deficiencies are extremely rare because all the trace elements are present in compost, manure, and other bulky organic matter. Problems can occur when the action of trace elements such as iron, manganese, and boron is inhibited by alkaline, or limy soil, resulting in yellowing of rhododendron leaves and between the leaf veins in raspberries. It is best to prevent trace-element deficiencies occurring at all, normally quite easily achieved by continued use of bulky organic matter. Where deficiencies have occurred, treat soil annually with seaweed meal fertilizer.

Iron
Needed to make chlorophyll. Deficiency shows as yellowing between leaf veins, especially younger ones. More likely on alkaline soils, sometimes looks like magnesium deficiency.
Treating deficiency
Spray with liquid seeweed, apply seaweed meal and/or manure.

Zinc and copper
A deficiency of either makes younger leaves mottled yellow; citrus trees develop "little leaf".
Treating deficiency
Dress with seaweed meal, compost, or manure.

Manganese
Necessary for chlorophyll and protein. Deficiencies (stunting and yellowing of younger leaves) show more on akaline soils.
Treating deficiency
Spray with liquid seaweed; apply seaweed meal, compost, or manure.

Boron
Important to growing tissue. Deficiencies more likely on alkaline soils: lead to a tissue breakdown: internal "corkiness", especially in apples and many root crops, and brown-heart in celery and brassicas.
Treating deficiency
Once apparent, it is too late to save the crop. To protect next crop, apply seaweed meal, compost, or manure.

Molybdenum
Used in protein production; deficiency shows as deformed growth, causing "whiptail" in brassicas (leaves become thin and straplike). Deficiency due to acid soil conditions (*see page 81*).
Treating deficiency
Add lime to raise pH. Spray plants with liquid seaweed fertilizer, dig in seaweed meal, and/or compost or manure to the soil.

Soil nourishment

As emphasized by the various cultivation techniques described on pages 64–65, all soil types benefit by the addition of bulky organic matter such as well-rotted compost or manure. This is the key to soil fertility and a healthy, fertile soil is the basis of the organic approach to gardening, and indeed the basis of all good gardening, organic or not.

What should you use to improve your soil?

But where is all this manure to come from, particularly if you live in a town? Compost is the alternative. But is that realistic? Certainly it looks good during early summer when you start your compost container with grass cuttings. After a couple of mowings, it fills up to overflowing and you have to start another. Yet by the time it has rotted down completely, it has shrunk to no more than a few bucketfuls.

Using bought-in material
In fact, a normal-sized garden with a productive vegetable plot will simply not produce enough compost. You will have to buy in some form of organic matter, and be constantly on the look-out for suitable composting material. The more you can gather the better, because you will have to buy less. Even in an urban area there are ways of doing this (*see page 74*).

Unfortunately, it is almost impossible to garden totally organically, because virtually everything that you might use is polluted with some chemical or other. Straw has been sprayed with pesticides; cows have been force-fed with hormones; even the leaves swept from the pavements are polluted with lead from petrol. So you may feel safer by composting all imported material for at least a year, hoping to leach out the toxins.

Feeding the soil

Plants need the nutrients described on pages 66–67 to be present in the soil in specific proportions. These nutrients will be supplied by the addition of sufficient compost or manure, but you may have to use organic fertilizers as well for the required balance. The techniques of feeding and the type of fertilizer will vary depending on your soil type, and how much organic matter is available. The degree of acidity or alkalinity, or pH, of your soil will also affect the availability of some nutrients (*see page 81*). So, you may find that, having established the pH level and adjusted it if necessary, you release more nutrients, increasing the fertility of your soil.

The four phases of soil improvement

The first phase of soil improvement is analysing the soil; the second is general soil conditioning and replacement of nutrients with organic matter; phase three is the general application of fertilizer; the fourth phase covers more specialized application of fertilizers for specific plant needs.

1 Analysing your soil
If you are starting out, especially on virgin soil, it is a good idea to have it analysed. Soils uncultivated for many years are often grossly deficient in one or other necessary nutrients.

It is best to send a sample of your soil away for professional analysis. The kits available to amateur gardeners (*see pages 62–63*) are not accurate enough for this all-important first stage. Used regularly, they indicate a trend but no more. There are plenty of reputable companies who will analyse your soil. They advertise in gardening magazines. They will be able to tell you the exact chemical make-up and exactly how much fertilizer you need to correct a deficiency. Ask them to recommend *organic* fertilizers. After this first analysis, annual home pH testing is probably sufficient.

2 Using soil conditioners

This stage deals with the general soil improvement and replacement of plant nutrients removed by previous crops. It is here that there will be variation because it depends on how much, and what type, of organic material you have available to you.

First of all, it should be taken as read that all organic material not actually taken for the kitchen is returned to the soil as compost, and that this should be supplemented by manure or some other bought-in soil conditioner (*see page 77*) as necessary. Organic matter should be dug in during the autumn and spread over the soil as a mulch in the growing season. This will increase the water-holding capacity of light soils and open up very heavy soils, as well as supplying all the nutrients. Spread over the surface of the soil in thick layers as a mulch, it also acts as a weed suppressant (*see page 217*) and will eventually be worked into the soil by the action of weather and soil organisms.

The amounts required and whether it is dug in or mulched will vary slightly depending on your soil, the time of year, and the plants you want to grow. Ideally, use at least two 9-litre (2-gallon) buckets of well-rotted compost or animal manure for every square metre/yard of soil in the vegetable garden, one bucket per square metre/yard as a mulch round trees and shrubs, in the ornamental borders and for fruit trees and bushes. If you can afford to use more, do not be afraid to do so. And you can always supplement your compost or manure with green-manure crops whenever the beds are empty for any length of time (*see page 79*).

3 Adding general fertilizer

Not everyone can get sufficient supplies of compost or manure. This is, therefore, where concentrated fertilizers come in. If, for any reason, the composting or manuring falls below the recommended levels, you will have to make up the nutrients "out of the bag" with a general fertilizer such as blood, fish, and bone meal. The application rates vary according to the soil and the plants you want to grow, so recommendations have been made in the relevant sections of the book. Where any trace element deficiencies have occurred in the past, give the soil a light dressing of seaweed meal at the beginning of each season.

4 Using specific fertilizers

Some crops such as greenhouse tomatoes and raspberries always need special treatment even when the manure and fertilizer levels are sufficient to start with. Apply extra phosphorus, or phosphate, before planting trees or sowing to encourage root growth. All recommendations are discussed in more detail in the relevant chapters of the book.

Digging in manure
The best way to incorporate organic material into soil is to dig it in during autumn. Dig out a trench, taking the soil to the end of the plot. Put a layer of manure in the bottom of the trench; half fill with soil dug from the next trench. Add more manure, then fill in.

Mulching
This involves spreading a layer of organic matter over the soil where it cannot be dug into the ground because plants cannot be disturbed. Mulching is normally carried out in spring. Make sure the soil is moist before you apply the mulch because it absorbs surface water.

Compost

Every garden must have one or preferably two compost heaps. Compost is the ideal way to return organic matter to the soil, following nature's example. Decomposing vegetation provides a home for millions of soil organisms, it opens up the soil, improving drainage and easing the way for root growth, and it helps over-drained soils hold water and therefore nutrients.

Plant remains all contain much plant food. The rotting process is carried out by bacteria. Millions of them begin to feed on anything recently removed from the soil. To carry on the decomposition, these bacteria need nitrogen. If the garden waste is dug in "green" (unrotted), the bacteria draw the nitrogen from the soil, leaving plants desperately short of food. Turned into compost, the material actually adds nitrogen to the soil. After the initial rotting, a species of bacteria known as *Azotobacter* is attracted and can "fix" nitrogen from the air into a form usable by plants.

The rotting process takes time and a successful, well-planned organic garden should therefore have at least two compost heaps, one left to rot down while the other is filled.

Compost containers

Although you can pile compost up in a corner of the garden, compost in a container rots right up to the edges of the heap. In an open heap, the edges dry out so you must turn the whole heap at least twice during the rotting process to push unrotted material to the centre.

The size of your container will depend on the size of your garden. There are plenty of containers at garden centres. The most useful is a wooden box with slatted sides, more sections easily being added. Some suggest you can add material to the top while shovelling out the compost at the bottom, but this is not realistic. Whether you build or buy a bin, make sure you can get at the compost easily.

SOME HOME-MADE COMPOST CONTAINERS

It is quite easy to build your own bin. Apart from wood (*see opposite*), you can also make compost bins from brick, or stakes and wires. Large plastic barrels used for fruit concentrates are also ideal, with both ends cut off and 2.5 cm (1in) holes drilled around every 30 sq cm. (1 sq ft).

Brick-built compost bin
Suitable if you are never going to move the heap. Stagger the bricks so that air can get into the compost heap. Make the front of wooden slats as the home-made wooden bin opposite. Fix battens down the inside of the walls and slide the slats in.

Wire-and-post container
Hammer four stakes into the ground in a 1m (3ft) square. Staple 4m (12ft) of wire netting, 1m (3ft) deep, to the outside. Tie pieces of cardboard to the inside of the wire.

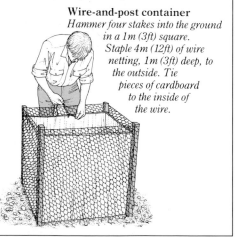

MAKING A WOODEN COMPOST CONTAINER

It is not difficult to make a wooden compost container. You do not need to buy new wood. A demolition contractor will always have suitable timber at half the price of new wood. Old floorboards are particularly good for the sides, while 7.5×10cm (3×4in) floor joists make ideal corner supports.

You need:
- 4×1m (3ft) lengths of 5×10cm (2×4in) wood for the uprights
- 19×1m (3ft) lengths of wood for the sides
- 5×75cm (2ft 6in) lengths of wood for the front panels (you may need to check this measurement when you have completed the main part of the bin)
- 4×75cm (2ft 6in) battens
- 2 small pieces of wood
- 1cm (½in) piece of wood between the side panels
- Strong nails about four for each side panel

More battens - 3 removable sides.

1 Place two of the uprights on the ground to lie parallel to each other and 75cm (2ft 6in) apart. Place one of the side planks across them, 7.5cm (3in) from the bottom of each post and nail it into position. Using a 1cm (½in) piece of wood as a spacer, nail five more pieces of wood between the two uprights, at right angles to the uprights and parallel to each other.

2 Make another wall to match. Stand the two walls up parallel to each other and at right angles to a garden wall. Nail a piece of wood to the top of each upright to hold them in position. Working from the bottom upwards, nail six pieces of wood across the back, ensuring that they are level with those pieces of wood on each side.

3 Remove the support panel. Turn the box round. For the front wall, nail a board across the front of the uprights 7.5cm (3in) from the bottom. Nail two battens on to the side edge of each upright, far enough apart to slide the front panels between them. Nail a small piece of wood across the bottom of the battens to prevent the front panels sliding out as you fill the bin.

4 Slide all the front panels into the bin to make sure they fit; cut them down as necessary for a good fit. Paint the entire container, including the cut edges and the front panels, with a water-based wood preservative. Leave to dry.

5 Slide all the front panels into position. Tie a piece of string across the top of the container to prevent the sides bulging outwards when you fill it with layers of compost. The compost container should be stood on a level surface, preferably on a soil base.

m - removable.   getting steps in?

How to make good compost

Obviously, the first requirement for good compost is something to compost. Then the heap needs air, nitrogen, lime, water, heat, and bacteria. There are a great many old wives' tales about what can and cannot be used, but the rule is very simple: anything entirely organic in origin can be composted – with a few exceptions (*see opposite*).

Air circulation
Air is of vital importance in the compost heap. Without it, the material is worked on by a different group of micro-organisms, known as anaerobic bacteria, which turn grass cuttings and the like into a stinking, useless slime.

So, first of all, the container itself should have plenty of air circulating through it. Secondly, never let the compost material pack down solid, but mix fine material with larger weeds or shredded newspaper.

Nitrogen
Because bacteria in the compost heap require nitrogen as a fuel, you must add a certain amount to the heap. Ideally, use animal manure (*see pages 75–76*). Alternatively, buy organic compost fuels, or activators, in a garden shop. Dried sewage sludge can often be obtained from the local sewage works – ideal also as a fertilizer. Seaweed meal is excellent, and dried blood, the best form of nitrogen fertilizer, makes a very good, if slightly expensive, activator (*see pages 82–83*).

Whatever you use, you do not actually need very much – and not as much as the manufacturers say. A fine dusting every 30cm (12in) of compost is sufficient.

Lime
Adding lime will keep the compost "sweet" – helping to neutralize the acidity (*see page 81*). Apply a slightly heavier dusting of lime than of the nitrogen activator every 30cm (12in).

On chalky soil, you may feel that it would be better to omit the lime and use very acid compost instead. You *can* do this, but the bacteria involved actually prefer conditions that are not too acid, so rotting will take longer.

Water
This is an essential ingredient of any compost heap. Generally, there will already be enough in the green material you put on the compost heap, certainly in grass cuttings. It is possible, in a hot summer, for the edges to dry out, in which case you may need to apply extra water. Straw is an excellent aerating material, especially mixed with grass cuttings, and it composts well, but you must wet it first.

Heat
Decomposition is much faster when the material is warm. In summer you will have usable compost in two to three months; in winter, the process slows down considerably and the compost will not be usable until spring.

You can cover the heap with black polythene weighted at the edges; this keeps the heat in and prevents it becoming too wet, a problem particularly in winter. A piece of old carpet will not need weighting down and also "breathes", allowing more air into the heap.

Bacteria
Finally, you need the bacteria themselves. There are millions in just one crumb of soil, so there should be plenty in the crumbs of earth that cling to the roots of the weeds you put in the heap. It is completely unnecessary to add layers of soil throughout the heap: not only is it hard work, but it also makes the compost less concentrated.

Managing your compost
Really good compost is supposedly brown and crumbly with the sweetest of smells, like woods in the autumn, but if your heap is small and you are using any organic material you can find, it often will not live up to that ideal. Generally, while some material is in an advanced stage of decomposition, other material will not have rotted down nearly as much. The compost is more likely to be very variable, with a lot of semi-rotted fibrous material. But that will still improve the soil and certainly do no harm; it will just take a bit longer to rot down.

BUILDING UP A COMPOST HEAP

Start with a 15cm (6in) layer of coarse material (horse manure, straw, or large weeds) to give a free flow of air at the bottom. Then add a layer of material 15cm (6in) deep. Sprinkle on some compost activator or nitrogen fertilizer, or add another layer of horse manure; the nitrogen in it will act as a compost activator. Add another 15cm (6in) layer of material, then cover with a dusting of lime, and so on. Always cover the bin to keep it dry. Compost rots down and shrinks quickly so that what seems like a finished heap one week, has sunk down to give room for more the next week.

Lime

Grass cuttings

Horse manure, or straw, then compost activator

Lime

Leaves from vegetable garden mixed with grass cuttings

Horse manure, or straw, then compost activator

Grass cuttings

Horse manure

Getting good quality compost takes care, and each composting material needs different treatment. For example, always mix grass cuttings thoroughly with some coarser material such as larger weeds, shredded newspaper, or straw, to prevent them turning to slime.

Newspaper can be difficult to rot down but is worth persevering with, particularly when mixed with grass cuttings. As a rough guide, use 1 part newspaper to 4 parts grass cuttings. Never put it on the heap folded into a thick wad; cut it into 2.5cm (1in) strips and keep it in a plastic bag until needed. Then put it in a bucket of dilute seaweed. Use only a small amount and never the paper from glossy magazines, which contains lead.

Potato peelings often cause problems because those tiny "eyes" will develop into potato plants either in the heap or when the compost is spread. But they are not difficult to pull up and provide that much more material for the next heap. Any old clothes made of natural fibre can be put on the heap as well. It is a good idea to cut them into strips beforehand, as they will rot down faster.

The amount of compost you can make in a year depends very much on the type of material you use but even more on the weather. From each bin you should, in a hot year, get two good binfuls in the summer – one in early summer and a second in late autumn – and another in the spring if you are lucky.

WHAT NOT TO INCLUDE IN THE COMPOST HEAP

- Any material diseased or infected with pests – always burn this.
- The top growth of maincrop potatoes may infect the heap with potato blight spores.
- Roots of pernicious weeds, for example, couch grass (*Agropyron repens*), bindweed (*Convolvulus arvensis*),

ground elder (*Aegopodium podagraria*), and creeping buttercup (*Ranunculus repens*): burn these roots at once as they will multiply in the compost heap.
- Coffee grounds tend to stick together, so are not suitable. Use tea leaves instead.
- Prunings from woody plants

take too long to rot, although chopping them into smaller pieces can speed up the process slightly.
- Cooked kitchen scraps often putrefy and attract vermin.
- Any weed seeds: the heap will "cook" them and render them unviable only if it reaches a *very* high temperature.

Alternative sources of compost

Few gardens can produce enough waste organic material to be self-sufficient in compost. But a remarkable amount of good stuff that is thrown away can be "harvested" by the organic gardener. The local greengrocer or street market after closing time on Saturdays is an excellent source of greenstuff. The local sports ground or golf club often have no means of disposing of massive amounts of grass cuttings and would be delighted to have them cleared away. Another excellent source of free soil conditioner could be a tomato nursery which grows in peat bags and has surplus at the end of the season.

Leaf mould

Leaves are slow to rot down. Be prepared to wait at least a year, and possibly even two or three, for a good, crumbly compost ready to use. Leaf mould is really much too good for mulching or digging in: use it as a potting or seed-sowing compost (see page 101).

The decaying process is quite different from compost-making. Leaves are broken down by fungi which need more light and less air than compost bacteria. So build the container in a corner where it can be left undisturbed.

Building a leaf-mould container
Drive four wooden stakes at least 1m (3ft) tall into the ground to make a 1m (3ft) square. Staple about 4m (12ft) of wire netting around the outside.
Make sure that the netting reaches right to the ground, so that small animals cannot penetrate the container.

You will need at least two heaps because of the length of time involved. You do not need elaborate containers: make them out of stakes and wire netting. Pile the leaves into the container as you collect them, treading down each time. They may need a little water in a dry summer; otherwise, leave them alone.

The local council is often a good source of leaves, possibly "polluted" with cigarette packets or other rubbish, but these are easily removed while stacking. They could contain lead from car exhaust emission, but all you can do is hope to reduce it to an acceptable level, if it is not leached out entirely by composting.

Sheet composting

Making good compost takes time and trouble – time which may be difficult to spare, and as organic matter should never be thrown away, you may find it more convenient to "sheet compost". This simply involves spreading a thin layer of organic matter on the soil between rows of vegetables or on a vacant area, and allowing it to rot down there. Naturally, this method is useful only in productive parts of the garden where aesthetics are not important. Sheet compost can be particularly useful on areas regularly trodden, like paths between rows, or as a mulch around fruit trees.

Ensure weeds have wilted beyond recovery, or you may find them re-rooting and growing away in your carefully tended vegetable patch. Also ensure that they are not about to shed seeds. Grass cuttings are ideal for sheet composting, but watch out for sprouting annual meadow grass seeds in summer.

Whatever organic matter you use, it will rot down into the soil much more slowly than well-rotted garden compost. It may also cause nitrogen deficiency in the soil, so you may need to add a little nitrogen fertilizer first.

An alternative, certainly speedier, method is to dig the sheet compost into the top few centimetres. Even better, chop it up with a rotary cultivator, after which earthworms will make short work of it. In this case, extra nitrogen is definitely necessary: so sprinkle a handful of dried blood per square metre/yard.

Animal manure

Animal manures are the very best sources of organic matter for your soil, though more difficult to obtain than compost. Manure can be used on any soil, not only to improve its condition, but also to feed it with nutrients. Use some, like poultry manure, with care because of their high nitrogen content.

There is little point in trying to beg manure from organic farmers because they need it themselves. In the meantime, we have to use what is available. Unfortunately, much bought-in animal manure is likely to be adulterated with hormone fatteners, herbicides, insecticides, and fungicides. However, if it is stacked for at least a year, there is little evidence to show that these chemicals pollute the soil or make their way into harvested vegetables and fruit. Leaving the manure for a year does lose some of the nutrients, but these can always be made up in other ways.

USING MANURE

All manure is used neat unless otherwise specified – but avoid putting it on young shoots because it will scorch them. Make sure that it is well-rotted. General manure levels are given with each description; recommendations for specific plant needs are described in the relevant chapters.

Cow manure

Many beef cattle are kept in the cruellest of battery conditions where they never move about or see the daylight. Their droppings are washed away through the slatted floors and disposed of as slurry. It is still sometimes possible to find a farmer who grazes cattle outside some of the time and brings them into yards in the winter. So cow manure can sometimes be obtained after the cows have been turned out for summer. Compared with other forms of organic material, it is very cheap, and excellent as a soil conditioner and source of nutrients. Store for twelve months before use to leach out impurities and prevent scorching of roots.

Cow manure does not contain a very high percentage of plant nutrients when compared with an inorganic fertilizer, but you will be using a far greater volume of manure than of an inorganic fertilizer, so the mineral concentration is less significant.

Moreover, manure will hold water and maintain that high level of fertility that organic growers continually try to achieve.

Nutrient content	
Nitrogen	*0.6 per cent*
Phosphorus	*0.2–0.3 per cent*
Potassium	*0.3–0.5 per cent*
Trace elements	*Full range*
Coverage 9	*15kg (20–30lb) per sq metre/yard*

Horse manure

An excellent source of organic matter, horse manure is often more readily available near urban areas. Large stables generally have a contract with commercial mushroom growers to remove manure, but there are plenty of smaller stables who are pleased to sell it. Use manure only from stables where straw or peat is used as bedding; wood-shavings may be a source of plant disease.

Fresh horse manure must not be used directly around plants since it can cause scorching. Moreover, if put unrotted on the soil, much of the nutrient value will be lost and the straw mixed in with the manure will take a long time to decompose. If you have access only to small quantities of manure, put them on the compost heap where the high nitrogen content will assist the decomposition.

Large quantities are best stacked, if possible on a concrete base and, since there is a lot of air space in the straw, and thus a danger of it drying out, tread the heap down as you stack it. In winter, cover with polythene to protect from excess rain. Horse manure will be ready for use in two months unless you are concerned that any straw may be contaminated with pesticides, in which case leave it for a year.

Nutrient content	
Nitrogen	*0.6 per cent*
Phosphorus	*0.6 per cent*
Potassium	*0.4 per cent*
Trace elements	*Full range*
Coverage	*9–15kg (20–30lb) per sq metre/yard*

Pig manure

Somewhat colder and wetter than horse or cow manure, pig manure has a very high nutrient content. Treat the same way as horse manure but, since it is heavier, you usually need not tread it down.

Nutrient content	
Nitrogen	*0.6 per cent*
Phosphorus	*0.6 per cent*
Potassium	*0.4 per cent*
Trace elements	*Full range*
Coverage	*9–15kg (20–30lb) per sq metre/yard*

Chicken manure

This is very powerful manure indeed, with an extremely high nitrogen content, and should not be used neat. If you can find a farmer who keeps hens in an old-fashioned deep-litter house, where the birds are housed on straw, take as much manure as you can get and stack it as described for horse manure. If you keep your own hens, use their manure as a source of nitrogen for the compost heap. As a crop finishes, move the hens' wire-netting run onto the space. They will devour all the green matter there, recycling it as fertilizer.

Chicken manure from a battery-hen unit can be used to compost straw. Put a layer of straw in the bottom of a compost container, soak it with water, then cover with a sprinkling of chicken manure. Add more straw, water it, then cover with manure. Continue until the bin is full, ending with a layer of manure. Leave this type of compost to rot for at least a year because the manure will contain all the hormones that are fed to battery chickens.

Nutrient content
Fresh, wet chicken manure
Nitrogen *1.5 per cent*
Phosphorus *1.5 per cent*
Potassium *0.5 per cent*
Trace elements *Full range*
Coverage *3.25–4.5kg (7–10lb) per sq metre/yard*
Dry chicken manure
Nitrogen *4 per cent*
Phosphorus *4 per cent*
Potassium *1.5 per cent*
Trace elements *Full range*
Coverage *20–30g (8–12oz) per sq metre/yard*

Sheep manure

Because sheep are not normally housed inside, you do not get a mixture of straw and muck as with cow, horse and pig manure. However, the manure itself is so high in nutrients that it is well worth going round the fields collecting it. Half a sackful will provide enough liquid manure to last the average-sized garden a whole year. You can easily make liquid manure (*see below*).

Nutrient content
Nitrogen *0.8 per cent*
Phosphorus *0.5 per cent*
Potassium *0.4 per cent*
Trace elements *Full range*
Use as liquid manure (*see below*).

Other manures

Pigeon droppings contain even higher concentrations of nitrogen than chicken manure, so contact local pigeon-racing enthusiasts. The manure can be used in the same way as chicken manure.

Rabbit manure is also ideal, though likely to be available in only small quantities. Use in the same way as chicken manure.

Goat manure is similar to horse manure, but of better quality. If you can find any, or, if you keep a goat yourself, compost the manure and use as horse manure.

Before leaving manures, one suggestion that is not as crazy as it sounds: when the circus leaves town it is often left with a manure problem, so it could well be worth contacting it as soon as it arrives!

HOME-MADE LIQUID MANURE

It is very easy to make your own liquid manure which will be as nutritious as any you can buy. All you need is a large metal or plastic drum that holds water, a hessian sack and some animal manure. Sheep manure is the best because it is particularly high in nutrients, but cow, pig, horse, or goat manure can be used. About half a sackful will give a year's supply. Home-made liquid manure can be used neat, provided the soil has first been watered. This is essential because there are two possible problems with dry soil. The first is that the manure will simply run off the soil, rather than penetrate it. The second is that it will disperse through the soil more slowly, and therefore remain in more concentrated amounts that could cause root damage to delicate plants.

1 *Fill the drum with water. Collect up half a sackful of animal droppings. Tie up the sack with a double loop of string.*

2 *Put a stout stake across the top of the drum and loop the string over it to suspend in the water. Leave for a fortnight, until the water is a rich dark brown colour. Remove the sack and leave the drum covered, far right.*

Alternative soil conditioners

Apart from compost and manure, many other organic materials can be dug into your soil or used as a mulch to help improve drainage or water-holding capacity, depending on the soil type. These materials should be looked upon only as soil conditioners: although some contain plant nutrients, they are not present in large enough quantities.

Spent mushroom compost

Use instead of manure, but leave at least a year to leach out insecticides and get rid of pests. Put directly but sparingly round plants: it can scorch badly. Alkaline (being a mixture of peat and chalk), so never use on acid-loving plants. Ideal on heavy clay soils.

Nutrient content
Nitrogen   *0.71 per cent*
Phosphorus   *0.3 per cent*
Potassium   *0.26 per cent*
Trace elements   *Full range*
Coverage *1–1.5kg (2–3lb)*
per sq metre/yard

Spent hops

Difficult to get, but try asking the local brewery for a few bags. Dig in fresh or use as a mulch. Keep well away from young plants to avoid scorching. Can be bought dry, but then more of a fertilizer high in nitrogen (of which it has 2.5–3.5 per cent).

Nutrient content
Nitrogen   *0.5 per cent*
Phosphorus   *1–2 per cent*
Potassium   *0.5 per cent*
Trace elements   *Full range*
Coverage *1–1.5kg (2–3lb)*
per sq metre/yard

Seaweed

Collect from the beach. Particularly rich in trace elements. Its alginate content binds soil particles together, improving the structure. Most effective if composted for a while, though it can be dug in fresh. With small quantities only, use it as a compost activator.

Nutrient content
Nitrogen   *0.3 per cent*
Phosphorus   *0.1 per cent*
Potassium   *1.0 per cent*
Trace elements   *Full range*
Coverage *1–1.5kg (2–3lb)*
per sq metre/yard

Wool shoddy

An excellent soil-conditioner, although unfortunately only available in wool-producing areas. Nutrient content varies considerably, and trace elements may or may not be present, depending on diet of animals. Dig in wet in autumn.

Nutrient content
Nitrogen   *3–15 per cent*
Phosphorus   *0.5–10 per cent*
Potassium   *0.1–12 per cent*
Trace elements   *–*
Coverage *0.25–0.5kg (½–1lb)*
per sq metre/yard

Composted pine bark

Normally sold part composted. No nutrients, and very expensive. Best used as mulch for organic weed control (*see page 217*): if dug in as a soil conditioner, the bacteria that rot it down take large amounts of nitrogen from the soil, a definite disadvantage.

Nutrient content
Nitrogen   *–*
Phosphorus   *–*
Potassium   *–*
Trace elements   *–*
Coverage *5–7cm (2–3in) layer*
if using it as weed suppressant.

Worm-worked compost

Earthworms can be put to work by the organic gardener in the soil, compost or manure with highly beneficial results.

Worms feed mainly on organic matter and, in the process, break the waste down and eject it as pellets. The resulting crumb structure helps to improve soil drainage and aeration and therefore provides a superior environment for root growth. Pellets also change nutrients in organic matter into a form readily available to roots. At the same time the water-holding capacity of the soil is increased considerably. The worms also produce enzymes which enable bacteria to work more efficiently, so the presence of worms in the compost or manure heap accelerates the decomposing process.

Adding worms to the soil

This is not quite as easy as it sounds. First, you need to build a wormery; secondly, to employ the right variety of worm, commonly known as a "brandling" or "tiger worm", and used in many parts of the world by fishermen as bait. These worms do not live for long in soil, but you can generally find some in compost or manure heaps. If not, buy some from a fishing tackle shop or specialist supplier.

The worm has the convenient habit of working upwards. Once it has digested one layer of organic matter, it will move up to the next layer. Design the wormery to take worm-worked material from the bottom, leaving the worms working on the upper layers.

The most useful task performed by the worms is the breaking down of compost. They work through almost anything from grass cuttings to kitchen scraps, even soaked newspapers used in moderation. Mix it all together, never adding more than a few centimetres in a week. You can, however, put animal manure in the wormery on its own.

Using worm-cast compost

The resulting material is high in nutrients and micro-organisms and should be used sparingly. It is an admirable and easily handled mulch. Sprinkle a little into your seed drill before sowing, especially if the soil is very dry. Rake into the top few centimetres of soil in a seed bed to provide a good crumbly surface and add vital nutrients. Use to make seed compost by mixing one part worm-cast compost and two parts coir, or potting compost with equal parts of coir and worm-cast compost.

MAKING A WORMERY

Make a wooden box at least 60cm (2ft) high and about 60cm (2ft) by 90cm (3ft) – slightly wider and longer than your wheelbarrow. Support the box on legs so that you can wheel the barrow underneath. Staple a piece of strong 5cm (2in) mesh across the bottom of the box. Make two holes in one side of the box and slide two lengths of wood through. Fix pieces of metal or wood on the ends to make the scrapers. Lay newspaper over the mesh floor and soak with water. Cover with a layer of old compost or manure, if you have it, and a handful of

brandling worms. Put a thin layer of uncomposted material over the top.

Place the wormery in a sunny, sheltered part of the garden: worms will not work if the temperature is lower than about 7°C (45°F) – in freezing weather they will die. The optimum temperature is 20–24°C (68–75°F). In cold weather, cover the wormery with a piece of old carpet to keep as much heat in as possible. In very hot weather it may be necessary to water the material to keep it cool. It is better for the compost to be too wet than too dry.

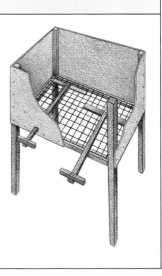

Green manure

This is a crop grown to add organic matter to beds that are empty for a period of time. It is sown specifically for digging into the soil to provide organic matter and plant food. It is also able to make plant nutrients available, so that when it is dug in they are nearer the surface and accessible to the next crop of plants.

In addition, leguminous plants like beans and lupins have the ability to "fix" the nitrogen in the soil through bacteria living in tiny nodules in their roots. When the plant is dug in, the nitrogen becomes available to the next crop.

Green-manure crops provide shade and competition for water and soil nutrients that will discourage all but the most tenacious weeds. The manure crops will not cause a nuisance by re-growing after being dug in.

Sowing crops for green manure

Sow a winter crop in late summer or early autumn and dig it in before planting or sowing vegetables the following spring. Some crops of green manure are fast-growing enough to allow sowing between ordinary crops in the growing season. Choose a plant that will mature in the time available, preferably unlike the crop just harvested or the one you intend to sow. The soil needs to be in good condition. If low in nutrients, apply a fertilizer before sowing.

Working green manure into soil

Do not let the crop flower or become too woody before you dig it in or the rotting process will take nitrogen from the soil. If the crop is fairly large, it may be best to cut it up finely with a mower before cultivating the soil.

Allow a period of wilting before digging the material under. Low-growing crops can simply be cut down with a spade and allowed to wilt for a few days, then dug in, while taller plants can be worked into the surface with a rotary cultivator and then, after a few days, rotavated more deeply. When digging in, do not bury the material deeper than about 15cm (6in).

TYPES OF GREEN-MANURE CROP

NITROGEN-FIXING PLANTS

Medicago sativa
Alfalfa (lucerne)
Deep rooting perennial. Provides much green matter. Needs to grow for whole season, so it needs much space. Sow spring/autumn, dig in autumn or spring.

Vicia faba
Broad or fava bean
Stands the winter almost everywhere, much green matter, beans can be eaten. Sow autumn or early summer. Leave row to seed for later crop.

Trifolium pratense
Red clover
Low-growing, extensive roots, much green matter. Sow spring/late summer, dig in when land needed.

Lupinus augustifolius
Lupin
Tall legume, adds phosphates. Sow spring, dig in summer; sow second crop eight weeks later.

Vicia villosa
Winter tare
Tall, much green matter, grows during winter. Sow late summer, dig in early spring.

PLANTS THAT DO NOT FIX NITROGEN

Fagopyrum esculentum
Buckwheat
Tall, much organic matter, attracts hoverflies. Sow when weather is warm, dig in autumn.

Secale cereale
Rye
Sow perennial variety late summer/autumn, dig in spring. Leave some to seed for next crop.

Phacelia tanacetifolia
Phacelia
Fast-growing; if dug in while soft, will not rob soil of nitrogen. Sow after frosts, dig in after eight weeks.

Sinapsis alba
Mustard
Low, fast-growing, shallow roots, good weed suppressor, but can harbour club root. Good where land cannot be spared long. Sow spring/summer, dig in before flowering.

Lolium multiflorum
Italian ryegrass
Fast-growing and bulky, sow early in summer. Germinates quickly even in cold soil. Dig in "Westerwolds" before it produces seed.

Fertilizers

The use of concentrated fertilizer is probably one of the most controversial areas in organic gardening. Some gardeners claim that additional fertilizer is unnecessary with correct cultivation methods. Others employ methods identical to the chemical grower except that the products used are organic in origin.

Plants need a wide and varied range of nutrients to be present. Chemical growers supply those needs as immediately available fertilizers. The soil simply holds the nutrients, but therefore becomes devoid of life, and lost nutrients must be replaced every year. Organic gardeners feed soil rather than plants. If high soil-fertility levels are maintained by regular additions of organic matter, the plants can simply draw on the material as required. All necessary nutrients will be added if you manage the soil as on pages 64–65. There is no danger of an overdose and a steady supply is ensured by all the various soil organisms.

Why use fertilizers at all?

Quite acceptable crops can be obtained without fertilizers, but feeding is normally required. Firstly, you may not be able to supply your soil with enough compost or manure for the necessary nutrients. Secondly, your soil may be grossly deficient in an essential nutrient. To correct this with bulky organic material can take several years; it is more realistic to add concentrated organic fertilizer as well. Thirdly, many gardeners make higher demands on their soil than even the hardest-working bacteria and fungi could provide.

Applying fertilizers

The application of organic fertilizers need not be quite as precise as for inorganic compounds. Most release nutrients slowly and are unlikely to scorch young plants.

How much fertilizer depends on your soil, the weather, and the plants you wish to grow. Use the "rule-of-thumb" method of simply adding general fertilizer if growth is poor, and specific fertilizers if deficiencies show up on the plants. Also, apply an annual dressing to the ornamental garden, and to the vegetables as in the relevant chapters.

Applying granular fertilizers

Granular fertilizers should always be used to provide general nutrients to supplement compost and manure. Apply in the spring or before planting. Sprinkle over and rake into the soil as recommended, avoiding the foliage. The application is normally given as "handfuls per square metre/yard". For a row, convert the square measurement to a linear one: if the rows are 30cm (12in) apart, spread the amount of fertilizer recommended for a square metre/yard along 3m (9ft) of the row.

Applying liquid fertilizers

Dilute according to the instructions and pour it on, but never on bone dry soil – you may scorch the roots. Water with clear water first and let it drain away before adding the fertilizer.

For plants in pots, simply fill up to the rim of the pot. For those growing in soil, water fertilizer on generously around a fairly wide area, until the soil is saturated. For plants that are regularly fed in this way, bury a flower pot in the soil near the plant and fill that (*see page 160*). The fertilizer penetrates deeper and you know exactly how much you are giving.

The advantage of liquid feeding is that, since plants can only take up nutrients in liquid form, the nutrients are available immediately; granular fertilizer has to be dissolved first. However, liquid fertilizer does not remain effective as long and is leached into the subsoil fairly quickly. It is used to supply short-term nutrients to plants and to correct deficiencies; it is *not* an alternative to solid feeding.

Foliar feeding

Spraying the leaves of the plant is faster-acting but shorter-lived than other methods, so really only of value for rapid remedial action. In warm weather, you could cause leaf scorch.

Lime

Before deciding on any soil-feeding regime, you must first discover whether the soil is acid or alkaline. Acidity or alkalinity of soil is determined by its lime content, measured in units using the pH tests (*see page 62*). pH is measured in units on a scale of 1 to 14. Neutral soil has a pH of 7; anything above that is alkaline and anything below it, acid.

It is easier to make an acid soil more alkaline by adding lime than the other way round. Adding lime to heavy clay soils will help bind the particles together (*see page 64*). However, too much lime can chemically "lock-up" some plant nutrients, particularly trace elements, so that they are unavailable to roots and result in nutrient deficiencies.

Raising soil pH

Make an acid soil more alkaline by adding lime. The effect is slow and, in any case, excessive quantities will scorch the roots. Simply apply small dressings regularly. The lime will gradually be washed through the soil into the drainage system, and the applications of compost and manure will have an acidifying effect.

When to apply lime
Apply lime several weeks before sowing or planting. Ideally, dig manure into the soil in the autumn and apply lime in the spring. Never apply lime to soil that has just been manured because they will combine to form ammonia gas, which releases nitrogen into the air.

How much lime?
The amount of lime will depend to some degree on your soil type. Heavy clay soils need more than light sandy ones. As a rough guide, to increase the pH of a sandy soil by one unit, apply 1kg (2lb) lime every 100 square metres/yards. A sandy loam will need 2kg (4lb), a medium loam about 3kg (6lb), and a heavy clay roughly 4kg (8lb), though the pH level is not so critical that plants will die if it is not exactly right.

Lowering soil pH

Few garden soils are likely to be so limy that they will not grow vegetables at all. In most cases liberal doses of compost and manure will lower the pH sufficiently.

However, a very chalky soil can cause problems because there may be nutrient deficiencies associated with the excess lime (*see page 66*). If so, grow vegetables on the deep-bed system (*see page 132*): raising the growing area slightly prevents alkaline water from draining into it. Then, by treating beds with heavy dressings of organic matter – digging in compost or manure annually and applying regular mulches – you will make the soil more acid. In the ornamental garden similarly raise the border above the level of the lawns or paths, preferably with lots of organic matter (*see page 52*).

TYPES OF LIME

Lime is available in several different forms. More expensive varieties, such as ground limestone or calcified seaweed, will usually last longer.

Slaked lime (*calcium oxide*)
Probably the most readily available, this is sometimes sold as "garden lime"; it lasts longer than builder's lime (hydrated lime).

Hydrated lime
Builder's lime, commonly sold for use with cement, is perfectly satisfactory for garden use but must be replaced at least annually.

Ground limestone
Often known as "Dolomite lime", this is undoubtedly the best type for garden use. More expensive than hydrated or slaked lime, it will last for several years. Ground limestone also contains magnesium.

Calcified seaweed
Containing magnesium and other plant foods, this lasts two to three years, but is expensive.

Organic fertilizers

There is no scientific evidence to suggest that yields will be significantly heavier or that fruit and vegetables will actually taste any better if the plants are fed with organic nutrients instead of inorganic ones.

The reason there is no scientific evidence is that, so far, there has been no research done on the subject. Most organic gardeners will assure any scientist, however, that he or she will certainly notice a difference in the taste of organically grown early potatoes and vegetables compared to the inorganically grown ones found in the shops.

Plants will take their nutrients in the form of the same chemical elements whether they are organically or inorganically derived. Organic gardeners do not suggest that plants actually take up different chemicals if they are grown naturally. What is true is that the chemicals in organic fertilizers will not harm the soil or its many inhabitants; the inorganic ones will. Indeed, organic feeding actually benefits soil micro-organisms as well as plants.

There are several compound fertilizers that are described as "semi-organic" or "organically based". These may be more powerful than the completely inorganic equivalent, but they are *not* the real thing. The main difference is usually in the potash content, which in "semi-organic" fertilizers is sometimes supplemented with potassium sulphate. The following products provide everything necessary.

Blood, fish, and bone meal

A general compound fertilizer, this is the basis of the nutrition plan recommended in this book. Regular dressings should maintain nutrient levels in all soils. The nitrogen contained in this fertilizer, however, is fairly quickly released, so do not spread more than two weeks before sowing or planting for best results.

Nutrient content	
Nitrogen	*3.5 per cent*
Phosphorus	*8 per cent*
Potassium	*0.5 per cent*
Trace elements	–

Fish meal

A useful fertilizer that also contains nitrogen and phosphate (phosphorus). Some fish meal manufacturers also add potash inorganically, hence you may find that it is on sale, labelled as "semi-organic".

Nutrient content	
Nitrogen	*9 per cent*
Phosphorus	*2.5 per cent*
Potassium	–
Trace elements	–

Bone meal

A popular phosphate fertilizer used for activating root growth. Buy bone meal that is clearly marked "steamed" (when it is safe) as in its raw form, it has, in the past, been found to carry the anthrax virus. Many gardeners wear gloves when spreading it as an extra precaution.

Nutrient content	
Nitrogen	*3.5 per cent*
Phosphorus	*22 per cent*
Potassium	–
Trace elements	–

Dried blood

A very fast-acting nitrogen fertilizer. Use it where a rapid nitrogen "tonic" or short-term boost is required, but not later than end summer or it will be washed into the subsoil. If you get frosts in your garden, do not apply later than mid summer to avoid soft foliage growth that would be damaged by frost.

Nutrient content	
Nitrogen	*12–14 per cent*
Phosphorus	*Small amount*
Potassium	–
Trace elements	–

Hoof and horn

One of the best sources of slow-release nitrogen. The ground hooves and horns are heated to 60°C (140°F) before being packed, so it is quite safe to use. It has to be broken down by bacteria before it becomes available to plant roots, so it must be applied a good two weeks before its effect is needed. Thereafter it will remain in the soil for some time.

Use hoof and horn fertilizer for a quick boost to overwintered plants, such as cabbages, in the spring, or for any plants that appear to have stopped growing. Hoof and horn is not, however, as fast-acting as dried blood (*opposite*), which provides a quick boost.

Nutrient content	
Nitrogen	*13 per cent*
Phosphorus	–
Potassium	–
Trace elements	–

Seaweed meal

An alternative to blood, fish, and bone meal, more expensive, but better balanced and with nutrients in a slow-release form. It contains 60 to 70 different chemical elements, including the complete range of trace elements. It can be raked into the soil before sowing or planting, but its cost means that it is generally used as a compost activator and to supply trace elements (*see page 67*). Apply at any time, but preferably on warm soil, so bacteria can break it down, thereby making nutrients available to plants.

Nutrient content	
Nitrogen	*2.8 per cent*
Phosphorus	*0.2 per cent*
Potassium	*2.3 per cent*
Trace elements	*Full range*

Rock potash

An invaluable source of potassium – the element missing from many organic fertilizers. Rock potash is insoluble and has the advantage that it remains in the soil for long periods, thereby enabling plants to take it up as required.

Nutrient content	
Nitrogen	–
Phosphorus	–
Potassium	*10.5 per cent*
Trace elements	–

Wood ash

A useful source of potassium and a small amount of phosphate. Put twigs and prunings, which contain useful quantities of minerals, through a shredder and use the chippings as a mulch, or burn them and compost the ash.

Nutrient content	
Nitrogen	*Varies*
Phosphorus	*according to*
Potassium	*material*
Trace elements	*burned*

Dried animal manures

These contain only small amounts of the major nutrients but are rich in trace elements. Mix them with composted straw or mushroom compost if you cannot get bulky animal manures.

Nutrient content	
Nitrogen	*1 per cent*
Phosphorus	*1 per cent*
Potassium	*1.5 per cent*
Trace elements	*Full range*

Liquid seaweed

Liquid seaweed contains nitrogen, potash, phosphate, all the trace elements and growth hormones, which help increase the efficiency of photosynthesis and also the production of protein. It is invaluable as a means of correcting deficiencies quickly. Many gardeners and retailers also claim that it helps reduce attack by fungus diseases and protect plants from frost.

Nutrient content	
Nitrogen	*1.5 per cent*
Phosphorus	*Min. amount*
Potassium	*2.5 per cent*
Trace elements	*Full range*

Liquid seaweed

Liquid animal manure

Liquid animal manures

These contain all the major nutrients in small quantities, but are rich in trace elements and so very useful for treating trace element deficiencies (*see page 67*).

Nutrient content	
Nitrogen	*1 per cent*
Phosphorus	*1 per cent*
Potassium	*1.5 per cent*
Trace elements	*Full range*

· CHAPTER FOUR ·

SETTING UP AN ORGANIC FRAMEWORK

When planning your organic garden, it is, of course, essential to prepare the soil extremely carefully. You can do this only once, since when you have planted the trees and shrubs, and laid the lawn, there is no opportunity to dig organic matter in at the lower levels. Then you can begin putting your plan for the garden into effect.
Your first considerations should be siting and planting the "permanent" or "semi-permanent" features, such as hedges, trees and lawns. Careful preparation of the ground, and a good choice of material will go a long way to ensuring success.
Next, think about where to site a pond – if you want one – and choosing a suitable size and shape, and plants that will thrive in the conditions you can offer.
Before you start to plan the ornamental, fruit and vegetable gardens, think about whether your garden, on its own, will provide enough space for all you have in mind. One solution, if it will not, is to buy or build a greenhouse. If you really do not have room for this, however, consider enhancing available space by planting material in containers.

Marking out the shape
The strong lines of this garden, with its formally clipped hedge and clearly defined lawn, are softened by loose mounds of planting and the informal shapes of the trees behind.

Hedges

Once the soil is well prepared, you can start laying out the framework of your garden. An early job is to plant a hedge, so it can become established and grow while you build up the rest of the garden. There are two main types of hedging plant: those that can be neatly clipped, creating a formal hedge, and those that are allowed to grow informally in their natural state.

Formal hedges can be clipped back to reduce the amount of space they take up. Though the essence of the small garden is informality, a well-clipped coniferous hedge, such as the Lawson cypress (*Chamaecyparis lawsoniana*) or yew (*Taxus baccata*), or the shiny foliage of laurel (*Prunus laurocerasus*), makes a fine background to the ornamental garden. As a windbreak, the close foliage of a formal hedge is unbeatable.

Informal hedges require a lot more room, as they are allowed to grow in their natural way. They have the advantage of flowers, which are not cut off as they would be with a formally trimmed hedge. Almost any tall-growing flowering shrub can be used: escallonia is particularly attractive. To keep out animals, choose a hedging plant with thorns, as, for example, the barberry (*Berberis* sp.).

Hedging plants can be bought bare-rooted, container-grown, or balled. Each type has advantages and disadvantages. Bare-rooted plants are grown in the open ground and dug up for sale. They are cheaper than container-grown plants; the disadvantage is that they can only be planted in winter when dormant. Generally, shrubs like beech, privet, and hawthorn are only available bare-rooted.

Container-grown plants can be planted at any time of the year provided the ground is not frozen. Ensure that they have actually been grown in the container; if they pull out easily, they will have just been lifted from the nursery and may well fail. Conifers are often sold balled, the soil left around the roots and wrapped in sacking or polythene. Plant them in spring or autumn.

Whichever type of plant you decide to buy, ensure that the roots are well developed and free from disease. Bare-rooted deciduous plants should have closed leaf buds.

1 *Mark out the hedge line with string and dig a trench at least 60cm (2ft) deep and 90cm (3ft) wide along the line. Take out the topsoil to the depth of the spade and break up the subsoil thoroughly.*

2 *Put a 7.5cm (3in) layer of compost or manure in the trench. Cover with a layer of soil, then more organic matter, and refill. Add two handfuls of blood, fish, and bone meal per metre/yard length.*

3 *Allow the soil to settle for a fortnight. Then, if the plants are container-grown, carefully disentangle any roots running around the bottom of the pot. This is especially important when planting conifers.*

4 *Plant each shrub at the recommended planting distance (see chart opposite). Use a planting board (see page 180) as a guide to ensure even planting. Water well after planting.*

Planting and maintaining a hedge

The essence of a good hedge is to provide effective cover quickly and time spent in preparing the soil will give it a good start. There is little point in spacing the shrubs too closely: planted at the distances recommended, they will quickly grow together, forming a close hedge at a much lower cost.

Some hedging shrubs, such as quick thorn (*Crataegus* sp.) and privet (*Ligustrum ovalifolium*), are best cut right back to within 2.5cm (1in) of the ground immediately after planting. This will encourage shoots to grow out from the base, and ensure that the overall growth is bushy.

Hedges tend to get neglected, but should be treated like any other shrub. Feed in early spring with blood, fish, and bone meal. Mulch with well-rotted compost or with manure immediately after feeding.

Trim conifer hedges only when they reach the required height, cutting out the top shoots to limit upward growth. Prune the sides annually in late summer. Faster-growing hedges, like privet, must be sheared regularly throughout the growing season.

The bottom of the hedge tends to catch all kinds of rubbish. This will trap frost-laden air and is an ideal place for pests and diseases to overwinter, so make a habit of cleaning out the bottom of your hedge when you do the annual garden maintenance in autumn.

Hedges can harbour pests and diseases on their leaves which may spread to other garden plants. Native species will attract more pests, but this is offset by a greater attraction to the pest predators. If your garden is planted with a wide variety of species, hedge-dwelling pests should not be a problem as their natural predators will control numbers.

RECOMMENDED PLANTING DISTANCES

Plant	Planting distance					Max height
	30cm (12in)	45cm (18in)	60cm (2ft)	75cm (2ft 6in)	90cm (3ft)	
FORMAL HEDGE SHRUBS						
*Lawson cypress (*Chamaecyparis lawsoniana*)				●←→		12m (40ft)
Leyland cypress (*Cupressocyparis leylandii*)				●←→		14m (45ft)
Western red cedar (*Thuja plicata*)				●←→		16m (50ft)
Yew (*Taxus baccata*)		←●→				4.5m (15ft)
Hawthorn (*Crataegus monogyna*)	●					7.5–9m (25–30ft)
Common laurel (*Prunus laurocerasus*)				●		4.5–6m (15–20ft)
Holly (*Ilex aquifolium*)					●	5.5–6.5m (18–22ft)
Privet (*Ligustrum ovalifolium*)	●					3.5–4.5m (12–15ft)
Beech (*Fagus sylvatica*)		●				12m (40ft)
INFORMAL HEDGE SHRUBS						
Barberry (*Berberis* sp.)			●			2.5–3m (8–10ft)
Escallonia (*Escallonia* sp.)			●			4.5m (15ft)
Griselinia (*Griselinia* sp.)			●			3–7.5m (10–25ft)
Pittosporum (*Pittosporum* sp.)			●			4.5m (15ft)

Lawns

New lawns can be made from seed or turf. Seed is cheaper but turf much quicker to establish. It is at least three months before a seed lawn can be used, whereas a turf lawn can be used within six weeks.

Preparing the site
Preparation is the same for seed or turf. This is the most important phase of the lawn's life in order to get the grass growing so well that it chokes out weeds or moss. This requires a healthy, fertile soil with an active animal community. Chemical gardeners who kill earthworms with chlordane poison then have to spend hours aerating the soil with a fork, because there are no worms to do it for them. Yet it takes only a few minutes to brush wormcasts over the lawn before mowing. Encourage earthworms by digging in at least 10kg (20lb) per square metre/yard of manure, compost or one of the alternatives. A layer of gravel under heavy soil will improve drainage. Do this job thoroughly as it will be your last chance to dig below the level of the grass.

Seed lawns

Choose a seed mixture to suit your needs. Very fine mixtures need regular maintenance for a high quality lawn. Coarse mixtures are hard wearing, ideal for children to play on.

Sowing a seed lawn
Sow in early spring or early autumn, when wet weather can be expected. Raise the lawn level above paving for easy mowing.

Rake a stale seed bed (*see page 185*) roughly level. If soil is light or lacks organic matter, rake in a 5cm (2in) layer of coir; if heavy, use coarse grit. Rake in two handfuls of blood, fish, and bone meal every square metre/yard. Tread the whole area with the weight on your heels.

Rake the soil level and sow seed at 25–35g (1–1½oz) per square metre/yard. Rake in, covering about half with soil; then cover with perforated polythene, removing when the first seed germinates.

Maintaining a new seed lawn
A new lawn is very vulnerable in dry weather. Water well with a fine sprinkler. Mow when grass is about 7cm (3in) high. First, roll with the mower, keeping the blades right off the ground. Raise the blades as high as possible and trim the tips of the new grass. Lower the blades progressively with each cut, until they are about 1cm (½in) above the soil surface. Weeds will be cut out regularly.

Turf lawns

A turf lawn is an "instant lawn", and looks good straight away. Buy turf from a reliable source to ensure that it is of good quality. Turf from uncultivated pasture may contain inferior quality grasses. Always buy turf sown for the purpose, cultivated to be fine and weed-free.

Improving drainage or water retention
Work over the lawn with a hollow-tined fork, removing cores of soil. If your soil is heavy, brush grit into the holes. For light soil, use garden compost.

Maintaining a new turf lawn

Only a little drying out shrinks turves and leaves ugly gaps. So water well with a sprinkler. The grass has rooted when it looks greener and stands up. Mow as a seed lawn.

Maintaining established lawns

You cannot dig in organic matter to an established lawn, but you can keep the grass in good condition. Improve drainage by incorporating grit or organic matter. Give blood, fish, and bone meal once or twice a year, in early spring and in early summer. For the instant greening of a chemical lawn fertilizer, use a liquid manure feed high in nitrogen.

Grass growing well and regularly cut will not have many weeds. Control rosetted weeds like dandelions and daisies by cutting out regularly with a penknife, or by dropping table salt on the growing point. They will die overnight.

To repair a coarse patch of lawn, score the patch in a criss-cross fashion with a penknife and reseed, using an equal-parts mixture of seed, garden compost, and good soil.

Never mow the lawn too close as this encourages bare patches which will be colonized by moss and weeds. Always leave the grass 1cm (½in) long and remove cuttings to prevent attack by fungus diseases.

Sowing a wild-flower meadow

For best results, choose a patch of land with low fertility if possible. Prepare the ground and sow as for a lawn, using a mixture of grasses and flowers that are suitable for your soil type (*see page 115*).

Cut the meadow only twice a year, once in early spring as growth starts, and after the flowers have set seed in late summer. Use the seed for next year's meadow.

LAYING A TURF LAWN

1 *Rake the prepared soil flat. Always work from boards. You should never walk on turves you have just laid, or on prepared soil. Place a board along the longest straight edge and lay first row of turf. Lay rows of turf all around the edge of the lawn area. With the back of a rake tap the strips close to the soil.*

2 *Lay a board – scaffolding boards are ideal, if you can get them – on the first row of turf. Standing on the board, lay a second row of turf parallel to the first and pull it into the first with the back of the rake. There is no need to bond the turves together. Continue in this way until you reach the edging turf.*

3 *At the end of a row, butt the last turf up to the edging turf by laying it on top and cutting off the excess with a penknife. When the whole lawn is down, you can shape the edges with an edging knife. Water with a sprinkler. Keep the turves well watered to prevent shrinkage. Once the lawn is established, water less often.*

Trees

Like hedges and lawns, the sooner you plant the trees in your garden, the better. All trees take at least a few, and often many, years to reach their full height and spread and to achieve the effect you planned for them.

The first consideration should be the ultimate height and spread of the tree. Some of the most popular garden trees, such as Leyland cypress (*Cypressocuparis leylandii*), can grow up to 15m (50ft) tall, so are not an option in a small garden, but there are many suitable small trees, like the Kilmarnock willow (*Salix caprea* "Pendula"). Ask your local nursery if you are unsure. (*See also pages 92–95.*)

Do not plant vigorous trees less than about 12m (40ft) from the house. Roots of trees like willows (*Salix* sp.) and poplars (*Populus* sp.) will seek out cracked drains, quickly blocking them. Worse still, they can cause soil shrinkage, cracking, and subsidence, particularly dangerous on clay soils.

Trees can be bought container-grown or bare-rooted and should come from a reputable nursery. Container-grown trees are smaller and more expensive than bare-rooted ones, but can be planted at any time. Bare-rooted trees can only be planted when dormant.

Planting trees

Never plant in freezing or waterlogged conditions. If the trees arrive when the ground is frozen, leave them unpacked, in a frost-free building, until better weather, or "heeled-in" temporarily in a slit trench (*see page 110*).

Never plant in uncultivated soil. A hole in hard ground acts as a sump for all the surrounding water; in winter, the tree's roots will then be cold and deprived of air. So prepare the soil properly. Even if planting trees in an area of grass, dig as big a hole as you can – at least 90cm (3ft) square. Break up the subsoil to improve drainage and work in plenty of organic matter. Do not use spent mushroom compost as it contains lime and most trees (and shrubs) prefer a slightly acid soil. Add two handfuls of blood, fish, and bone meal fertilizer.

PLANTING CONTAINER-GROWN TREES

1 *Dig a hole large enough for the root ball. Water the tree while in the container. Place the tree in the hole, leaving the roots undisturbed. Check the hole is deep enough by laying a spade across the top.*

2 *Cover root ball with soil and firm down. Water retention round the root ball is vital. Use some of the dug-out soil to make a small retaining wall around the tree, so that the soil around the roots can be really soaked later.*

3 *Hammer two 5×5cm (2×2in) stakes 45cm (1ft 6in) into the ground and one-third of the way up the trunk. Tie trunk to a crossbar nailed between the stakes. Four to six weeks later. Mulch with compost or manure.*

Keep roots of bare-rooted trees covered with sacking until the planting area is ready. Water container-grown trees in the container. Put the tree in the hole at the level of the old soil mark on the stem. For container-grown trees, refill the hole, firm down, and stake a bare-rooted tree as shown below. Mulch with compost or manure – bare-rooted trees immediately after planting, container-grown ones four to six weeks later.

All young trees need staking when first planted. The type of stake is different for bare-rooted and container-grown trees (*see below*). Movement of the trunk in the wind thickens the base and improves the root system, so the stake should anchor the base and the roots and leave the rest of the stem free to move. Secure the tree with a special tree tie or strip of plastic, never wire or nylon twine which will cut through the trunk and possibly cause irreparable damage as the tree grows.

Watering, especially in dry weather, is the most important aspect of planting container-grown trees; lack of water is the main cause of failure. The roots will not spread out into the soil for several weeks.

Maintaining trees

Trees growing in ornamental borders will normally be fed every year when the other plants receive fertilizer. In addition to two handfuls of blood, fish, and bone meal every spring, spread a layer of compost or manure around the roots every autumn (avoid spent mushroom compost because of its lime).

If trees are growing in grass, they should be fed in the same way, but just a little earlier – say mid winter – so that the fertilizer is washed down into the soil before the grass starts growing and using up nutrients.

Ornamental trees need little pruning during the first years after planting; it is generally only a case of removing branches that are dead, diseased, crossing, or overcrowding during the dormant season. Take out straight away any branches growing towards the centre of the tree, or beginning to grow across other branches. This avoids removing very large branches later, spoiling the shape of the tree.

Check tree ties at least every autumn. They may be too loose to hold the tree in winter storms or so tight that they restrict further growth. Replace as necessary.

PLANTING BARE-ROOTED TREES

1 *Drive a stake 45cm (18in) into the soil. The stake should be at least twice as thick as the stem and one-third of the way up the tree's trunk. Be sure to hammer the stake well down into the ground so that it is really firm.*

2 *Sprinkle two handfuls of bone meal fertilizer over the soil you have dug. Place the tree in the hole and put a little fine soil over the roots. Gently jerk the stem up and down a few times to settle the soil around the roots.*

3 *Refill half the hole and tread down the soil. Complete filling and re-tread. Tie the stem to the stake with a tree tie or length of thick plastic, tied in a figure-of-eight. Mulch with compost or manure immediately.*

Choosing deciduous trees

These are trees that shed their leaves before the cold or dry season, usually after they have turned orange, red, or yellow. New leaves appear in spring. There are many different shapes and sizes; those shown here are just a tiny selection. When choosing, check the height and spread and remember that most trees cast shade, affecting nearby plants.

Gleditsia triacanthos
Honey locust
The leaflets are bright yellow in spring and autumn, and light green in summer. The branches bear spines. Green flowers are produced in spring, and brown seed pods in autumn. Height 10m (30ft), spread 4.5m (15ft).

Prunus avium "Plena"
Wild cherry
Grown for its plentiful, double, white flowers which open at the same time as the leaves and are followed in autumn by small, shiny, plum-coloured fruits. The leaves turn red in autumn. Height 12m (40ft), spread 10m (30ft).

Acer griseum
Paperbark maple
Grow this tree for its beautiful autumn colouring: orange-red leaves and brown outer bark peeling away constantly to reveal attractive new, orange bark beneath. Height 6m (20ft), spread 2.5m (8ft).

Pyrus salicifolia "Pendula"
Willow-leaved pear
This ornamental pear tree has, as its name suggests, grey-green, willow-like leaves covered in fine, downy hairs. Ideal for smaller gardens. Height 4.5m (15ft), spread 2.5m (8ft).

Acer platanoides
Norway maple
Large, handsome trees grown for their leaves, which turn yellow, and sometimes red, in autumn. The several attractive forms have various foliage colours including white-and-green variegation. Height 10m (30ft), spread 6m (20ft).

Prunus subhirtella "Autumnalis"
Autumn cherry
An ornamental cherry tree producing no fruit but white, semi-double flowers intermittently from late autumn to spring. Most autumns, the leaves turn an attractive red. Height and spread 10m (30ft).

Betula platyphylla
Birch
Birches are grown for their beautiful bark which, on some species, constantly peels to reveal the new, lighter bark beneath. The leaves turn yellow in autumn and the trees bear catkins in spring. Height 10m (30ft), spread 4.5–6m (15–20ft).

Sorbus "Joseph Rock"
Mountain ash
A small tree with glossy green leaves turning deep, fiery red in autumn. In spring, clusters of cream-coloured flowers appear, developing by early autumn into amber-yellow fruits. Height 5.5m (18ft), spread 2.5m (8ft).

Salix caprea
Sallow
The leaves have dark-green upper surfaces with grey undersides. Male plants bear yellow catkins in spring, female plants silver. Height 3m (10ft), spread 8m (25ft).

Laburnum vossii
Laburnum
A small tree suitable for most soils and situations. The three-lobed leaves are deep green, and the tree is covered with a profusion of bright-yellow flowers in late spring and early summer. All parts are poisonous. Height 5.5m (18ft), spread 4m (12ft).

Eucalyptus gunnii
Gum tree
This tree is, in fact, an evergreen, constantly shedding and replacing a few leaves at a time. Like all eucalyptus, it should be planted in a sheltered position. The young leaves are round. Height 15m (50ft), spread 6m (20ft).

Choosing coniferous trees

Conifers are available in a wide variety of colours, shapes, and sizes – from dwarf forms for the rock garden or tubs, to large specimen and hedging varieties: a small selection is illustrated here. Always try to buy conifers in containers as they do not move well when bare-rooted, unless they are lifted with a sizeable root ball.

Cedrus deodara
Deodar
Best grown as a specimen tree in a large lawn. When young, the needles are light green, darkening with age. The branches droop as the tree matures, giving it a weeping habit. Height 12m (40ft), spread 3m (10ft).

Taxus baccata
Common yew
The narrow, waxy leaves are dark green. The red berries are the only non-poisonous part of the tree. Height and spread 4.5m (15ft).

Juniperus virgineana
"Skyrocket"
Pencil cedar
One of the narrowest junipers, an ideal specimen for adding interest to a low planting. It has mid-green leaves loosely arranged on the shoots. Height 4.5m (15ft), spread 30cm (1ft).

Tsuga canadensis
Eastern hemlock
The branches of this graceful conifer grow to rest on the ground. Shoots are covered with small, dark-green needles and oval-shaped cones. Best as a free-standing specimen tree. Height 10m (30ft), spread 6m (20ft).

Pinus mugo
Mountain pine
The long narrow needles of this pine are arranged in pairs around the stems. The brown, oval cones are about 5cm (2in) long. Its prostrate habit and slow growth rate makes it an ideal subject for the rock garden. Height and spread 4.5m (15ft).

Ginkgo biloba
Maidenhair tree
An unusual deciduous conifer. Leaves are dark green in summer, transparent yellow in autumn. Height 10m (30ft), spread 3m (10ft).

Picea pungens
"Koster"
Colorado spruce
A very popular blue spruce, used as a specimen tree and ideal on a lawn. The needles are arranged spirally. The brown cones are 10cm (4in) long. Height 8m (25ft), spread 3m (10ft).

Chamaecyparis obtusa
"Nana Gracilis"
Hinoki cypress
This conical bush is very slow-growing, and is popular in the rock garden, taking many years to outgrow its space. Height 3m (10ft), spread 2m (6ft).

Thuja plicata
Western red cedar
Fastest-growing of the thujas, a tall, conical tree when fully mature. The flattened sprays of scale-like leaves have a distinctive fruity scent. The cultivar "Atrovirens" makes an excellent hedge. Height 16.5m (55ft), spread 6m (20ft).

Cupressocyparis leylandii
Leyland cypress
One of the fastest-growing conifers available and can grow very tall. It makes an excellent dense hedge growing, in good soil, 60–90cm (2–3ft) a year. Height 15m (50ft), spread 4.5m (15ft).

Chamaecyparis lawsoniana "Allumii"
Lawson cypress
As the tree ages, it widens at the base, making an attractive "candle-flame" shape. Height 6m (20ft), spread 1.5m (5ft).

Ponds

The simplest way of making a pond is to buy a ready-made fibreglass shell and dig a hole for it. Alternatively, dig a hole the size you want and line it with polythene (perishable), or a butyl-rubber liner (slightly more expensive, but much more durable). Dig the hole with a slope on one side, and cut out a shelf at the edge for the marginal plants. This should be 7–12cm (3–5in) deep and wide enough to allow sufficient space for a plant container. Include an area not more than 5cm (2in) deep, where smaller fish can escape from predatory adults. The deep water area should be at least 45cm (18in) deep.

CONSTRUCTING AND PLANTING A POND

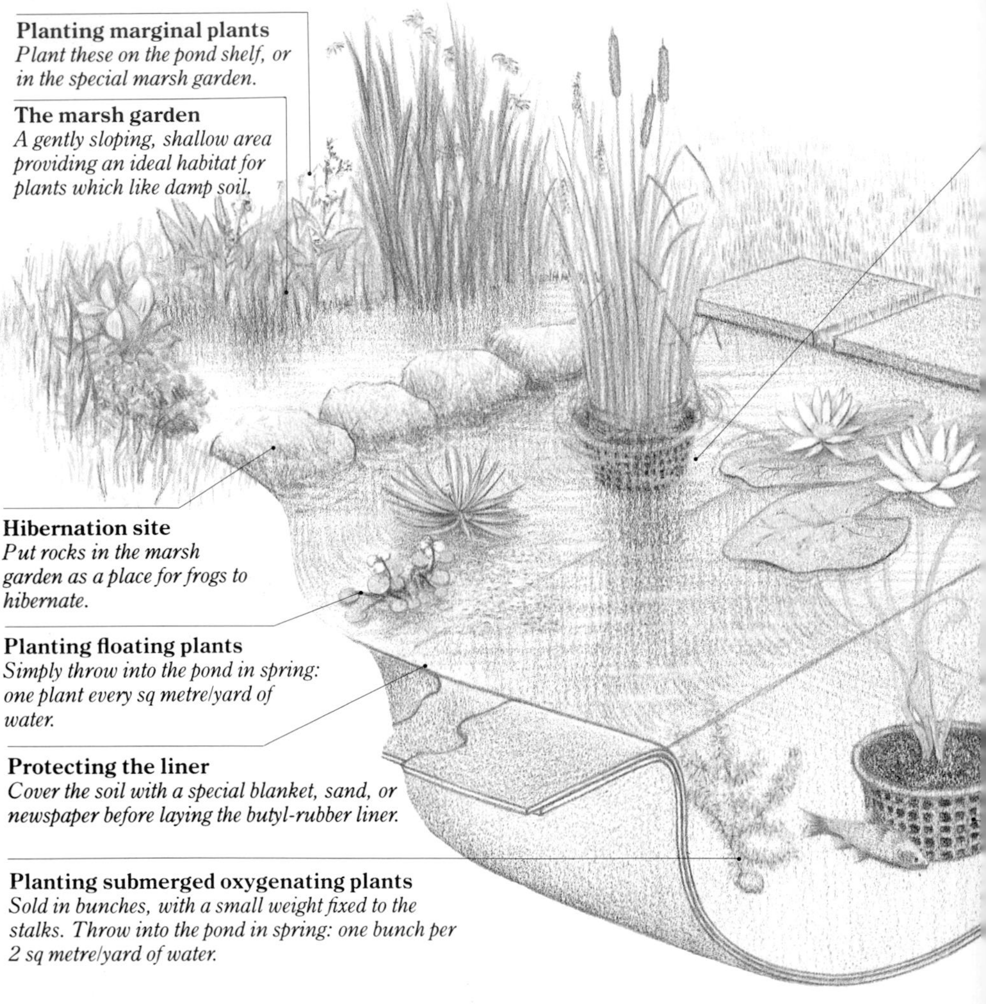

Planting marginal plants
Plant these on the pond shelf, or in the special marsh garden.

The marsh garden
A gently sloping, shallow area providing an ideal habitat for plants which like damp soil.

Hibernation site
Put rocks in the marsh garden as a place for frogs to hibernate.

Planting floating plants
Simply throw into the pond in spring: one plant every sq metre/yard of water.

Protecting the liner
Cover the soil with a special blanket, sand, or newspaper before laying the butyl-rubber liner.

Planting submerged oxygenating plants
Sold in bunches, with a small weight fixed to the stalks. Throw into the pond in spring: one bunch per 2 sq metre/yard of water.

Line the hole with a thick layer of soft material to protect the liner from sharp stones. For a waterfall or fountain, run the electricity cable underground before laying paving or lawns.

Soon after filling, algae growth may turn the water pea-green. If you empty out the water and refill, the algae gain another meal of mineral salts; leave the water in the pond, the mineral supply will soon diminish, the algae will die, and the water clear.

The marginal shelf
A planting area for plants which like to grow in shallow water. Make it very shallow in places as a refuge for fish fry and frog spawn (you may have to guide the latter there yourself).

Edging the pond
Paving stones make planting and maintenance of the pond easy. They also help to secure the butyl-rubber liner.

Planting deep-water aquatics
Plant during late spring and summer. Cut off all the old leaves and lower the container to the bottom of the pond. New leaves will soon grow up to the surface.

Planting in pots
Use heavy soil or rotted turf, but not soil rich in organic matter: it will putrefy as it rots down. A thin layer of gravel on top prevents the soil from floating to the surface and stops inquisitive fish disturbing it. Put plants into the pond in plastic buckets of soil.

Aquatic plants
Aquatic plants can be divided into four groups – deep-water aquatic plants, floating plants, submerged oxygenating plants, and marginal plants. Try to include plants from each group.

Deep-water aquatics are plants that root at the bottom of the pond but whose leaves float on the surface. This group includes the water lilies (*Nymphaea* sp.), not only very decorative but also useful in reducing the growth of algae: the more leaf cover on the surface of the water, the better. Attractive deep-water aquatics include the white water lily (*Nymphaea alba*) and water crowfoot (*Ranunculus aquatilis*).

Floating plants also reduce the amount of sunlight that reaches the surface and include the water hyacinth (*Eichornia crassipes*) and the water chestnut (*Trapa natans*).

Submerged oxygenating plants aerate the water, and are essential to the health of the pond. They include spiked water milfoil (*Myriophyllum spicatum*), Canadian pondweed (*Elodea canadensis*), and curly pondweed (*Potamogeton crispus*).

Marginal plants grow in the shallowest water and the boggy soil around the edges. Some must be planted in water a few centimetres deep, like the sweet-scented rush (*Acorus calamus*); others, like the primulas, in marshy soil.

Maintaining the pond
Thin plants by hand and add compost, returning any animals to the pond. Regular removal of blanket weed prevents infestation of this slimy, ugly, green weed. Keep leaves out of the pond or they will sour the water as they rot. Try to avoid building the pond near deciduous trees, or cover it with netting in autumn, to prevent leaves from falling in.

The pond in cross-section

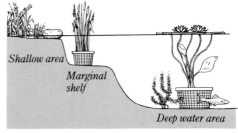

Shallow area

Marginal shelf

Deep water area

Greenhouses

A greenhouse is an asset in any organic garden as it enables you to sow and harvest crops months earlier than otherwise possible in temperate or cold areas. Many frost-tender plants can be "overwintered". You can raise a great many plants from seed, and cultivate tender plants normally grown outside only in sub-tropical or tropical conditions.

Greenhouses come in an assortment of shapes (*see page 57*), sizes, and materials. Appearance is important, but practicality more so. Check advantages and disadvantages of each greenhouse carefully before buying.

Size

Even a tiny greenhouse can accommodate a large quantity of plants, especially if you add a cold frame (*see page 57*), or cloches (*see page 131*). Buy the biggest you can afford, or one designed to take additional sections, because a greenhouse of any size will always be full! Ensure that the height to the eaves is sufficient for comfortable working, and the design will not restrict the range of plants to be grown.

Materials

Greenhouse frames are usually aluminium or wood. Aluminium houses let in more light because the glazing bars are thinner. Wooden houses are perhaps slightly cheaper to heat, because the wood itself is warmer; they certainly look more attractive, but must be painted regularly to protect against decay.

Glass is most commonly used for walls and roof, but greenhouses can be made from sheet polythene stretched over metal hoops or a frame (much cheaper, although the polythene has to be replaced every two years).

Ventilation

It is vital to control temperature accurately by regulating the passage of air through vents in the roof or sides of the greenhouse. Polythene greenhouses have open-mesh panels or a mesh "skirt" to reduce condensation; these make it impossible to control temperature, so you can grow only crops that need no extra heating.

Heating

Even an unheated greenhouse will produce yields considerably earlier than outside, but providing just enough heat to keep frost at bay allows half-hardy perennials to be overwintered, and tender plants planted much earlier than otherwise possible.

Controlling temperature

The vital statistics are the minimum temperature at night and the maximum during the day: ideally, these should vary by not more than 10°C (18°F). Use a maximum/minimum thermometer to record the extremes and try, by careful ventilation and heating adjustment, to even out differences as much as possible.

Reducing heating costs

Locate the house in a bright place to benefit from free solar heat, and provide shelter from strong winds. Insulate to prevent heat loss, and heat the minimum area needed.

Connection to the mains is initially expensive but more economical in the long run than using portable heaters. Most modern heaters are thermostatically controlled, to keep a constant temperature. Fuels can be gas, oil and paraffin, electricity or solid.

Using polythene inside the greenhouse

Divide the greenhouse with a polythene curtain so you need only heat a small area. Line roof and sides with polythene sheeting to keep in the heat. A "thermal" screen can be drawn at night to retain the heat and pulled back to admit light during the day.

Using a propagator

A propagator restricts the area to which heat has to be supplied for seed germination. You can buy them, or easily make your own. Cover a shallow wooden box with a perspex lid, line with polythene and fill with polystyrene granules. Lay an electric heating cable in a serpentine fashion among the granules and connect it to the mains supply through a hole in the box. Or, morning and evening, fill with boiling water a small tin standing in a larger one.

THE GREENHOUSE

Shading
Special compounds can be painted on to the outside of the glass in summer (cheaper than blinds).

Ventilation
Panels in the roof and walls control greenhouse temperatures.

Insulation
Sheets of bubble polythene can help prevent heat loss.

Capillary mat
Plants can be watered automatically using absorbent matting.

Blinds
These protect against sun scorch in hot weather. Best on the outside; remove each winter and store indoors.

Measuring temperature
A maximum/minimum thermometer records the highest and lowest temperatures reached during a specific period.

A permanent water supply
Keep a tank of water inside the greenhouse, under the staging if space is limited. Refill after watering each day, so that water is always at greenhouse temperature.

Propagator
Seeds can be germinated in a specially heated container.

Watering can
Use a rose attachment when watering delicate seedlings.

Raising seedlings
After germination, seedlings are grown in trays and pots on the greenhouse staging.

Greenhouse borders
Many crops, such as lettuce, can be grown to maturity in the greenhouse borders.

Hot bed
Fresh straw horse manure is used as an organic means of heating the soil around plants growing in the borders.

Storage space
The space below the staging is used to store greenhouse equipment.

Staging
Many greenhouse plants are cultivated on benches that raise the plants up nearer to the light, ensuring healthy growth.

Heating
A variety of permanent and portable systems are available.

Potting bench
Use a portable bench for messy jobs such as repotting.

Growing bags
A range of plants, such as tomatoes, can be grown in self-contained beds.

MAKING A HOT BED

1 *A hot bed is a cheap alternative to cable heating. Break up the border soil and stack a 23cm (9in) layer of fresh manure. Cover this with a 5cm (2in) layer of soil and a dusting of lime.*

2 *Add two more layers of manure, with a second layer of soil and lime between them. This layer neutralizes the acid manure and provides a suitable medium for young plants.*

3 *Make a series of holes, and fill them with soil-based compost. Cover the bed with a layer of soil. Transplant young plants into the holes. The manure warms the roots, encouraging growth.*

Heating the soil

Heating plant roots reduces the need to heat the air. Install an electric soil-heating cable, or make a hot bed. A hot bed heats the roots of plants by surrounding them with a horse manure mixture, and it also gets them off to a good start. It is a cheap, organic alternative to undersoil cable heating.

Maintaining your greenhouse

After eight weeks, give plants either home-made liquid manure, proprietary liquid seaweed, or animal-manure feed. Feed subsequently according to the crop – see separate entries on pages 75–79. Too much fertilizer is worse than too little.

Most greenhouse plants do better if given a thorough soaking and then left for a while. In early spring, tap water is probably much too cold for tender young seedlings. Leave a can of water overnight in the greenhouse to warm to greenhouse temperature, or keep a water tank inside the greenhouse.

A moist, humid atmosphere is achieved by wetting the paths, the staging, and often the plants themselves early in the morning, and sometimes in the evening, a process known as "damping down". By keeping the greenhouse spotlessly clean, you will discourage pests and diseases that might otherwise thrive in the warm, humid environment. Remove any plant debris in which pests and diseases may hide and, at the end of the season, wash the house thoroughly with warm, soapy water, brushing it into every corner. Wash pots or seed trays thoroughly in boiling water to kill any lurking disease spores or insect eggs.

Soil-borne pests and diseases may build up when you grow the same crop, such as tomatoes, year on year in the same border. One solution is to grow a different crop in the borders and plant the tomatoes in growing bags on the other side of the greenhouse.

Potting composts

Trial and error is the only way to evaluate bought organic composts. Once you have found one that suits your plants, it is best to stick to it. Or you can make your own.

Making potting composts

To make soil-less potting compost, add 30g (1oz) Dolomite lime to every 9-litre (2-gallon) bucket of coir. Moisten before sowing with a half-strength solution of liquid seaweed, and the same at seedling stage, full strength after potting up. Or mix one part worm-worked compost with two parts coir, adding 30g (1oz) lime to every bucketful. Soil-based composts are best for plants grown in containers outside, but the loam must be fibrous and crumbly, from freshly cultivated grassland or stacked turf. You can make your own.

For sowing, mix two parts loam with two parts coir and one part coarse grit, adding 60g (2oz) of bone meal and 30g (1oz) garden lime to every bucket. For potting, use seven parts loam to three parts coir and two of coarse grit, adding 30g (1oz) garden lime and 150g (5oz) of blood, fish, and bone meal.

To make loam, grass in the space around rows of raspberries, soft-fruit bushes, or apple trees. Use as a path for at least a year. Strip off the grass with a 2.5cm (1in) layer of soil and stack it, grass side down, for a year. Replace the soil with the once-used compost after greenhouse crops have finished, and resow immediately with grass. The process takes three years in all, so you need three plots for a succession.

As a safeguard against pests and diseases, you may sterilize your loam with an electric sterilizer or by heating in an ordinary oven to 100°C (212°F) for 15 minutes.

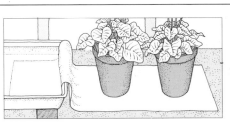

Home-made growing bags
A cheap alternative to buying commercially prepared growing bags is to fill old compost bags with worm-worked compost or animal manure. Tape up the end of the bag and cut holes in the top.

AUTOMATIC WATERING

An automatic watering system will save you much time. There are many types of automatic watering systems for greenhouses. The capillary matting and the trickle irrigation system are efficient as well as simple.

Watering with capillary matting (above)
Stand potted plants on the mat and place one end in a container of water. The water is gradually drawn out to moisten the whole mat and the plants take it up as required. Replenish the water in the container as necessary.

Watering with a trickle irrigation system (left)
The main hose leading from the overhead tank rests flat on the staging. From it, lengths of narrow-gauge tubing spaced at regular intervals are fixed into each pot with staples. The system can also be used to water plants grown in border soil.

Containers

Containers are particularly useful in small organic gardens because they can increase your growing area. They are attractive too – for example, place a hanging basket against a wall or an old stone trough filled with alpines over an unsightly drain cover.

Good garden centres stock a wide range of containers – from simple wire baskets to plastic and "Greek" urns, wooden barrels and concrete vases. Any container, bought or home-made, will do, as long as it has adequate drainage holes and is raised slightly off the ground on bricks. Terracotta clay pots blend very well with organic cottage gardens, but are not frostproof. Most softwoods need treating with preservative. Window boxes are available in wood and plastic, or you can make your own. Secure the box safely to windowsill or wall, as it is very heavy when filled with soil.

Hanging baskets must be watered and fed particularly regularly. To create a complete ball of flowers, you need a deep basket planted on top and through the sides – shallow baskets will not hold enough plants. You can buy baskets of coated wire or plastic mesh, or make your own from wood. Fix basket brackets firmly.

Filling containers with compost

Never use a soil-less compost – it dries out very quickly. Fill with a soil-based compost (*see page 101*). For acid-loving plants, make up the same compost but with acid soil and no lime, or, instead of acid soil, two-thirds soil and coir or soil and sharp sand, one-third sharp sand, and fertilizer.

Cover the holes with crocks (broken pots), laid concave-side down, then a little gravel and a piece of turf or old sacking. In a tub at least 30cm (12in) deep, add a layer of compost or manure before the potting compost. Leave at least 3.5cm (1in) at the top for watering.

Planting containers

Fill containers with permanent plants, or eye-catching seasonal displays, or a combination – say, small shrubs surrounded by annuals and biennials for winter and summer colour. Most spring bulbs, except tall ones, are suitable.

Traditional urn
This is made from reconstituted, frost proof stone and filled with bedding plants. Position it before filling with soil: it will be very heavy afterwards.

Half-barrels
Most wooden half-barrels are made of oak, which does not need treating, although the metal hoops will need painting to prevent rust. Avoid buying barrels that have contained poisonous substances.

In temperate regions, plant seasonal subjects in spring for late spring and summer display, once all danger of frost has passed. In early autumn, remove the summer display, take out the top 23cm (9in) compost and mix in some well-rotted garden compost or manure. Refill and plant with your early spring show.

Dwarf conifers make good tub plants. Small shrubs also last a long time in containers, the root constraint forcing them into regular and prolific flowering; water acid-lovers like camellias with rain water. Most low-growing perennials are suitable. Ivies (*Hedera* sp.) trail beautifully over the sides and break up any hard lines. Ferns, grasses, and other foliage plants like plantain lilies (*Hosta* sp.) make an attractive change. Low-growing alpines are interesting in shallow containers with good drainage, and a compost of equal parts of loam, coarse grit and garden compost or ground bark, plus 30g (1oz) lime per bucketful.

Herbs are an obvious choice for containers, especially if sited close to the kitchen door. Also for limited spaces, fruit trees on dwarfing rootstocks are ideal. Gooseberries and redcurrants make splendid tub plants, and strawberries do quite well in strawberry pots (*see page 172*). Most shorter-growing vegetables will grow in containers, mixed with a few flowers, not just to improve their looks, but to attract useful insects.

Maintaining container plants

Feed weekly with liquid seaweed or animal manure during the growing season. Water regularly – daily in the summer, in the winter only when the weather is very dry. Dead-head as blooms die back in order to extend the flowering season.

Hanging baskets

It is quite possible to have spring, summer, and winter colour in hanging baskets with plants similar to those used in tubs. A few bulbs such as crocus liven up a winter or early spring hanging basket. Vegetables are not recommended, but baskets make ideal, if fairly temporary, quarters for low-growing herbs.

In autumn when flowers start to look tired, reline the basket, fill with fresh soil, and replant for winter.

Seasonal trailing baskets
The colourful summer basket, left, is planted with geraniums and other pendulous plants. The more subdued but equally decorative autumn basket, right, holds winter heathers, pansies, and ivies.

Maintaining hanging baskets

Feed spring and summer baskets once a week with liquid seaweed or animal-manure fertilizer. Winter baskets need no feeding.

Water spring and summer baskets once or even twice a day. Unless weather is very dry, winter baskets may not need watering.

PLANTING HANGING BASKETS

Hanging baskets are simple and inexpensive to construct yourself. They should always be lined – preferably with polythene and moss – before you start to fill with plants.

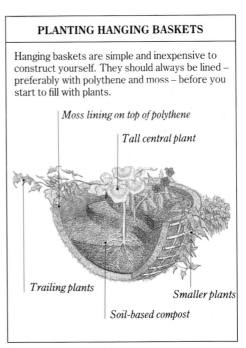

Moss lining on top of polythene

Tall central plant

Trailing plants

Smaller plants

Soil-based compost

CHAPTER FIVE

CREATING ORNAMENTAL BORDERS

After completing the basic construction of your garden layout, it is time for the fascinating task of planning the detailed planting. Consider your type of soil, the aspects of your garden, and its amount of sun – all these govern the type of ornamental plants you can grow. Pages 12–27 and 108–9 give you some ideas. With chalky or alkaline soil, avoid acid-loving plants like azaleas, unless you grow them in raised beds (*see page 120*) with special acid soil. To create a real balance you need flowers and fruits for as long as possible to attract wildlife, so you may have no place for "sophisticated" planting of, perhaps, single-colour borders or areas that peak at one particular time.

When you have a general idea of your planting plan, to avoid costly mistakes put it down on paper, not necessarily to follow religiously but to give you a starting point. There is no need to plan all the borders at once – collect the plants slowly, learning about them from visits to nurseries, garden centres, and other gardens.

Mixed planting scheme

Flowers and vegetables in the same border can look very attractive, especially backed by profuse climbers scrambling over a wall or fence. A small apple tree or other fruit tree also adds height.

Planning and maintaining a colourful border

When you are planting a new border, it is best to start with the shrubs. You can slot in herbaceous plants later: they can easily be dug up if you feel you have made a mistake – they may actually benefit from being moved occasionally. Shrubs, on the other hand, need to establish themselves and will be set back every time they are lifted. Shrubs such as roses can also be included. They give an opportunity for companion planting to keep pests at bay (*see page 195*).

Filling between shrubs
Intermingle perennials with shrubs to fill up the spaces. Perennials grow quite fast, so do not allow them to overcrowd and inhibit the shrubs.

For instant colour, particularly in the first few years, annuals and biennials are ideal for the spaces around young shrubs. Do not plant them too close or they will compete for light: if they encroach, trim them back. Even when borders are mature, leave some space for annuals and biennials to brighten the garden.

Also useful in the mixed borders are bulbs, including tubers, corms, and rhizomes. By choosing species carefully it is possible to have bulbs in flower all the year round. Spring-flowering bulbs planted amongst shrubs and herbaceous plants will make a show when other plants are still dormant. When the herbaceous plants or shrubs are in full leaf, the messy, post-flowering, bulb foliage is hidden from view. In a fairly young mixed border, plant the bulbs quite near the shrubs. As you should never dig near the roots of shrubs for fear of damage, the bulbs will not be dug up accidentally when planting other subjects.

Giving a border height
Climbing plants can be included in informal borders to add height – especially in front of a wall or hedge. They can also be used to cover any ugly features, such as a garage or central-heating oil tank. And some plants, like the less vigorous cultivars of the clematis, are invaluable scrambling over shrubs and in trees. Choose a variety that flowers when the tree or shrub does not. (*See also pages 116–17.*)

General maintenance
Maintain a regular supply of nutrients by mulching annually with well-rotted compost or manure. Dress with blood, fish, and bone meal in early spring. Every three years, dress with seaweed meal to ensure that the trace elements are in plentiful supply.

Give plenty of water in dry weather, and ensure border plants, particularly container-grown shrubs, do not dry out after planting.

Ornamental plants are susceptible to many of the general pests and diseases on pages 200–1. Constant vigilance and companion planting will keep problems to a minimum.

Covering any exposed soil with bark chippings or ground-covering plants will suppress weed growth, greatly reducing the workload. Bark chippings look good but are quite expensive and need to be replaced every few years. Low-growing plants quickly cover the soil and suppress weeds. Plant several different species to make a tapestry of colours and leaf textures under and around the taller plants. In the early stages, before dense cover is established, a great deal of hand weeding will be necessary. For other forms of weed control, *see pages 216–17.*

Mulching with bark
A covering of pine bark chippings controls weeds by blocking the light. Here the heathers will eventually take over by growing together as ground cover.

CREATING A COLOURFUL INSTANT BORDER

1 *To create an instant border of summer colour, prepare the soil in the normal way, digging out any perennial weeds and working in plenty of well-rotted compost or manure through the top as well as the lower levels.*

2 *Sprinkle a light dusting of blood, fish, and bone meal, at the rate of one handful per square metre/yard, over the surface of the soil before planting. Be sure to choose plants that are suitable for your soil type.*

3 *Plant the annuals in "drifts". Leave plenty of room for the permanent plants to grow. A tomato plant will not look out of place in this border. French marigolds (Tagetes) attract predatory hover-flies.*

The finished border
By using annuals, the border will be a blaze of colour all summer. By mixing the productive with the ornamental vegetable plants are camouflaged from insect pests attracted by sight and scent; the diverse planting creates a natural balance of pest and predator.

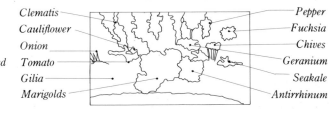

Clematis
Cauliflower
Onion
Tomato
Gilia
Marigolds

Pepper
Fuchsia
Chives
Geranium
Seakale
Antirrhinum

Choosing suitable plants

It is important to choose plants that suit the type of soil in your garden. The charts below show a selection of ornamental plants for each soil type. The lists are divided according to the different plant types and further divided to indicate sun/shade tolerance. Bulbs, annuals, and biennials are not listed because they are tolerant of most soil conditions and light levels.

Pages 110–17 give cultivation details for the many different groups of ornamental plants which can be included in a border. You will find advice on choosing and buying, and on the method of planting each type of plant. Sections on maintenance give general information on looking after each type of plant once it has been planted.

CLAY AND SILT SOILS

Many plants will grow very well in heavy clay and silt soils if drainage is reasonable, and organic matter is applied regularly to improve the heavy texture. The following plants grow particularly well on clay and silt soils.

SHRUBS
Sun
Rose (*Rosa* sp.)
Flowering currant (*Ribes* sp.)
Snowberry (*Symphoricarpos* sp.)

Shade
Spotted laurel (*Aucuba japonica*)
Skimmia (*Skimmia* sp.)
Oregon grape (*Mahonia* sp.)

Tolerant
Witch hazel (*Hamamelis* sp.)
Honeysuckle (*Lonicera* sp.)
Hazel (*Corylus* sp.)
Aronia (*Aronia* sp.)

PERENNIALS
Sun
Bear's breeches (*Acanthus* sp.)
Marigold (*Tagetes* sp.)
Bugle (*Ajuga* sp.)
Pearl everlasting (*Anaphalis* sp.)

Shade
Solomon's seal (*Polygonatum* sp.)
Comfrey (*Symphytum* sp.)
Brunnera (*Brunnera* sp.)

Tolerant
Day lily (*Hemerocallis* sp.)

Primula (*Primula* sp.)
Hellebore (*Helleborus* sp.)
Hepatica (*Hepatica* sp.)

CLIMBERS
Ivy (*Hedera* sp.)
Wisteria (*Wisteria* sp.)

Primula (*Primula* sp.)

SANDY SOIL

A light, free-draining soil. Most plants will grow on sandy soil provided plenty of organic matter is incorporated regularly to improve water-holding capacity. The following are examples of plants that grow particularly well in sandy situations.

SHRUBS
Sun
Artemisia (*Artemisia* sp.)
Broom (*Cytisus* sp.)
Cinquefoil (*Potentilla* sp.)
Rock rose (*Cistus* sp.)

Shade
Shrubby germander
(*Teucrium fruticans*)
Ornamental bramble (*Rubus* sp.)
Barberry (*Berberis* sp.)

Tolerant
Eleagnus (*Eleagnus* sp.)
Rose of Sharon (*Hypericum* sp.)
Barberry (*Berberis* sp.)
Cotoneaster (*Cotoneaster* sp.)

PERENNIALS
Sun
Yarrow (*Achillea* sp.)
Aubrieta (*Aubrieta* sp.)
Campion (*Lychnis* sp.)

Shade
Bergenia (*Bergenia cordifolia*)
Liriope (*Liriope muscari*)
Pick-a-back plant
(*Tolmeia menziesii*)
Cranesbill (*Geranium macrorhizum*)

Tolerant
Cranesbill (*Geranium* sp.)
Phlomis (*Phlomis* sp.)
Euphorbia (*Euphorbia* sp.)
Phygelius (*Phygelius* sp.)

CLIMBERS
Honeysuckle (*Lonicera* sp.)
Rose (*Rosa* sp.)

CHALKY SOIL

A chalky, or alkaline, soil tends to be dry as it drains quickly. It has quite a high pH and many plants will not tolerate this as it leads to certain nutrient deficiencies. The following are examples of plants that grow well on chalky soil in various light levels.

SHRUBS
Sun
Wintersweet (*Chimonanthus* sp.)
Lilac (*Syringa* sp.)
Butterfly bush (*Buddleia davidii*)

Shade
Periwinkle (*Vinca* sp.)
Oregon grape (*Mahonia* sp.)

Tolerant
Spiraea (*Spiraea* sp.)
Forsythia (*Forsythia* sp.)
Yucca (*Yucca filamentosa*)

PERENNIALS
Sun
Peruvian lily (*Alstromeria* sp.)
Paeony (*Paeonia* sp.)
Dutch iris (*Iris* sp.)
Anemone (*Anemone* sp.)

Shade
Bergenia (*Bergenia cordifolia*)
Dicentra (*Dicentra* sp.)
Primula (*Primula* sp.)
Primrose (*Primula vulgaris*)
Plantain lily (*Hosta* sp.)

Cinquefoil (*Potentilla* sp.)

Tolerant
Hellebore (*Helleborus* sp.)
Columbine (*Aquilegia* sp.)
Cinquefoil (*Potentilla* sp.)

CLIMBERS
Honeysuckle (*Lonicera* sp.)
Clematis (*Clematis* sp.)

ACID SOILS

Most plants prefer a very slightly acid soil, although most of the ones listed below will not tolerate anything but an acid soil. Acid soils are often moisture-retentive, so incorporate plenty of organic matter to improve drainage. The following are examples of plants that grow well on acid soil.

SHRUBS
Sun
Broom (*Cytisus* sp.)
Bearberry (*Arctostaphylos* sp.)
Rock rose (*Helianthemum* sp.)
Gorse (*Ulex* sp.)
Pernettya (*Pernettya* sp.)

Shade
Magnolia (*Magnolia* sp.)
Rhododendron
(*Rhododendron* sp.)
Azalea (*Rhododendron* sp.)
Snowy mespilus
(*Amelanchier* sp.)
Pieris (*Pieris* sp.)

Tolerant
Witch hazel (*Hamamelis* sp.)
Heather (*Erica* sp.)
Dogwood (*Cornus* sp.)
Camellia (*Camellia* sp.)
Kalmia (*Kalmia* sp.)

PERENNIALS
Sun
Carex (*Carex* sp.)

Lily (*Lilium* sp.)
Lupin (*Lupinus* sp.)
Ornamental onion (*Allium* sp.)

Shade
Solomon's seal
(*Polygonatum* sp.)
Gentian (*Gentiana* sp.)
Japanese primrose
(*Primula* sp.)

Tolerant
Woodrush (*Luzula maxima*)
Campion (*Lychnis* sp.)

CLIMBERS
Trumpet vine
(*Campsis radicans*)
Wisteria (*Wisteria* sp.)

Heather (*Erica* sp.)

Lily (*Lilium* sp.)

Campion (*Lychnis* sp.)

Shrubs

Shrubs form the framework of any border as well as attracting birds and insects. Some plants, including the beautiful butterfly bush (*Buddleia davidii*), prove irresistible to butterflies. Birds, on the other hand, particularly appreciate dense, berried shrubs like the snowberry (*Symphoricarpos doorenbosii*).

When choosing shrubs, cast your mind forward at least ten years, when the shrubs have grown to their maximum height and spread. Think about a colour scheme, not forgetting the shrub's flowering season and any others near it. Also check preferences for shade or sunshine, soil, and acidity tolerance.

Shrubs can be bought bare-rooted or container-grown. Container-grown plants tend to be smaller and more expensive, but can be planted at any time of the year instead of having to wait for the dormant season. However, a container-grown plant is more likely to suffer from the root ball drying out, so it is still safer to wait until autumn. Check all shrubs for signs of pests or disease and make sure they have healthy root systems.

Planting shrubs

Dig a hole large enough for the roots or root ball. Mix the dug-out soil with a bucketful of organic matter. Water the plant well and carefully cut away the plastic container.

Plant at the level of the old soil mark on the stem. Sprinkle a little fine soil over the roots. Refill the hole and firm the soil, mulching with some organic matter. In an exposed spot protect shrubs with a windbreak.

Maintaining shrubs

If possible, mulch shrubs annually with well-rotted compost or manure. If not, dress the border with blood, fish, and bone meal in early spring, and with seaweed meal every year.

Always pay particular attention to watering, especially the first year while the shrubs are becoming established (particularly important with container-grown plants).

For many shrubs pruning should be carried out regularly. All shrubs can be shaped and, to some extent, kept smaller by regular cutting

back, and many, such as forsythia, are pruned annually to produce flowering stems. Trim heathers (*Erica* sp.) and lavender (*Lavendula* sp.) after flowering to keep them compact. Plants like broom (*Cytisus* hybrids) are pruned after flowering to prevent them producing seed. Some shrubs like the butterfly bush (*Buddleia davidii*) flower late in the summer on wood made the same season. In early spring cut back hard all previous year's shoots.

It is an advantage to remove the dead flower heads from many shrubs to increase the flower yield the following year (called deadheading). Plants like the heathers can be trimmed with shears immediately after flowering. Other shrubs like rhododendrons have to be dead-headed by hand.

Winter frosts can lift autumn-planted shrubs out of the ground again, so check at regular intervals and, if necessary, tread them back in.

Pests like greenfly and diseases such as leaf spot attack a wide variety of shrubs, so check and treat plants regularly.

TEMPORARY PLANTING

If you cannot plant immediately, set the plants in a temporary, V-shaped trench at an angle of 45°. Cover roots, lower stem with soil and firm down. This is called "heeling in". Shrubs can be kept in this way for several weeks; trees for several months.

Roses

A particularly popular shrub is the rose. There are many types of rose and classification can be confusing. Species roses are the original ancestors of modern, hybrid roses and should be grown in the same way as other shrubs. The modern, hybrid roses can be grown as bushes or standards (bush roses budded on to a long stem to make a short tree). Many varieties of climbing and rambling rose are also available.

With the wide variety of shapes and colours available, choosing roses can be difficult. Bush standards may look too formal for mixed borders in very small gardens, though "weeping standards" (rambler roses on a long stem, shoots hanging down) fit in quite well.

Roses can be bought bare-rooted in winter or container-grown at any time of the year. Check for mildew and black spot (*see page 201*).

Planting roses
Unlike other shrubs, bush roses should be planted a little lower than they grew at the nursery to encourage new shoots from below ground. About 2.5cm (1in) deeper is generally sufficient, but make sure that the point at which the variety is budded on to the rootstock is below ground to discourage unwelcome shoots called suckers (*see right*). Roses planted in autumn should be pruned back hard immediately after planting.

Maintaining roses
Feed as other shrubs, mulching annually with well-rotted compost or manure. Water well in the first year after planting. Thereafter, ensure the roots do not dry out in warm weather.

Prune hybrid bush roses every year in spring, just before growth starts, so you can assess and cut out frost damage. The principle of pruning is that the harder you cut back, the more vigorously the shoot will grow. So, always cut back weak shoots further than the stronger-growing ones to balance the bush. Weak shoots should be pruned to leave one or two buds, while stronger ones can have three or four. Prune bush standards like the bush hybrids; weeping standards after flowering.

Rose varieties have usually been grafted on to a rootstock. Occasionally this will send out a vigorous shoot (a sucker), with no ornamental merit, but easy to spot, being light green and usually covered with more thorns. If they are allowed to develop, suckers will sap the plant's energy, so must be removed.

Removing fading flowers of continuous-flowering varieties will ensure a supply of blooms all through summer and autumn and often into early winter. Using your thumb and forefinger, break the stem about 1cm (½in) below the fading flower.

Check all roses regularly for pests or diseases, particularly mildew, black spot, or greenfly.

Pruning rose bushes (right)
Cut all the shoots back to an outward- or downward-facing bud to encourage them to grow outwards, away from the centre of the bush.

Removing a rose sucker (far right)
Scrape away a little soil where the sucker arises from the root, and pull it off if you can. If not, cut it as near to the stem as possible.

Perennials

Perennials are plants with soft stems that generally die down every winter and produce new growth in spring, persisting for many years. There are many hundreds available, providing a good selection for every soil type and sun preference.

Confusingly, perennials may be sold as "herbaceous perennials", "herbaceous plants", "hardy plants", "hardy perennials", and "hardy herbaceous perennials", although these are all the same thing! Half-hardy perennials need to be overwintered indoors.

Try to include as varied a selection of plants as possible. With a large area to fill, plant in groups of three to five to create blocks of colour.

Perennials can be bought all year round as container-grown plants, or bare-rooted in spring and autumn. Most can be raised from seed or propagated by division (*see page 188*).

Staking a delphinium
Stick a 2.5m (8ft) bamboo cane into the ground next to the plant and tie the stem to it with soft string. Add further ties as the plant grows.

Planting perennials
Unlike shrubs, perennials are better planted in spring, just as new growth is starting. They will make roots straight away and, provided you water them, will never look back. Planted in autumn, they may suffer from cold, frozen soil, or from waterlogging, which can rot the soft parts of the plant.

Remove the plant from its pot and dig a hole large enough to accommodate the root ball. Sprinkle a handful of a general fertilizer, such as blood, fish, and bone meal, around the rim. Once the plant is in the prepared hole, gently firm the soil down. Give the plant enough water to form a puddle on the soil surface. It is important to ensure that the root ball of container-grown perennials does not dry out. "Puddling in" ensures that the plants obtain enough water when first planted.

Maintaining perennials
General border feeding should be sufficient to maintain perennials (*see page 106*). They should be well watered when they are first planted. Afterwards, water as necessary.

Many perennials need supporting. Stake tall perennials such as delphiniums fairly early in the season, using a bamboo cane and tying the stems to the stake as they grow longer. Hold medium-sized perennials like hellebores erect with a few twiggy sticks, less obtrusive than canes. Some shorter perennials like oriental poppies (*Papaver orientale*) need staking to stop them flopping. Either use a special wire support, or put a piece of wide-mesh wire netting over the young plants. As the plants grow up through it, the mass of new leaves soon hide the mesh.

To propagate, lift, divide, and replant most perennials every three to five years, or they will form large clumps with bare or died-out centres. Propagate half-hardy perennials by cuttings in late summer or early spring.

Some perennials – for example, Michaelmas daisies (*Aster novi-belgii*), delphiniums, and poppies (*Papaver*) – are susceptible to mildew in dry conditions. Pull out any affected plants as soon as you notice the problem, and increase watering around the others, particularly if the weather is very dry. Throw diseased plants away; never compost them.

Annuals and biennials

Annuals are plants that grow from seed, flower, and die in the same year. They need to be replaced each year, but provide a very bright display of colour all summer and can be very useful in a new bed until you have planned your permanent planting. They also attract many beneficial insects.

Biennials are sown one year and flower the next, after which they die. Some, such as pansies, are really perennials, but best grown as biennials as they flower better the first year.

There are so many different varieties of annuals that it is often difficult to choose which to grow. They are divided into those that can stand a certain amount of frost and those that cannot, known as "hardy" and "half-hardy" annuals respectively.

Both annuals and biennials can be raised from seed or bought in trays as small bedding plants. Avoid all plants with diseased or blemished leaves, and check that your choice is suitable for the soil type and amount of sun your border has.

Growing hardy annuals

Preferably the soil for any kind of annual or biennial should not be too rich. In poor soil, they will make more flower and less leaf growth. Avoid fertilizer at planting time, but add compost or manure. In the small mixed border, fertilize for shrubs and perennials and let the seasonal subjects take their chance.

Hardy annuals, the easiest annuals to grow, can be raised from seed sown in open ground in the spring, as soon as the soil is dry and warm enough at 7°C (45°F). Sow seeds in shallow seed drills 15cm (6in) apart. When large enough to handle, carefully thin out to about 15–20cm (6–9in). Alternatively, sow in a seed tray. Grow without thinning out and plant in clumps when tall enough. This is also better on heavy soil that lies wet in early spring.

Growing half-hardy annuals

These are much more difficult to grow than hardy annuals, but generally worth the extra effort. Sow in a heated greenhouse or propagator, on a windowsill, or in the airing cupboard, usually at 18°C (65°F). After germination, grow on in a light place until the delicate stems can be handled without damage. Transfer to another seed tray at a wider spacing and grow on. "Harden off" (acclimatize them to lower temperatures outdoors) in a cold frame, increasing ventilation gradually over a week or so. After all frosts are gone, plant out in soil prepared with compost or manure (but not fertilizer). Cover with a cloche if frost threatens.

Growing biennials

Biennials are very easy to raise from seed sown outside in early summer. When sturdy enough to handle without damage, transplant 10cm (4in) apart in rows; in early autumn transplant again to their final positions in soil enriched with well-rotted compost or manure. Spring-flowering biennials will flower until early summer; then replace with summer-flowering annuals.

Maintenance

Do not feed annuals unless they have stopped growing completely, or they will make leaf growth instead of flowers. Water carefully when first planted, and in very dry weather.

Some annuals are prone to fungus diseases such as botrytis (see page 201) in cold, damp weather. Remove affected leaves immediately.

Planting hardy annuals
Sow the seeds fairly thickly in a seed tray in early spring. When the seedlings are 2.5cm (1in) or so tall, take the block out of the tray and cut into small squares with a penknife. Plant out the clumps.

Bulbs

Bulbs are ideal for filling spaces between shrubs with colour. Do not consider them merely as spring-flowering plants – with careful planning a year-round display is possible.

Corms, rhizomes, and tubers are included here with bulbs as they are all types of food-storage organs. After flowering, the foliage dies down and food is stored in the bulb through the dormant season.

When buying, inspect each bulb carefully. Check that the skin is intact and the bulb feels firm. If not, it is rotten or shrivelled inside.

Planting bulbs

Plant spring-flowering bulbs in late summer, and autumn- and summer-flowering types in spring or early summer. Most bulbs look best in groups, but do not mix different varieties as they flower at slightly different times.

Plant bulbs in any well-drained soil: bad drainage quickly leads to rot. Make sure heavy soil is deeply dug and, ideally, raised above the surrounding levels; plant bulbs on a layer of grit. Depth of planting varies with each bulb, but generally, in light and normal soil plant twice as deep as the depth of bulb, and at the same depth in heavy soil. Some bulbs will not produce flowers if planted too near the surface. Make sure they are the right way up – the "nose", or pointed end, is at the top. Some summer-flowering bulbs, such as lilies, like their heads in sunshine and feet in shade; plant them under a low-growing shrub.

You can also grow bulbs in grass – known as "naturalizing", especially attractive where the grass is cut only two or three times a year. For a regularly mown lawn, choose bulbs that flower very early, or mowing will be delayed several weeks. Naturalized bulbs are best planted informally – scatter haphazardly on the grass and plant with a bulb planter (a tool that removes a core of soil, so you can plant the bulb and replace soil and grass in one go).

Maintaining bulbs

You cannot just leave bulbs to their own devices. The first year's flower is the result of the grower's efforts the previous year. To achieve as good a result the following year, you have to do what he did. After flowering, ensure a plentiful supply of potash. Bulbs in borders will obtain sufficient manure or fertilizer when you feed the other plants. Bulbs planted on their own, in tubs, or under trees, will benefit from a couple of liquid feeds of seaweed or liquid manure after flowering. Once foliage has died down, mulch with compost or manure.

It is essential, after bulbs have flowered, to allow foliage to remain attached so that it can build up a flower for next year. Remove leaves only after they have turned yellow; then cut off and compost them. If you cut them off too early or tie them in neat little knots, the plant cannot use sunlight to make food, the bulb gets smaller, and eventually disappears. Bulb foliage in borders is fairly quickly masked by other leaves, especially of foliage plants like hostas.

If you want to move bulbs after flowering, make space for annual flowers, dig them up with as much root as possible and intact foliage. Then, in a sheltered corner, replant them in a row in a V-shaped slit trench, known as "heeling in" (*see page 110*). Give a couple of liquid feeds before foliage dies down.

Lift some tender summer-flowering bulbs like gladioli and dahlias just before heavy frosts threaten, dry them off, clean and store them over the winter in a cool, frost-free shed.

Planting bulbs in heavy soil
Dig a hole about 60cm (2ft) diameter and 30cm (12in) deep. Put a bucketful of grit in the bottom, sit the bulbs on the grit, then cover with soil.

Wild flowers and alpines

Wild flowers grown in a wildlife meadow (*see page 89*) associate very well with naturalized bulbs. Wild flowers can be also grown in the borders, where, manured and fertilized with the other plantings, they grow much bigger, with many more flowers.

There are several specialists who sell wild flower seeds, and most retail seed catalogues carry a selection. Mixtures are available to attract butterflies, bees, or birds. Other mixtures may include old-fashioned cornfield flowers such as the corncockle (*Agrostemma githago*) and cornflower (*Centaurea cyanus*). Some wild flower suppliers sell rooted plants; never lift plants from the wild – this is how they become rare or even extinct. Check soil and habitat preferences before planting.

Planting wild flowers

Sow directly in well-drained ground in spring, or in seed trays in an unheated greenhouse. Ideally, choose a piece of soil uncultivated in the recent past; in a new garden, subsoil thrown up by builders is suitable. Wild flowers thrive on poor land, so do not add fertilizer or the coarser weeds will take over. Harden off greenhouse seedlings.

ALPINES

The choice of alpines is enormous, providing attractive flower colours and shapes and interesting foliage. Many alpines need an alkaline soil; others, such as some of the gentians, are lime-haters and need an acid soil.

Planting alpines

Plant alpines in spring or autumn, but sow seeds in winter because they need a period of cold to germinate. Good drainage is vital to replicate their natural mountain environment, where they grow in rocky cracks or in scree (gravel that has broken off and rolled down the mountainside). Use a mixture of soil, coarse grit, and garden compost or coarse bark. When planting in old stone sinks, put plenty of drainage material in the bottom. Plant in walls in autumn. Fill gaps in a patio with soil and plant with prostrate alpines.

Maintaining alpines

Fertilizer is rarely required. Only feed alpines if they look as though they have stopped growing – not more often than every five or six years. Dust lightly with blood, fish, and bone meal. Water only in very dry weather. Weeding can be time-consuming, especially when alpines are very small. Cover bare soil with coarse grit to prevent weeds from growing. Many alpines, especially with grey, woolly foliage, are not happy in the wet climate of lower areas. Cover with glass supported on wire legs.

A rock garden for alpines
A rock garden is often a way of growing plants on an awkward, sloping site, with the rocks arranged in horse-shoe shapes to form planting pockets which offer protection from the wind.

Growing alpines in a wall
Cut a piece of turf large enough to cover the root ball. Leave upside down until the grass dies, then soak in water. Roll around the root ball and push into the hole.

Climbing plants

Some climbers, especially clematis and roses, can be trained to grow through trees and shrubs as a contrast in flower colour and height, or to bloom when the tree has finished: avoid vigorous types like *Clematis montana* and Russian vine (*Polygonum baldschuanicum*) which will swamp the tree. Other climbers, such as ivy (*Hedera* sp.), are useful ground-cover plants, or disguises for unsightly barriers and buildings. Many, like the ornamental vines (*Vitis* sp.), are grown for their colourful foliage.

Climbers are normally bought as container plants. Choose a plant with short, strong shoots growing from the base rather than a long, bare stem with shoots at the top.

Planting climbers

Good preparation is essential, especially if the plant is to grow against the house wall, which is often the driest spot in the garden, protected from rain by overhanging eaves. Generously enrich the planting site with well-rotted compost, manure, or an alternative. Double dig an area of at least 1.2m (4ft) square, and work

in at least a barrowload of organic matter, plus two good handfuls of blood, fish, and bone meal. Plant most climbers at the level of the soil mark on the stem, but clematis about 10–15cm (4–6in) deeper. Cover the soil with a layer of coarse material such as bark to shade the roots (they like to be cool), prevent evaporation, keep slugs at bay, and suppress the growth of weeds.

Training climbers

True climbers cling on with tendrils, curling leaf stalks, adventitious roots, or by twining. Many shrubs can also be trained to climb by regularly tying their shoots on to supports.

Self-clinging climbers include ivy, climbing hydrangea (*Hydrangea petiolaris*), and Virginia creeper (*Parthenocissus quinquefolia*). Just plant them by the wall and point them in the right direction. They will not grow quickly until they attach, but they soon make up for it.

Twining climbers need supporting with wires, trellis, or netting. They include honeysuckle (*Lonicera*) and wisteria, which

SUPPORTING PLANTS AGAINST WALLS

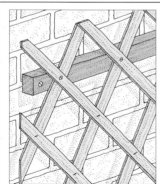

Wooden or plastic trellis
Can be screwed to wooden battens fixed on to the wall, so a gap is left to enable the plants to be tied in. The trellis itself is more decorative than a wire support.

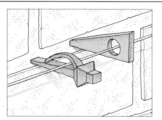

Vine eyes and wall ties
Used to secure wire supports to a brick or stone wall and ensure that there is a gap between the wall and the wire. Vine eyes are small, flat steel tags with a hole at one end; wall ties are lead nails with a "tie" at one end. Both can be knocked into the wall quite easily and do not damage the mortar. Use brass eyes if the mortar is crumbly.

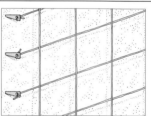

Horizontal wires
Fixed to the wall about every 30cm (12in) to help support climbing plants; tie the shoots into them as they grow. Twining plants such as clematis may need a few vertical wires as well. Fix these at the same spacings to make a wide mesh. Train fruit trees by fixing wires at required heights and canes to the wires to prevent chafing.

twist round any kind of support, and clematis (which holds up the stem by clinging to supports with tendrils or leaf stalks). Tie in new shoots of wall shrubs like climbing roses, cotoneaster, and firethorn (*Pyracantha* "Lalandeii") to the wall, pergola, or arch.

Supporting climbers
The neatest and least obtrusive way to train climbers that do not stick to the wall or fence is with horizontal wires fixed to the wall with vine eyes driven into the mortar joints. This beautiful fast-growing clematis (Clematis montana "Rubens") has tendrils which will twist around the wires and very quickly disguise them from view.

Maintaining climbers
In well-prepared soil, water climbers only in very dry weather. Climbers under overhanging eaves need extra watering. On well prepared soil, general border feeding should be sufficient.

Self-clingers only need to be prevented from straying where they are unwelcome, cutting them away from windows or they will block out the daylight quite quickly. Do this with shears or secateurs when necessary, ideally spring.

Prune climbers annually to improve flowering. Early-flowering plants should be pruned and dead-headed immediately after flowering; those that flower later in the season should be cut back the following spring.

GROUPING CLIMBERS FOR PRUNING	
Early-flowering climbers	**Late-flowering climbers**
Clematis montana	*Clematis jackmannii*
Clematis macropetala	*Clematis* "Ville de
Clematis "The	Lyon"
President"	*Clematis* "Hagley
Wisteria	Hybrid"
Summer jasmine	Trumpet vine
Honeysuckle	Russian vine
(Woodbine)	Winter jasmine
Chinese gooseberry	Chilean glory flower
Akebia quinata	*Lapageria rosea*

Making a rose-covered pillar
A pergola or pillar will add height to your plantings as well as making an attractive feature. Carefully wind the rose stem around the pillar and tie in with soft string. As you are doing so, try to pull the shoots down to form a flat spiral, to increase the number of flowers produced. Check the string regularly to ensure that it is not too tight.

· Chapter Six ·

Growing Organic Herbs

The range of herbs you grow will depend on personal priorities. You may base your selection on culinary value, decorative qualities, or a combination of these and other factors.

Herbs like the variegated sages and the thymes make superb ground-cover plants, swamping weeds and providing a splash of colour as well as attracting pollinating insects. Grow some of the "cultivated" forms of herbs especially for the flower garden, for example, several varieties of giant chives with large, dramatic flowers.

There are also golden and variegated balms and some highly attractive coloured hops, all as useful in the kitchen as their more commonly grown counterparts. However, you must also consider the practicalities of your choice, such as size, whether the plant is frost-hardy, and so on. So, before you buy your seeds or young plants, ensure you can provide the space and conditions needed to grow them successfully.

The essential herb garden
Always include herbs in an organic garden, as they attract many insects and have innumerable uses in the kitchen. As this abundant planting shows, a herb garden can be extremely decorative, as well as useful.

Planting and harvesting herbs

In traditional herb gardens, the plants are arranged in formal patterns and the herbs are enclosed by a low hedge like box or by lavender. To attain this effect along with the casual abundance of an informal herb plot, and to ensure also that plants of contrasting height and foliage sit well alongside one another, a written plan can prove to be quite indispensable. Consider the potential height and spread of each plant, as well as its rate of growth and how much sun it prefers. Some, such as lovage, grow to enormous proportions and are only suitable for the back of a large herb garden. Plants like borage need a great deal of sun, while mint, for example, will thrive in semi-shade; both are fast spreading. The maximum height of the basic herb collection is given on pages 28–29.

Soil preparation for herbs

Ideally, the soil in which herbs are grown should be well drained and light, though, with good preparation, they will grow happily in heavier soils. Double dig the area, breaking up the subsoil and working in plenty of well-rotted compost or manure, or an alternative. Since most herbs like a soil pH of between 7.0 and 7.5, spent mushroom compost is ideal.

The one thing most herbs cannot abide is bad drainage so, if your soil is wet and heavy and cannot be improved by deep digging or the inclusion of coarse grit and organic matter, it is best to build a raised bed. If you can, use hard-wearing brick or stone to raise the sides, although wood can also be used. Old railway sleepers are ideal and can raise the bed by about 30cm (12in), which is all that is needed.

The first essential is to ensure the soil is completely free of weeds. If there is so much as a sprig of ground elder root or a slip of couch grass, it will thrive unnoticed amongst the sprawling herbs. Then the only option is to lift the plants again and thoroughly clean the soil.

If you decide to grow your herbs in a special herb garden, delay planting for a year. Dig the area thoroughly, removing any trace of a weed; then cover the whole area with black polythene, dug into the ground all round to prevent it blowing away, and leave it for a year.

If you are going to plant out pot-grown herbs in the spring or summer, rake in two handfuls of blood, fish, and bone meal per square metre/yard, about a fortnight before planting. Use a similar quantity of bone meal alone before planting out herbs in autumn and winter.

Sowing and planting herbs

Details of sowing and planting are given in the individual entries on pages 122–25.

Maintaining a herb garden

A mulch of well-rotted compost or manure applied over the top of the whole garden will maintain fertility. Spread a layer about 5–7.5cm (2–3in) thick in mid or late winter, but guard against slugs (*see pages 198–99*).

Some watering may be necessary in dry weather. Use a sprinkler for at least two hours to ensure that the water permeates through to the lower levels. During the early stages of cultivation, it is important to remove weeds by hand. Established plants will spread and inhibit weeds themselves.

Some herbs, like lavender and thyme, must be trimmed back after flowering to keep them compact and within bounds. Regular harvesting

---

MAKING A RAISED BED

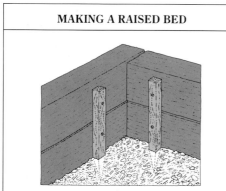

Mark out the area for the bed and lay one row of sleepers on their sides along the edge. Hammer stakes into the ground at the corners, and where two sleepers meet, and nail them to the sleepers; the wall can be one or two sleepers high.

will keep most herbs in check, but all respond well to being cut back from time to time. Some herbs need to be watched carefully and self-sown seedlings removed at an early stage: plants like borage, mint, and especially feverfew can completely take over the garden, if their seedlings are allowed to grow unchecked. Mint, in particular, needs to be confined to a bucket or other container sunk in the ground.

Perennial herbs can be propagated by lifting and dividing; the ideal time for this is in autumn and early winter, though it can also be done in early spring. Propagate the shrubby herbs, like rosemary, bay, and lavender, from softwood cuttings in early summer.

Harvesting and storing herbs

The leaves of many herbs, including thyme, can be harvested fresh throughout the growing season. Many herbs can also be preserved by drying. This enables them to be used throughout the year and can sometimes actually improve the flavour. Pick leaves for drying before the plant comes into flower to get the best results, and only ever take young, healthy leaves. Do not harvest more stems than you have room to dry immediately, and avoid handling the individual leaves. Most of the herbs are dried quite simply in the way shown. If a different method is required, this is explained under the relevant herb entry.

Harvesting herbs
Cut the leaves fresh all through the growing season for kitchen use. For drying, cut before flowering.

Drying herbs
Tie the stems in small bunches and hang them in a dry, airy shed. Large bunches will slow down the drying process by restricting air circulation. Any damage to the leaves causes essential oils to be lost and has a detrimental effect on the aroma and flavour of the herbs, so be very careful when handling them. Crumble the dried leaves into an airtight jar.

Saving seed
Harvest stems just as the seeds ripen and hang them upside down in small bunches, in a dry, airy shed. Place a cloth or bowl beneath to catch the seeds as they fall. Apart from the seeds used in cooking – such as lovage (shown here) – save those of annual herbs for sowing the following year.

Cultivating herbs

The following pages explain how to grow a basic selection of herbs, but there are hundreds of different kinds with culinary and decorative attributes (such as pot-pourri, flower arranging, and cosmetics), so you may well want to experiment with others.

Many herbs will grow from seeds and readily self-seed once established. A large proportion can also be grown from cuttings and division. Herbs are mainly disease-free, but over-crowding or too much water can weaken plants, so look out for physical conditions that might require attention. When you buy or are given a plant, check that no pests such as scale insects are lurking on or under leaves. For treating pests and diseases, see pages 198–205.

SAGE
Widely used as a culinary herb, though the several variegated and flowering forms are worth growing for their decorative qualities alone.
Soil and site Sun, well-drained soil: dig in plenty of organic matter. Add grit to heavy soils to improve drainage.
Sowing and planting Seed sown in spring often does not breed true, so it is better to plant container-grown or bare-rooted shrubs 60cm (2ft) apart. Easily propagated by layering, potting up, or replanting in spring, or also by softwood cuttings taken early summer.
Maintenance Pinch back growing shoots to keep plant compact. Layer leggy shoots (*see below*).
Harvesting Pick young leaves all summer. Dry in airy shed.

Layering sage
Peg down some shoots into the soil. When new roots develop, cut the shoots away from the parent plant.

BALM
Decorative variegated and yellow varieties are available.
Soil and site Water-retentive soil enriched with organic matter. Sun or semi-shade.
Sowing and planting Sow outside mid/late spring, 45cm (18in) apart, or divide established plants and plant at same distances.
Maintenance Trim to maintain bushy habit and retain colour of variegated/yellow varieties. Lift and divide every three years.
Harvesting Cut fresh leaves all summer. Does not dry well; freeze in plastic bags or ice-cubes.

COMFREY
This prolific perennial is useful to cultivate as compost material: its foliage is very rich in potassium and contains some trace elements.
Soil and site Prefers soil rich in organic matter; shade, and damp.
Sowing and planting Buy a plant (takes long time from seed); plant offsets from outside of root each autumn, 90cm (3ft) apart.
Maintenance Needs no encouragement for vigorous growth. Divide every three years.
Harvesting Cut fresh leaves with shears as required. To make a liquid manure high in potash, steep leaves of Russian variety (these can grow up to 30cm (12in) long) in bucket; dilute the resulting liquid by about 10:1. Use leaves and bell-shaped flowers for dyeing – producing a yellow or orange colour.

SAVORY
Summer savory is a rather floppy annual, winter savory an erect perennial, both good in borders.
Soil and site Sun; well-drained soil rich in organic matter.
Sowing and planting *Summer savory:* sow plenty outside mid/late spring, 15cm (6in) apart: low yield. *Winter savory:* softwood cuttings summer, or sow outside late summer, 45cm (18in) apart.
Maintenance *Summer savory:* weed and water. *Winter savory:* keep pinching back top growth to encourage base shoots. Cover with cloches in cold weather. Replace plants every three to five years.
Harvesting *Summer savory:* for immediate use, pick leaves all season; for drying, just as flowers begin. *Winter savory:* pick leaves fresh all year.

CHERVIL
One of the most useful herbs.
Soil and site Shade, moist soil essential: runs to seed in sun.
Sowing and planting Sow outside early/mid spring, 23cm (9in) apart. Allow to reseed; thin to 23cm (9in). Or let a few plants run to seed, resow late summer/early autumn (cover last sowings with cloches).
Maintenance Water well in dry weather. Pick flowers to delay seeding until last flowering.
Harvesting Pick from outside of plants. Freeze or dry.

BASIL
Sweet basil is taller, with larger leaves and a better flavour, than bush basil.
Soil and site Sunny, sheltered spot, best possible soil.
Sowing and planting Sow inside early spring in small pots. Harden off in cold frame. Plant out 30cm (12in) apart when frosts are gone.
Maintenance Keep well watered. Pinch off flower buds as they appear, for more growth.
Harvesting Pick fresh leaves all summer. Use fresh, or dry in sun and store in airtight jars, though not as flavoursome as when fresh. Can also be frozen.

TARRAGON
French tarragon has a very strong flavour; the more vigorous Russian type stands lower temperatures.
Soil and site Sun, shelter, and good drainage essential.
Sowing and planting *French:* will not grow from seed; plant bought plants 45cm (18in) apart. *Russian:* sow outside spring, 60cm (2ft) apart.
Maintenance Weed and water. Protect French type from frost with light mulch of straw or bracken. Divide both types every four years for vigour and flavour.
Harvesting Pick fresh leaves all season. Dry spring-cut ones.

Attracting pollinating insects
The decorative lilac-pink flowers of thyme attract bees and other insects necessary for plant pollination.

MARJORAM
Wild and pot marjoram are hardy perennials, but sweet marjoram (the most aromatic and tasty) must be grown as a half-hardy annual except in warm areas.
Soil and site Best in sun. Prefers well-drained soil, but dislikes dryness at roots, so work in plenty of organic matter before planting.
Sowing and planting *Wild and pot marjoram:* sow outside in spring, or plant young or divided plants 30cm (12in) apart. *Sweet marjoram:* in temperate areas, sow inside early spring; plant out 20cm (8in) apart when frosts gone. In warmer areas, sow directly outside as *wild and pot marjoram (above).*
Maintenance Pinch regularly for bushy, compact plants. Weed and water. Pot up and bring inside, pot marjoram end of summer. Divide perennials every three years.
Harvesting Pick fresh leaves from early summer. Sweet marjoram dries well, and its flavour is improved, but with a winter supply from potted plants drying may not be worth it. All types freeze well.

THYME
Both low- and high-growing varieties of thyme make pretty border edgings or ground cover. Common and lemon thyme are the most used kitchen varieties.

Soil and site Sun, well-drained soil. pH 7.0.
Sowing and planting *Common thyme:* sow outside 30cm (12in) apart mid spring. *Both types:* take cuttings or divide summer. Plant thyme bought in pots at any time, at same distances. Plants spread considerably, so set them further apart if you are prepared to wait a little longer for ground cover.
Maintenance Pinch out regularly to prevent legginess. Cut back hard after flowering.
Harvesting Pick leaves fresh all season (leaves have more flavour dry than when fresh). Cut sprigs before flowering; dry in airy shed.

Pinching out thyme (above)
You can encourage bushy growth, prevent legginess, and keep thyme plants compact by regularly pinching out the growing tips between your finger and thumb.

CHIVES

An attractive border edging with distinctive globular flowers.
Soil and site Moist soil.
Sowing and planting Sow outside early spring 30cm (12in) apart. Or divide existing clumps spring or autumn.
Maintenance Divide with knife every three years early/mid autumn; replant in fresh soil, or, if in same place, with well-rotted compost or manure dug-in.
Harvesting Thrives on being cut back: cut leaves with scissors to leave about 1cm (½in). Does not dry well; freeze in ice-cubes.

Growing chives
Chives are ready in early spring and also play a decorative role in the flower or vegetable garden.

FENNEL

Not to be confused with Florence fennel (*see page 32*), this tall, vigorous perennial enhances flower borders.
Soil and site Good soil, plenty of sun, away from coriander, caraway, and dill to avoid cross-pollination.
Sowing and planting Sow outside autumn or spring 60cm (2ft) apart. Or plant young or divided plants mid spring or autumn, 60cm (2ft) apart.

Maintenance Keep trimmed for succession of young leaves; allow some flowers to make seeds. Divide every three years.
Harvesting Pick fresh leaves as needed. Tend to lose much of flavour if dried. Hang plants up to dry flower heads and collect seeds.

JUNIPER

This shrubby conifer makes a good background plant, but needs plenty of room. Both male and female plants are needed to produce berries.
Soil and site Sun will give berries a fuller flavour. Well-manured soil best. pH 7.0.
Sowing and planting Sow outside late winter, or plant out young bought plants or softwood cuttings early summer.
Maintenance Weed. Feed with blood, fish, and bone meal late winter. Clip late summer if necessary to check growth.
Harvesting Pick berries when fully ripe, plump and black. Freeze, or dry very slowly on open trays at room temperature. When berries have lost their moisture, store in airtight jars.

LOVAGE

A shrubby perennial that dies down each year, but needs a lot of space. Its yellow flower clusters make it attractive enough for the back of borders. All parts of the plant have a strong flavour.
Soil and site Tolerates partial shade, better in sun. Moist soil, plenty of dug-in organic matter.
Sowing and planting Sow outside in spring, or plant divided clumps early spring or autumn, 90cm (3ft) apart (but probably only one plant needed).
Maintenance Needs no further encouragement for vigorous growth. Divide after four years when it is full size.
Harvesting Pick fresh leaves all season. Dry as on page 121.

ROSEMARY

This evergreen shrub, with several named varieties, makes a fine border or hedging plant.
Soil and site Prefers sun; well-drained soil enriched with organic matter. Lighten heavy soils with coarse grit.
Planting Set container plants 60–90cm (2–3ft) apart at any time of year; for hedging, 45cm (18in) apart. Or increase by taking cuttings early summer.
Maintenance Trim after flowering to prevent legginess and sprawling (once this happens, you should replace plants).
Harvesting Fresh leaves available all year, so no real point in preserving; but prunings can be dried in an airy shed and crumbled into airtight jars.

PARSLEY

The crisp type (*Petroselinum crispum*) or the plain-leaved French variety are generally grown. Grow these biennials as annuals to prevent seeding.
Soil and site Some shade; soil enriched with well-rotted compost or manure.
Sowing Sow an early crop inside in late winter (germinates slowly); plant out mid spring, 15cm (6in) apart. Or, for continuous supply, sow outside mid spring, and again mid summer; then sow another crop mid summer in pots to grow inside in winter. Remove outside crops at end of season.
Maintenance Remove weeds. Water during dry weather.
Harvesting Cut leaves when needed (but not all, so plant can regrow). Dry quickly in hot oven, or freeze in ice-cubes.

BAY

Bay trees can be left to grow naturally, or be clipped into various shapes. Frost-tender, so can only be grown in soil in warm areas; elsewhere, grow in tub and

bring inside in winter.
Soil and site Dry soil, semi-shade. Soil-based compost in tubs.
Planting Buy container-grown plants, or take softwood cuttings early summer.
Maintenance Water adequately at all times. Let top of compost in tubs dry right out before you rewater; never let pots become waterlogged. Feed monthly during summer with liquid manure. During summer, train by regularly pinching out tips of shoots growing out of place. In frost areas, bring tubs in for winter; if left outside, wrap tub in sacking and cover with woven polypropylene.
Harvesting Pick fresh leaves during summer. Dry in sun and store in airtight jars.

DILL
A widely used culinary herb with feathery leaves and yellow flowers.
Soil and site Well-drained soil, sun.
Sowing and planting For seeds: sow outside mid spring in short rows 30cm (12in) apart. Thin to 30cm (12in). For leaves: sow outside monthly until mid summer. Plant bought plants at same distances. Do not sow near fennel, as they may cross-pollinate.
Maintenance Weed. Water well in dry weather.
Harvesting Pick fresh leaves as needed. Dry and store.

BORAGE
A decorative border subject with arching sprays of blue flowers.
Soil and site Sunny, open site: not good in shade. Most soils.
Sowing Sow outside mid spring. Thin to 35cm (15in). Dies down in winter, but seedlings grow freely the next year. Remove seedlings growing where not wanted.
Maintenance Trim regularly.
Harvesting Pick young leaves in summer. Freeze: does not dry well. To crystallize flowers, first paint them with egg white; then dip in caster sugar.

SORREL
Both broad-leaved and French types (smaller-leaved and shorter) are hardy perennials.
Soil and site Moist soil enriched with organic matter; partial shade.
Sowing and planting Takes long time to mature from seed, so a root may be preferable. Plant seeds or roots outside in autumn 30cm (12in) apart.
Maintenance Remove flower heads to delay seeding until final flush of flowering. Weed. Make sure plants never go short of water. Divide and replant outer young offsets every three years.
Harvesting Pick fresh leaves hard all year: will soon regenerate. Dry and store in airtight jars. Does not freeze well unless puréed.

Drying sorrel
Lay fresh leaves flat on wire cake tray. To hasten drying, space so air circulates freely around each leaf.

HORSERADISH
Horseradish's tap root will reproduce from any small piece left in the ground, so beware!
Soil and site Rich soil; sun or semi-shade. For a large crop, contain roots in raised bed 60cm (2ft) above a concrete path.
Planting Buy roots; take cuttings 15cm (6in) long; plant vertically 30cm (12in) apart, early spring.
Maintenance None needed.
Harvesting Dig up whole plant each year to keep in check. Store roots in boxes of damp sand, bark, or compost in shed until required. Save some for spring replanting.

MINT
Apple mint and spearmint are best for cooking (the former resists mint-rust disease).
Soil and site Any soil; prefers semi-shade.
Planting Plant root cuttings taken in autumn, 60cm (2ft) away from other herbs. Very invasive, so plant in plastic bucket sunk in ground, rim above soil level.
Maintenance Water in dry weather. Check growth by regular picking.
Harvesting Pick spring/summer. Freeze leaves, or store in compost. Pot some in greenhouse.

STORING MINT

As an alternative to potting up mint, you can store the herb to ensure that you always have a fresh supply during the winter months.

1 Dig up a clump of mint and carefully remove a few sprigs with roots. Replant the remaining mint.

2 Lay sprigs in layer of moist compost in wooden box; cover them with more compost.

· CHAPTER SEVEN ·

GROWING ORGANIC VEGETABLES

This chapter contains advice to help you organise your vegetable growing, whether in vegetable beds, or as part of a mixed cottage garden planting plan. Pages 30–43 give you some idea of what you can choose. You should grow only what you need. If space is limited, eliminate vegetables such as maincrop potatoes that are easy to obtain. Instead, grow vegetables, such as sweetcorn, that deteriorate rapidly after harvesting and the so-called "gourmet" vegetables such as asparagus, which are so expensive. Pages 134–55 include cultivation details for over 50 different vegetables. All planting distances and pH numbers are approximate. If your soil is far removed from the pH number recommended, refer to page 81. In the cultivation sections each vegetable is assigned an ideal plot (A, B, C, or D) that applies if you use a three year crop rotation plan (*see page 128*). Pests and diseases indicated are specific ones that attack the particular crop. If you have any other problems with these crops or with those marked "trouble free", refer to pages 196–205.

Harvest time
The most rewarding part of growing vegetables is harvesting them. Onions grow particularly well in the organic garden.

Crop rotation

Grouping crops with similar needs and planting them in a different place each year makes better use of your resources. This is known as crop rotation. It also helps against pests and diseases, though it does not always prevent them.

Divide your vegetable plot into three, manure only a third of it each year and grow there those vegetables that most appreciate it. Slightly less demanding crops move to that plot the next year, those happy in poorer soil the third year. A fourth plot is used for permanent crops. Though the suggested plan provides for only one plot to be manured, treat the whole patch if you have enough manure. With the deep bed system (*see pages 132–33*), manure all plots every year before sowing or planting.

Ensuring a continuous supply
Many modern vegetables are bred to remain in the ground for some time after maturing. Others can be stored all winter. Pages 134–55 show where you can achieve a continuous supply by successional sowing and planting. Keep a diary to compare your plans with what actually happened.

THE THREE-YEAR CROP ROTATION PLAN

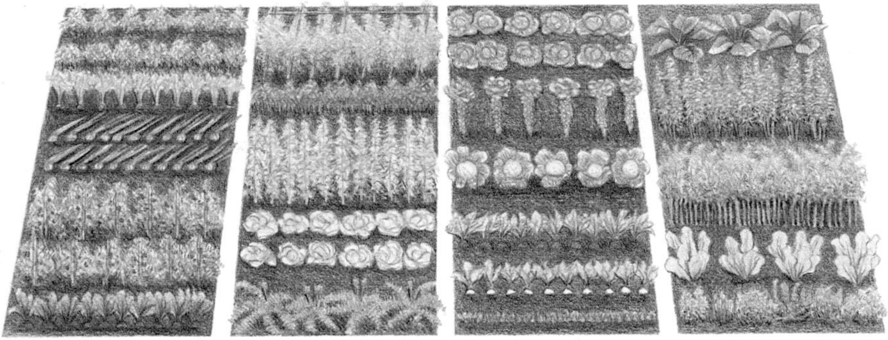

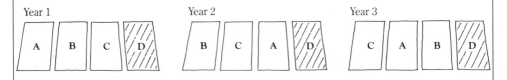

PLOT A
Cultivation: Double digging (*see page 182*); manure both levels: two handfuls of blood, fish, and bone meal per square metre/yard. Some crops may need extra feeding.
Suitable crops: Bulb, fruiting, squash, shoot, most root vegetables.

PLOT B
Cultivation: Single digging (*see page 181*); blood, fish, and bone meal (two handfuls per square metre/yard), two/three weeks before sowing.
Suitable crops: Pod and seed vegetables, salads, spinach, spinach beet, Swiss chard.

PLOT C
Cultivation: Single digging; blood, fish, and bone meal (as Plot B). Lime to pH 6.5–7.0. Some crops may need extra feeding.
Suitable crops: Leaf vegetables, swedes; turnips, kohlrabi, radishes.

PLOT D
Permanent crops, which occupy a plot of their own and do not come within the rotation plan, are: rhubarb, globe artichokes (grown as perennials), Jerusalem artichokes, asparagus, and herbs.

Year 1   A   B   C   D

Year 2   B   C   A   D

Year 3   C   A   B   D

Sowing vegetable seeds

The vegetable-growing season begins with seed sowing, either directly into the ground, or into pots or trays from which the developed seedlings are transplanted after a period of "hardening off". A good harvest depends on how well the seeds are sown initially. To make the best use of available land, aim for the maximum yield per square metre/yard and to extend the harvesting period as much as possible. Deep beds increase the yield (*see pages 132–33*), and cloches (*see page 131*) allow you to plant earlier in the season and continue later. Some crops can be multiple sown as below, or pre-germinated (*see page 130*).

Buying seeds

In most countries, the quality of vegetable seeds is controlled by legislation, so you are unlikely to find one grower's products better or worse than another's. However, seeds are expensive, so shop around. Avoid "dressed" seeds treated with fungicide. Some seeds, like peas and beans, are easy to save yourself – nearly all those you buy will be just as good sown the second year (*see page 185*).

There are several F1 vegetable hybrids available now, all much more expensive than open-pollinated types; most are bred with commercial growers in mind, whose needs are often very different from yours. The advantage of F1 hybrids is that they are often more vigorous, nearly always heavier-cropping, and sometimes resistant to disease and pest attack. If so, and all their flavour has not been bred out of them, they are an excellent proposition. Otherwise, stick with the older, open-pollinated varieties.

Multiple sowing

The very earliest crops are best started inside, either in a heated greenhouse or on a windowsill, to be well-established before they go out under the cloches, so they can be harvested earlier still. In the interests of economy, you will want to keep heating costs down, so the less space these early vegetables take up, the better. The best way of achieving this economy is multiple sowing (sowing up to six or eight seeds together in cells, rather than singly). Leave to grow as a clump and do not thin. When planted out, they simply push and jostle for space. Commercial growers have been using this method successfully for years.

Buy trays of small polystyrene or plastic cells. Fill with a good open compost like coir and worm casts, or a proprietary animal-manure compost. The plants are easily removed at planting-out time. Or use cardboard strips to divide a seed tray into squares about 4cm (1½in) across, or use very small pots. Not all vegetables are suitable for multiple sowing and there is no advantage with others.

HOW TO MULTIPLE SOW

1 *Make depressions in compost. Scrape six or seven seeds into each cell. Cover with silver sand. Water thoroughly, cover with opaque polythene, place near heat. At germination, remove polythene. Grow on in a cooler place.*

2 *When 2.5cm (1in), high, plants are ready for planting out. Water thoroughly. Press the block of cells down on a peg tray to push the compost and plants out. Plant the clumps in staggered rows, using a board. Water.*

Pre-germinating seeds

Sometimes it is beneficial to pre-germinate really slow germinators, like parsnips, before sowing. Otherwise, they may just sit in the ground doing nothing and even rot in cold, wet soil. Pre-germinated in optimum conditions, and sown when soil is slightly warmer, they will grow straightaway and easily catch up on a normal season.

Other seeds can fail to germinate because the soil temperature is too high: lettuces will not germinate in a soil warmer than 20°C (68°F). Pre-germinated in slightly cooler conditions, then planted out, they will grow normally, provided they have sufficient water.

Spread the seeds out on damp paper. You can buy a special kit with a germinating dish and absorbent filter paper, but it is cheaper to put some kitchen paper into a plastic sandwich box. Water and drain off excess.

Germinate seeds in the airing cupboard or kitchen cupboard, depending on temperature required, and check them daily. They should sprout a small root much quicker than outside. When a few roots are 3mm (⅛in) long, they are ready to sow. If it is impossible to sow them straightaway, put them in the refrigerator (not the freezing compartment); they will keep for three or four days without harm.

It is difficult to transfer the germinated seeds to the soil without breaking the tiny roots. They are at their most delicate stage and will not survive damage. Large seeds, like peas and beans, can be handled with ease; even the medium-sized ones, like parsnips, can be carefully picked up with tweezers and infinite patience. But smaller seeds, like lettuce, are impossible to sow in this way.

The answer is "fluid sowing" where the seeds are suspended in a "jelly". Special kits are available with an alginate gel which is mixed with water, heated up and allowed to cool before use. Equally effective is ordinary wallpaper paste, mixed to a stiff consistency. This does not need to be heated. Make sure you buy a paste without fungicide.

If you are fluid sowing in the summer, water the newly sown seeds straightaway, or the wallpaper paste may harden and trap the seeds inside. Gentle stirring distributes the seeds evenly through the paste. They can then be sown evenly, so only minimal thinning is needed.

FLUID SOWING WITH WALLPAPER PASTE

This method of sowing fragile pre-germinated seeds can be used for a number of vegetables including parsnips, as shown here. Stir gently to distribute the seeds evenly throughout the paste. They can then be sown evenly so only minimal thinning is needed at germination.

1 *Pre-germinate seeds. When ready to sow, carefully wash them off the kitchen paper into a flour sieve with cold running water.*

2 *Put seeds into a jar of wallpaper paste, making sure you do not damage the shoots. Stir gently; pour mixture into a polythene bag and tie a knot in it.*

3 *Rake soil to a fine tilth, make drills using the edge of a draw hoe and water with a liquid seaweed or animal-manure fertilizer.*

4 *Cut off corner of bag; squeeze gel and seeds down the row. Cover and gently consolidate the soil by tapping with the back of a rake. Water.*

Protecting crops against cold

In temperate climates, the earliest crops have to be grown in a heated greenhouse, but many vegetables can be brought forward at least a month by using cloches – simple plastic or glass covers – outside, with no heating.

After raising an early crop, cloches can cover tender vegetables like courgettes, beans, and tomatoes. Since you will harvest these well before outside-sown crops are ready, you will be eating them while shop prices are still high. At the end of the season, use the cloches again to grow late vegetables when those outside are finished. Once you have used cloches, you will not want to be without them – they will pay for themselves easily in the first season.

Types of cloche
Glass is now too expensive for commercial cloche-making, but some old panes can make a simple cloche using special cloche clips. As the cost of glass has risen, the price of plastics has fallen. Polythene is ideal cloche material but, for best results, it should be replaced each year. There are three main types of cloche: tunnel cloches (*see right*), traditional rigid tent or barn cloches, and floating cloches (sheets of plastic or woven polypropylene that "float" up on the growing plants).

Using cloches
Cloches are most useful for early planting out of multiple-sown seedlings or early sowings. On heavy soil, incorporate compost into the top few centimetres to aerate and warm the soil and, later, retain moisture. Position the cloche a month before sowing and planting. Measure the soil temperature – which should be 7°C (45°F) – before sowing and planting any of your plants.

The soil under the cloche will dry out faster than the open ground. If possible, install a length of seep hose (*see page 179*) along the length of cloche, and fit the end to the garden hose. Cloches can also exclude any pollinating insects. So, for a crop like peas that is pollinated by insects, open the cloche during the flowering period, at least during the day.

Start by raising plants on the windowsill or in the heated greenhouse: sow in late winter, and plant out under the cloches in early spring. In warm climates, sow directly into the soil in late winter, depending on the soil temperature.

You will only need small amounts of very early pickings, so either grow several different vegetables in the same row – if you have room for a full-length cloche – or split the cloche into several lengths for adjacent rows.

Organic methods of increasing fertility are even more important under cloches. Every time you change crops, dig the soil and work in as much compost or manure as you can spare.

MAKING YOUR OWN TUNNEL CLOCHE

The technique described here can be adapted to make a cloche of any size; the measurements will give you a cloche 45cm (18in) wide.

1 *Fix bolts 15cm (6in) from one end of a 1.35m (54in) long piece of wood, 30cm (12in) from the other. Cut pieces of stout wire the same length as the wood. Wind wires around bolts to leave loops and 15cm (6in) at each end. Peg two parallel planting lines 45cm (18in) apart. Bend wire into hoops; push into soil every 60cm (2ft).*

2 *Remove lines and cover hoops with polythene. Dig a small hole and bury one end under the soil. Pull polythene tight over all the hoops and bury the other end. Tie nylon twine through one of the wire loops; pull tightly over the cloche and secure to the opposite loop. Repeat with the other loops. Slide the polythene up to water.*

The deep bed system

The deep bed method of cultivating many vegetables has been practised around the world for centuries. It is very simple: instead of vegetables being grown in long rows, with an access path between each row, the crops are grown in beds 1.25m (4ft) wide, and all your work can be done from narrow paths at the sides. By cutting out unproductive paths, it is possible to double the amount of land. By digging deeply, breaking up the subsoil and incorporating plenty of bulky organic matter, plants draw nutrients from a much greater depth and can be planted closer together than otherwise possible, producing up to four times the yield of a normal bed.

Deep beds on heavy soils drain more easily if they are raised; light soils retain water better if you work extra bulky organic matter into the top few centimetres. Never tread on the bed once dug as this compacts the soil. If it is too awkward to work from the paths, use a wooden board to spread your weight evenly.

Fertilizing deep beds
Before sowing, rake into the top few centimetres of soil about two handfuls of blood, fish, and bone meal per square metre/yard, and cover with 5cm (2in) of well-rotted garden compost. Overwintering crops, such as spring cabbages, need an extra boost in the spring: a

little dried blood sprinkled round the base of each plant. Vegetables such as tomatoes and marrows that use a lot of nutrients – known as gross feeders – benefit from a fortnightly feed of liquid seaweed.

Sowing and planting in deep beds
Most vegetables can be sown so that they just touch their neighbour when mature. The relevant planting distances are shown under each separate entry on pages 134–55. Plant crops in blocks, rather than rows, setting out the plants in a series of staggered lines. Some, such as radishes, can be sown in a wide band. Make the drill with a draw hoe, and scatter the seeds thinly within it. You need not thin, but harvest some seedlings when quite small, allowing the rest to develop fully. Sometimes, vegetables sown at a wide spacing can be "intercropped" with a fast-maturing crop, say, broad beans combined with radishes. You can harvest the radishes long before the beans are big enough to deprive them of sunlight.

The increased drainage can make the top few centimetres of soil drier than usual, so water the drill before sowing in dry weather and cover the seeds with dry soil.

Deep beds are ideal for cloches – if you cannot buy a cloche wide enough to fit the bed, it is not difficult to make your own (*see page 131*). It should be 1.5m (5ft) wide.

Weeding deep beds
This is comparatively easy once the plants have matured, because their close spacing effectively smothers weeds. In the early stages, weeding can be time-consuming, especially by hand. Always start with a stale seed bed (*see page 185*), cover with a thick layer of well-rotted compost or manure, or plant through sheets of paper or polythene.

Tending plants in a deep bed
Plants can be spaced very close together if they are grown in deep beds of loose, organically enriched soil. To avoid treading on and compacting the soil, the crops are easily reached and tended from paths that run beside the narrow beds.

DIGGING A DEEP BED

To achieve optimum results with a deep bed, it is essential that the soil should be loose and deeply dug, so roots can penetrate to the required depth rather than spreading sideways. The soil must also be enriched with plenty of organic matter such as compost or manure.

1 *Mark one edge of the bed with a planting line. Measure 1.25m (4ft) across using the planting board and set up another planting line parallel to the first.*

2 *Using canes, mark a trench 60cm (2ft) wide. Dig out the trench one spade deep; take the soil to the other end of the bed in a wheelbarrow to fill the last trench.*

3 *Break up the exposed subsoil in the bottom of the trench with a fork, so roots will penetrate more deeply into the subsoil.*

4 *Put a 5–8cm (2–3in) layer of well-rotted manure into the bottom of the trench to enrich the soil and improve its texture.*

5 *Leaving a cane in the corner of the first trench, measure another 60cm (2ft) section with the other cane, so it contains the same amount of soil.*

6 *Start digging the soil from the second trench and transfer it into the first trench, spreading it to cover the layer of manure.*

7 *Put another 5–8cm (2–3in) layer of manure into the first trench. Because of the bulk of the added manure, the bed will be raised as you work.*

8 *Continue to dig out the soil from the second trench and cover the new layer of manure, leaving a deep bed of loose, organically enriched soil in the first trench.*

9 *Scrape all soil from the bottom of second trench. Break up exposed soil. Repeat steps 4–8. Use soil taken to end of plot to cover manure in final trench.*

Cultivating salad vegetables

Salad crops such as home-grown lettuces taste infinitely superior to even the freshest shop produce. Most can be harvested all year, with protection. You can often tuck salad vegetables in as "catch-crops" between slower subjects: they grow fast, and take up little room. They are ideal among flowers in ornamental borders, or even in containers such as window boxes. Most salad vegetables are grown in Plot B (*see page 128*).

LETTUCE

In most climates lettuce can be grown outside almost all year and, with a heated greenhouse or cloches, all year. For earliest sowings, use *Tom Thumb* or *Buttercrunch*; for successionals, *Great Lakes* or *Avoncrisp* or the cos varieties *Paris White* or *Lobjoits Green Cos*. For a loose-head lettuce, try *Salad Bowl* or the red-leaved *Red Sails*. For cut-and-come-again lettuce, use *Saladisi* or *Valmaine*. In greenhouses use *Magnet, Dandie*, or *Kellys*.

Soil and site Water-retentive soil. pH 6.5. Grow in soil manured for previous crop (too rich if freshly manured). Relatively cool site, so sow in semi-shade in a very hot garden. Plot B.

Sowing and planting *Earlies:* sow inside in tray of compost in heated greenhouse late winter at 15–18°C (60–65°F). When large enough to handle, transfer to larger tray, 5cm (2in) apart. Grow on at 10°C (50°F). When 5cm (2in) tall, plant under cloches 15cm (6in) apart in rows 15cm (6in) apart.

Successional crops: at same time, sow row of later variety outside under cloche. Leave some to grow on under cloche; transplant rest to open ground 23cm (9in) apart, 30cm (12in) between rows. Sow outside fortnightly until mid summer. Thin to 23cm (9in); plant out. Final sowing mid summer; plant out; cover with cloches early autumn. *Cut-and-come-again lettuce:* first outside sowing early spring; scatter seed thinly in wide band. *Deep beds:* Sow as above, but in blocks, seeds 15cm (6in) apart for early sowings, 23cm (9in) for successionals. *Greenhouse:* raise under cloches or in borders. Raise beds to drain; dig in plenty

of compost. Handful of blood, fish, and bone meal per sq. m/yd. In heated greenhouse, sow late summer to mid winter. In cold greenhouse, sow late summer to harvest late autumn; late winter to harvest from mid spring. Sow groups of three, 23cm (9in) apart, thin to one plant. Or sow in boxes; transplant 23cm (9in) apart when 4cm (1½in) high.

Maintenance Weed and water.

Harvesting When heart is hard, pull plant; compost root. Leave cut-and-come-agains in ground; cut leaves near base, more will grow.

Pests and diseases Millipedes, cutworms, slugs, aphids, botrytis, downy mildew fungus.

Lettuce	SPRING			SUMMER			AUTUMN			WINTER		
	Early	Mid	Late	Early	Mid	Late	Early	Mid	Late	Early	Mid	Late
Sow inside						•	•	•	•		•	
Plant out	•											•
Sow outside	•	•	•	•	•	•						•
Harvest	•	•	•	•	•	•	•	•	•	•	•	•

MUSTARD AND CRESS

A popular salad ingredient, garnish, and sandwich filler. No specific varieties.

Soil and site Will grow on very poor soil or damp paper. Plot B.

Sowing *Inside crops:* in winter scatter cress seed fairly thickly on moist soil, damp tissue, or cotton wool in a sandwich box. Drain away excess water. Cover with newspaper; place in warm spot. Sow mustard seed four days later for simultaneous harvest. After germination, remove newspaper;

place box in full sun. *Outside crops:* in summer, sow in corner of plot or in pot or tub, fortnightly for a succession of harvesting.

Maintenance None needed.

Harvesting Cut with scissors after 15–20 days.

Pests and diseases Trouble free.

Mustard and Cress	SPRING			SUMMER			AUTUMN			WINTER		
	Early	Mid	Late	Early	Mid	Late	Early	Mid	Late	Early	Mid	Late
Sow inside	•							•	•	•	•	•
Plant out												
Sow outside		•	•	•	•	•	•					
Harvest	•	•	•	•	•	•	•	•	•	•	•	•

CHICORY

For white-blanched "chicons" try *Witloof* and *Normanto*. Grow unblanched types *Crystal Heart* and *Sugarhat* to eat like lettuce.
Soil and site Sun; rich, moisture-retentive soil. pH 6.5. Two handfuls of blood, fish, and bone meal per sq. m/yd, two/three weeks before sowing. Plot B.
Sowing Sow outside early summer in shallow drills 30cm (12in) apart. Thin to 23cm (9in). *Deep beds:* sow blanching types in rows 20cm (8in) apart; thin to 20cm (8in) within rows. Sow non-blanching in rows 25cm (10in) apart. Thin to 25cm (10in).
Maintenance Weed and water

Chicory	SPRING Early	SPRING Mid	SPRING Late	SUMMER Early	SUMMER Mid	SUMMER Late	AUTUMN Early	AUTUMN Mid	AUTUMN Late	WINTER Early	WINTER Mid	WINTER Late
Sow inside												
Plant out												
Sow outside				•								
Harvest	•							•	•	•	•	•

non-blanching types.
Harvesting Cut unblanched types when hearts have filled out. Dig chicons in autumn to blanch in frost-free shed for all-winter supply. Trim leaves within 1cm (½in) of roots; lay in box of moist bark or compost. Every three to four weeks, plunge some roots upright into deep box one-third full of bark or compost. Cover with 23cm (9in) layer of same, well packed down. Put in warm place. Four/five weeks later, remove chicons, cutting away from roots.
Pests and diseases Trouble free.

WATERCRESS

Highly nutritious ingredient of salads, sauces, and soups. No individual varieties.
Soil and site Shade and moisture-retentive soil essential. Dig trench 30cm (12in) deep; half fill with compost or manure. Refill with organic matter and soil.
Sowing and planting Sow inside in trays mid spring at 12°C (55°F). Transplant to wider spacing in another tray. Plant out late spring/early summer 10cm (4in) apart. Or sow outside mid spring in shallow drills. Or plant rooted shoots from bought watercress.
Maintenance Hoe regularly. Water copiously. Pinch out leading shoots; remove flowers.
Harvesting Cut shoots as needed, thus encouraging more.
Pests and diseases Trouble free.

Watercress	SPRING Early	SPRING Mid	SPRING Late	SUMMER Early	SUMMER Mid	SUMMER Late	AUTUMN Early	AUTUMN Mid	AUTUMN Late	WINTER Early	WINTER Mid	WINTER Late
Sow inside		•										
Plant out			•	•								
Sow outside		•										
Harvest					•	•	•	•	•			

ENDIVE

Good varieties for late summer and autumn are *Moss Curled* and *Green Curled*, for winter, *Batavian Broad Leaved* and *Escarole*. Endives tend to be slightly tough if not cultivated well.
Soil and site Semi-shade (runs to seed and becomes bitter in hot sun). Rich, moisture-retentive soil. pH 6.5. Blood, fish, and bone meal as for chicory. Plot B.
Sowing Sow outside in shallow drills 30cm (12in) apart where they can be covered with cloches, early croppers in early summer, winter types in late summer. Thin to 30cm (12in) apart. *Deep beds:* sow in shallow drills 23cm (9in) apart. Thin to same distance.
Maintenance Weed and water. Late autumn, cover later-sown rows with cloches. To blanch: three months after sowing, cover with flower-pot (hole blocked), or black polythene (if leaves are dry). Or lift plants, tie leaves together to exclude light from hearts, and replant in box of moist soil in cool, frost-free place.
Harvesting Three weeks after blanching, harvest when hearts are creamy in colour and have lost their bitter taste.
Pests and diseases Trouble free.

Endive	SPRING Early	SPRING Mid	SPRING Late	SUMMER Early	SUMMER Mid	SUMMER Late	AUTUMN Early	AUTUMN Mid	AUTUMN Late	WINTER Early	WINTER Mid	WINTER Late
Sow inside												
Plant out												
Sow outside					•		•					
Harvest									•	•	•	•

Cultivating shoot vegetables

Most shoot vegetables take up a fair amount of room; in the three-year crop rotation plan, asparagus, rhubarb, and globe artichokes grown as perennials all need to be planted in Plot D (the space dedicated to perennial crops, *see page 128*), but these succulent "gourmet" vegetables are well worth the space and effort involved.

GLOBE ARTICHOKES

Faster-cropping and less demanding than many "gourmet" vegetables, best grown as an annual in deep beds. *Green Globe* is still the best variety.

Soil and site Sunny, sheltered site; plenty of dug-in organic matter to improve drainage of heavy soil (deep beds also help). pH 6.5. Plot C if grown as annuals (but manure the artichokes' area). Plot D if grown as perennials.

Sowing and planting Buy "suckers": plant them 1m (3ft) square mid spring. Or sow inside late winter in 7.5cm (3in) pots at 18°C (65°F). Plant out at 13°C (55°F). Plant perennials 1m (3ft) square mid spring. *Deep beds:* plant 45cm (18in) apart mid spring.

Maintenance Mulch with compost or manure; water in dry weather.

Harvesting Cut heads fairly tightly closed. Removing side shoots makes heads bigger but reduces overall yield. After harvest, cut stems to 30cm (12in). Tie together new shoots at 60cm (2ft) long; earth up like celery. A few weeks later, cook and eat.

Pests and diseases. Slugs.

Planting in a mixed border
Globe artichokes are decorative enough to mix with plants at the back of the ornamental border.

Globe artichokes	SPRING Early Mid Late	SUMMER Early Mid Late	AUTUMN Early Mid Late	WINTER Early Mid Late
Sow inside				•
Plant out	•			
Sow outside	•			
Harvest		• •	•	

ASPARAGUS

This perennial crop is improved by organic methods. *Mary Washington* is strong-growing, and resistant to rust. New varieties like *Lucullus* have only male plants, so yield is not reduced by seed production.

Soil and site Good drainage and sun essential. On light soil, dig in compost, manure, or alternative; grow plants "on the flat". On heavy soil, raise beds with organic matter as for a deep bed. Two handfuls of blood, fish, and bone meal per sq. m/yd. pH above 6.5.

Sowing and planting Some types can be raised from seed: sow outside mid spring 2.5cm (1in) deep in seed bed. When they germinate, thin to 7.5cm (3in). Transplant to Plot D, 30cm (12in) apart, the following spring. Or buy one-year-old roots ("crowns"), soak in water for an hour, plant 30cm (12in) apart in a trench 15cm (6in) deep, 30cm (12in) wide, and slightly raised in centre.

Maintenance Plants must never go short of water, especially first year. Each year, in early spring, dress with fertilizer; in autumn, mulch with compost or manure.

After seven/eight years, start another bed. When second bed is in full production, dig up first one.

Harvesting Cut lightly in second year, nearly a full crop subsequent years. Cut shoots 10cm (4in) above ground, tips tightly closed. Leave some shoots; cut for four weeks in third year, and six thereafter.

Pests and diseases Asparagus rust, asparagus beetles, slugs.

Asparagus	SPRING Early Mid Late	SUMMER Early Mid Late	AUTUMN Early Mid Late	WINTER Early Mid Late
Sow inside				
Plant out	•			
Sow outside	•			
Harvest		• •		

CELERY

Blanched types include *Giant Red* and *Giant Pink*. For self-blanching types try *Lathom Self-Blanching* and *Golden Self-Blanching*.
Soil and site Moisture retention and organic matter essential. pH 6.5. Trench for blanched types as shown right. Plot A.
Sowing and planting Sow inside late winter 18°C (65°F): do not cover seeds. At germination, transfer to wider spacing in second tray. Grow on at 13°C (55°F). Harden off late spring. Plant early summer: self-blanching in blocks, plants spaced 23cm (9in); blanched in trenches, plants 30cm (12cm) apart. *Deep beds:* grow self-blanching at same spacings.
Maintenance Weed and water self-blanching. Feed blanched with liquid manure mid summer and a month later. Blanch. Cover rows with tunnel cloches late autumn.
Harvesting Lift self-blanching before first frosts; then dig one blanched plant at a time.
Pests and diseases Slugs, celery fly, celery leaf spot.

Celery	SPRING Early Mid Late	SUMMER Early Mid Late	AUTUMN Early Mid Late	WINTER Early Mid Late
Sow inside				•
Plant out	•	•		
Sow outside				
Harvest		•	• •	• • •

BLANCHING CELERY

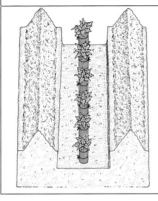

Dig trench one spade deep and 45cm (18in) wide, heaping soil either side. Put 5cm (2in) of compost or manure in the bottom; cover with 2.5cm (1in) of soil. Plant seedlings. Remove any suckers near the base mid summer. Wrap bunches of stalks with corrugated cardboard, brown paper, or newspaper. Fill trench to bottom of leaves. Repeat twice more at three-weekly intervals, sloping soil to drain off rain and prevent rotting.

RHUBARB

Frost-hardy, easy to grow, and can be harvested from late winter to mid summer. Try *Cawood Delight*, *Victoria*, *Canada Red*, *Ruby*, and *Sydney Crimson*.
Soil and site Well-drained soil; plenty of rotted compost or manure dug-in. Likes a soil of pH 7.0 (lime if necessary). Plot D.
Planting Generally, plant mature roots ("crowns") in winter; plants may be bought in pots all year, set at 75cm (2ft 6in) apart, 90cm (3ft) between rows (if more than the usual two/three plants grown). Cover with 2.5cm (1in) soil.
Maintenance Weed and water.

Every year mulch with compost or manure after leaves die down.
Harvesting Leave the first year; in subsequent years, pull thickest sticks when long enough: never strip plant. Remove flower spikes; place leaves on compost heap.
Pests and diseases Aphids, virus disease.

FLORENCE FENNEL

Not an easy plant to grow, but worth persevering with for its unique aniseed flavour. *Perfection* is very good, but the vegetable is normally sold just as *Florence fennel* or *Finocchio*.
Soil and site Sunshine; moisture-retentive soil rich in organic matter. pH above 6.5. Plot A.
Sowing Sow outside little and often for succession, mid spring to late summer, shallow drills 45cm (18in) apart. Thin to 20cm (8in).
Maintenance Must not dry out or will run to seed. When bases begin to swell to form golf-ball size bulbs, earth up to keep them sweet and tender.

Harvesting Cut heads two/three weeks after earthing up. Eat swollen stems raw or cooked.
Pests and diseases Slugs.

Florence fennel	SPRING Early Mid Late	SUMMER Early Mid Late	AUTUMN Early Mid Late	WINTER Early Mid Late
Sow inside				
Plant out				
Sow outside	• •	• • •		
Harvest		• •	• •	

Cultivating bulb vegetables

It is easy to grow these staple vegetables whose flavour adds so much to many dishes. As for soil and site requirements, all bulb vegetables prefer sunshine and a soil rich in organic matter: dig in plenty of compost or manure. If necessary, add lime to raise the soil pH above 6.5. If you are using the crop rotation plan, grow bulb vegetables in Plot A (*see page 128*).

GARLIC

One of the easiest of all vegetables to grow, given a sunny spot. Cloves (individual segments of the bulb) are widely available. Specific varieties are not usually given, but *Marshall's Long Keeper* is good.
Soil and site See above.
Planting Separate the cloves and plant, pointed end up, late winter in holes 2.5cm (1in) deep and 15cm (6in) apart. *Deep beds:* plant 15cm (6in) apart in staggered rows.
Maintenance Keep weed free.

On exposed sites, support stems.
Harvesting Dig bulbs in summer; clean and dry in sun before stringing, or storing in nets in frost-free place.
Pests and diseases Trouble free.

Garlic	SPRING Early	Mid	Late	SUMMER Early	Mid	Late	AUTUMN Early	Mid	Late	WINTER Early	Mid	Late
Sow inside												
Plant out	●											●
Sow outside												
Harvest					●	●						

SHALLOTS

Mild-flavoured bulbs much smaller than maincrop onions and harvested earlier, in summer. Shallots are easy to grow from sets (tiny bulbs specially treated to produce good-sized bulbs). *Dutch Yellow* and *Dutch Red* are the two most popular varieties. The exhibition variety *Hative de Niort* produces bigger bulbs, but they do not keep as well.
Soil and site See above.
Sowing and planting Remove dead foliage, plant sets 15cm (6in) apart early spring in drills 30cm (12in) apart, bulb tips just below soil level. Do not press sets into ground or they will push themselves out again when they grow roots. *Deep beds:* plant in staggered rows, 15cm (6in) between sets.
Maintenance Weed and water. In early summer, draw soil away from bulbs to assist ripening.
Harvesting Lift when foliage dies down in summer; clean and store bulbs in nets in frost-free place.
Pests and diseases Trouble free.

Drying shallots
Put harvested bulbs on a piece of chicken wire raised off the ground, so air can circulate around them.

Shallots	SPRING Early	Mid	Late	SUMMER Early	Mid	Late	AUTUMN Early	Mid	Late	WINTER Early	Mid	Late
Sow inside												
Plant out	●											●
Sow outside												
Harvest				●	●	●						

LEEKS

Hardy in all but the very coldest climates and a valuable winter source of fresh greens. The popular *Musselburgh* is very hardy, with thick stems; *Titan* has a very long stem. *The Lyon Prizetaker* is very hardy. Try *Titan* and *King Richard* for multiple sowing.
Soil and site See opposite.
Sowing and planting Multiple sow as for onions. No need to trench: leeks blanch each other by growing so close together. Alternatively, sow inside mid spring in seed boxes in greenhouse, 15°C (60°F), outside mid spring in seed bed, in shallow drill, 15cm (6in) apart. Plant out in deep furrow, so they can be blanched; starting early summer, make holes with dibber 15–20cm (6–8in) deep,

Leeks	SPRING Early Mid Late	SUMMER Early Mid Late	AUTUMN Early Mid Late	WINTER Early Mid Late
Sow inside	• •			
Plant out		•		
Sow outside	•			
Harvest	•		•	• • •

15cm (6in) apart, 30cm (12in) between rows. Trim roots by two-thirds and tops by half. Drop plant into each hole; do not refill, but pour a little water into each hole to wash soil over roots. *Deep beds:* plant the same way, in block of staggered rows, 15cm (6in) each way. Or multiple sow as above and plant 30cm (12in) apart each way.

Maintenance Hoe to keep weed-free. Pull some soil around base of each growing stem to blanch; do not get soil between leaves.
Harvesting Usually leave in ground until required. If expected cold weather may make soil too hard to dig, lift a few plants and store in box of moist bark or compost until required.
Pests and diseases Trouble free.

ONIONS

For continuity, grow a maincrop and a Japanese variety (harvesting much later). Maincrops that store well are *Rijnsburger, Southport Yellow Globe* and *Hygro*. A good Japanese variety is *Express Yellow*, ready early summer. *Hygro* and *Burpees Yellow Globe Hybrid* are especially good for multiple sowing. Small salad or "spring" onions such as *White Lisbon* and *Ishikuro* do not store. Try *White Lisbon* and *Evergreen Long White Bunching* for multiple sowing.
Soil and site See opposite.
Sowing and planting *Maincrop onions:* multiple sow late winter in heated greenhouse, 15°C (60°F), six/seven seeds per cell. After germination, lower to 10°C (50°F). Harden off in cold frame early spring. Plant out 30cm (12in) square mid spring. Or sow outside early spring, in shallow drills 30cm (12in) apart, on stale seed bed. Thin to 5cm (2in) apart. *Japanese onions:* sow outside late summer; spread handful dried blood per sq. m/yd in spring. *Deep beds:* sow or plant 5cm (2in) apart in staggered rows. For heavy, wet

Onions, Salad onions	SPRING Early Mid Late	SUMMER Early Mid Late	AUTUMN Early Mid Late	WINTER Early Mid Late
Sow inside				• •
Plant out	• •			•
Sow outside	• • •	•		•
Harvest		• •	• • •	• •

soil, buy onion sets. Cut off tips of old foliage; plant bulbs at above distances, tips just below soil. Do not push into ground.
Salad onions: multiple sow six seeds per cell late winter. Harden off. Plant out 15cm (6in) apart early spring. Or sow outside under cloches late winter; in open ground every three weeks from early spring. No need to thin. *Deep beds:* scatter in wide drill.
Maintenance Keep weed-free. Water in dry weather.
Harvesting Foliage turns brown and withers late summer. Lift and dry bulbs in sun. Remove tops and store in nets in frost-free shed. Or keep leaves on; tie in bunches.
Pests and diseases Onion fly, onion eelworm, neck rot, white rot, storage rot.

Multiple sown onions
The bulbs planted as a clump are forced to grow outwards as they compete for space.

Cultivating pod and seed vegetables

Apart from the pleasure in eating peas and beans and the like fresh from the pod, these leguminous plants have other benefits to the organic gardener. Their ability to "fix" nitrogen in the soil (*see page 79*) means that not only do they need little feeding, but that, if you dig the plants in after harvesting, the nitrogen becomes available for the next crop.

BROAD BEANS
The primary variety for early sowing is *Aquadulce Claudia*. Of maincrops, try *Express* and *Imperial Green Longpod*.
Soil and site pH 6.5. Plot B.
Sowing and planting *Earlies:* sow outside late autumn/winter in double rows 30cm (12in) apart and 5cm (2in) deep, 10cm (4in) between seeds, leaving 1m (3ft) between each double row. Or sow under cloches mid winter. *Maincrop:* open ground early spring at same distances. *Deep beds:* staggered rows, 15cm (6in) apart.
Maintenance Support winter and exposed sowings. Remove cloches when plants touch tops. Water. Mulch with compost.

Harvesting Pull before pods are leathery. In warm climates, cut plants back for a second crop. Dry beans in sun; store in bottles.
Pests and diseases. Blackfly, pea and bean weevils, chocolate spot.

Cutting down broad beans
Cut plants down to 5cm (2in) after harvesting. They will regrow.

Broad beans	SPRING Early	Mid	Late	SUMMER Early	Mid	Late	AUTUMN Early	Mid	Late	WINTER Early	Mid	Late
Sow inside												
Plant out												
Sow outside	•	•							•	•		•
Harvest				•	•	•	•					

SWEETCORN
New hybrids like *Early Xtra Sweet* are the sweetest of the fast-maturing types. Cross-pollination will occur near other varieties.
Site and soil Sun. Plot B. pH 6.5.
Sowing and planting Sow pairs of seeds inside mid spring in 8cm (3in) pots, 18°C (65°F). Thin out weaker seedlings. Harden off in cold frame late spring. Plant out early summer in blocks 60cm (2ft) apart. Or sow outside mid spring in furrows 60cm (2ft) apart and 15–23cm (6–9in) deep, two/three seeds every 60cm (2ft). Cover with 2.5cm (1in) soil, then with polythene. When seedlings touch polythene, cut slits in it. After flowering, cut polythene away.
Maintenance Keep weed-free. Mulch with compost, manure, or paper. Extra water at flowering.
Harvesting Pick when tassels turn brown and then black.
Pests and diseases Trouble free.

Harvesting sweetcorn
Break off ripe sweetcorn by pulling cob downwards with one hand, supporting plant with the other.

Sweetcorn	SPRING Early	Mid	Late	SUMMER Early	Mid	Late	AUTUMN Early	Mid	Late	WINTER Early	Mid	Late
Sow inside		•										
Plant out			•	•								
Sow outside		•										
Harvest						•	•	•				

RUNNER BEANS

Painted Lady is ideal for the ornamental border, with red and white flowers. *Romano* and *Polestar* are good. Grow *Pickwick*, the earliest, like French beans.
Soil and site Dig trench one spade deep, 60cm (2ft) wide. Break up bottom, half fill with compost, manure, screwed-up newspaper soaked in water or liquid manure. Replace soil and allow to settle. pH 6.5. Plot B.
Sowing and planting Sow inside one seed per 8cm (3in) pot in greenhouse or on windowsill. Harden off. Plant out late spring. Or, fortnight before last frost, sow outside against canes set at 30cm (12in) intervals in double row, 60cm (2ft) between rows. Or sow against a wigwam – four/six canes 45–60cm (18in–2ft) apart.
Maintenance Mulch with pine bark. Encourage plants to twist round canes. Pinch growing tips at cane tops. Plenty of water to roots at flowering helps pollination.
Harvesting Pick pods when young, to encourage more.
Pests and diseases Slugs, halo blight, blackfly, failure to set.

Runner beans	SPRING Early	SPRING Mid	SPRING Late	SUMMER Early	SUMMER Mid	SUMMER Late	AUTUMN Early	AUTUMN Mid	AUTUMN Late	WINTER Early	WINTER Mid	WINTER Late
Sow inside	●											
Plant out		●										
Sow outside		●	●									
Harvest					●	●	●	●				

TRAINING CLIMBING BEANS

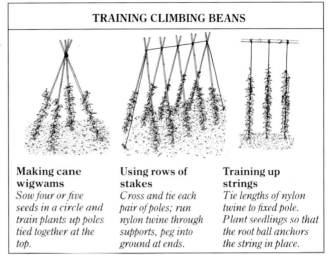

Making cane wigwams
Sow four or five seeds in a circle and train plants up poles tied together at the top.

Using rows of stakes
Cross and tie each pair of poles; run nylon twine through supports, peg into ground at ends.

Training up strings
Tie lengths of nylon twine to fixed pole. Plant seedlings so that the root ball anchors the string in place.

FRENCH BEANS

Limelight is the best flat-podded type. Of the round, pencil-podded kinds, *Tendergreen* is good. Climbing French beans like *Hunter* and *Largo* save space, crop for a long time, and are good for greenhouses. *Purple Podded* is very tasty and earlier than fleshy and stringless greenhouse *Romano*.
Soil and site Little extra feeding. Likes warm soil. pH 6.5. Plot B.
Sowing *Outside crops:* sow early spring in greenhouse. Plant out under cloches mid spring 20cm (8in) apart, in rows 30cm (12in) apart. Sow next crop outside early spring under cloches, two seeds every 20cm (8in) and 5cm (2in) deep, rows 30cm (12in) apart. Sow without cloches mid spring.

French beans	SPRING Early	SPRING Mid	SPRING Late	SUMMER Early	SUMMER Mid	SUMMER Late	AUTUMN Early	AUTUMN Mid	AUTUMN Late	WINTER Early	WINTER Mid	WINTER Late
Sow inside	●											
Plant out		●										
Sow outside	●	●	●	●								
Harvest					●	●	●	●				

Deep beds: sow bush types in staggered rows, 15cm (6in) apart. *Greenhouse crops:* sow two seeds in 8cm (3in) pots early spring, 18–21°C (65–70°F). Thin out weaker at first true leaf stage. Plant in borders late spring, 30cm (12in) apart: support with strings. Feed weekly with liquid seaweed. Pinch out tips at tops of strings. After first crop, remove lower leaves; drop plants to ground, coiling stems. New growth will climb strings for another crop.
Maintenance Hoe out weeds. Mulch with compost, bark, paper, or polythene. Water in dry weather.
Harvesting Regularly pick young pods before they become stringy. Leave some on plant to dry; pod and store in airtight jars. After harvest, leave roots in for nitrogen.
Pests and diseases Slugs, aphids, halo blight.

PEAS

For a succession, grow earlies (such as *Titania* or *Hurst Beagle*) and maincrops *Hurst Green Shaft* or *Onward*. Try *Oregon Sugar Pod* and *Sugar Bon* mangetout peas.
Soil and site Soil not too rich. pH 6.5. Little extra feeding. Plot B.
Sowing *Earlies:* sow inside late winter in plastic guttering in greenhouse at 5cm (2in) intervals. When 8cm (3in) tall, plant our entire contents of guttering early spring under cloches. *Second sowing:* sow outside early spring under cloches in wide trench. Scatter seeds 5cm (2in) apart in a drill 5cm (2in) deep; cover and firm. *Maincrop:* sow as second sowing in open ground mid spring, then fortnightly until early summer. *Deep beds:* most peas are difficult to support: grow *Bikini* (semi-lifeless and self-supporting

with tendrils) in blocks, rows 15cm (6in) apart and seeds 5cm (2in).
Maintenance Support all except leafless types with pea and bean netting or sticks. Hoe to weed. Mulch with compost or manure.
Harvesting Pick slightly young, and just before they are cooked for maximum sweetness. Cut foliage; leave roots in ground for nitrogen.
Pests and diseases Birds, mice, mildew, pea moths, pea and bean weevils.

Sowing peas in guttering
Sow peas in two staggered rows 2.5cm (1in) apart. Cover with soil.

Peas	SPRING Early Mid Late	SUMMER Early Mid Late	AUTUMN Early Mid Late	WINTER Early Mid Late
Sow inside				•
Plant out	•			
Sow outside	• • •	•		• •
Harvest	•	• • •	• •	

OKRA

To prevent a possible allergic reaction, avoid handling wet crop; if necessary, wear gloves. *Dwarf Green Longpod* and *Clemson Spineless* (with spineless pods and heavy yield) mature fast.
Site and soil Warm climates only: greatly decreased yield below 21°C (70°F). Sunny site. Plot B. Well-drained, fertile soil: dig in plenty of organic matter. If

soil is badly drained, grow in raised deep bed.
Sowing and planting Sow outside in shallow drills 90cm (3ft) apart, in spring when frosts have gone; early to mid summer for a second crop in autumn. Thin to 45cm (18in). Or sow inside in greenhouse or on windowsill in 8cm (3in) pots (roots resent disturbance). Plant out 45cm (18in) apart when frosts gone.

Maintenance Weed and keep plants slightly dry to prevent rotting. Two handfuls blood, fish, and bone meal per sq. m/yd a month after sowing. Mulch between plants with compost at the same time.
Harvesting Pick small pods every two/three days. To keep more than two days, cover with damp cloth in cool place.
Pests and diseases Aphids.

LIMA BEANS

Lima, or butter, beans are nutritious and delicious, but can only be grown in warm climates. *Burpee Improved Bush* and *Burpee Fordhook* are both recommended. Climbing varieties like *Prizetaker* and *King of the Garden* crop later and are more difficult.
Soil and site Sun and deep, rich soil with plenty of organic matter. Plot B.
Sowing Sow outside late spring, or when the soil temperature reaches 18°C (65°F), 2.5cm (1in) deep, 10cm (4in) apart in drills 60cm (2ft) apart. Sow climbers

against 2.5m (8ft) poles set in a tripod, 90cm (3ft) between pole bases, four/six seeds per pole; thin to three. Or start off inside in pots at 21°C (70°F) for rapid germination.

Maintenance Mulch with well-rotted compost or manure.
Harvesting Pick young pods regularly, to encourage more.
Pests and diseases Aphids, pea and bean weevils.

Lima beans	SPRING Early Mid Late	SUMMER Early Mid Late	AUTUMN Early Mid Late	WINTER Early Mid Late
Sow inside	•			
Plant out				
Sow outside		•		
Harvest		•	• •	

Cultivating fruiting vegetables

The fruiting vegetables – tomatoes, peppers, and aubergines – need a rich, moist soil and plenty of sunshine. In temperate climates, they mostly require the protection of glass in the form of greenhouse or cloche, but are still well worth growing. They are a rich source of Vitamin C and their brilliant fruits look as well as taste good.

AUBERGINES

If grown outside as perennials, aubergines need cloches in colder areas, and ideally a greenhouse or polythene tunnel. Early types are best: they crop longer. *Black Prince* is very early and heavy-yielding (good in greenhouses). *Early Beauty* is also quick-maturing.
Soil and site Shelter, with plenty of sun; well-manured soil. pH 6.5. In cold conditions, warm soil with cloches before planting. Plot A.
Sowing and planting *Outside crops:* sow inside early spring, in greenhouse or on windowsill, in polystyrene cells or seed tray, 18–21°C (65–70°F). Transfer to 8cm (3in) pots when large enough to handle. Harden off in cold frame mid spring. In warm climates, plant out late spring, 60cm (2ft) apart; in cold areas under cloches. Stake main stem firmly. *Deep beds:* plant out 45cm (18in) in staggered rows; in cold areas under cloches. *Cold greenhouse:* sow and pot on as above. Plant out in borders mid spring, 60–75cm (2ft–2ft 6in) apart, or three to a growing bag, or in 20cm (8in) pots of worm-worked compost. Support plants with canes.
Maintenance *Outside:* pinch out growing point at 23cm (9in). Tie side-shoots to canes. Remove extra flowers when five fruits per plant are swelling. Feed with liquid manure fertilizer weekly from mid summer. *Greenhouse:* Pinch out tops at 30cm (12in), side-shoot tips when fruits form. Only six fruits per plant. Feed at every watering as shown (*above right*).
Harvesting Cut late summer.
Pests and diseases Whitefly, aphids.

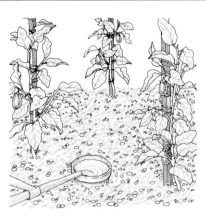

Feeding plants
Bury clay pot in soil between plants, and pour in liquid fertilizer. This enables the roots to get the maximum benefit from the feed.

Harvesting aubergines
To ensure the sweetest possible flavour, cut aubergine fruits when very shiny.

Aubergines	SPRING Early Mid Late	SUMMER Early Mid Late	AUTUMN Early Mid Late	WINTER Early Mid Late
Sow inside	• •			•
Plant out	• •			
Sow outside				
Harvest		•	• •	

PEPPERS

Peppers are slightly easier to grow than aubergines in cold climates, though they are still worthwhile growing under cloches. Of the "sweet" types (red and green peppers), *Gypsy* yields very well, although the fruits are a little yellow for some people. *Early Prolific* is earlier than most: good outdoors, and for unheated greenhouses and under cloches in temperate climates. *Bell-Boy* is reliable for the greenhouse. *Chili Serrano* is a very hot ("chilli") pepper for greenhouses or warmer climates. Grow the milder *Big Jim* under cloches in cooler climates. In greenhouses *Long Red Cayenne* is a prolific hot pepper.
Soil and site Shelter, sun; well-manured soil, pH 6.0–6.5. In cold conditions, cover soil with cloches before planting. Plot A.
Sowing and planting *Outside crops:* sow inside mid winter in heated greenhouse or on windowsill, early spring in cold greenhouse, 18–21°C (65–70°F). Peppers have a small root system, so not too much cold compost around their roots. When big

enough to handle, transplant to 8cm (3in) pots; pot on as roots fill pots. Space plants out early on to give plenty of light and air. From mid spring harden off in cold frame. Plant out under cloches or, in warm climates, in open ground late spring, 60cm (2ft) apart. *Deep beds:* plant out late spring in staggered rows, 45cm (18in) apart. *Greenhouse:* sow as above; plant mid spring in greenhouse borders, 35cm (15in) apart, or in growing bags, or (possibly best because they fruit better when roots are restricted) in 20cm (8in) pots of worm-worked compost.
Maintenance Pinch growing point at 15cm (6in) and tie in plant to cane. No stopping necessary; tie in growing side-shoots. Water regularly. Feed outside plants weekly with liquid seaweed or animal-manure fertilizer, and greenhouse ones at every watering.
Harvesting Pick sweet peppers when swollen, hot peppers when green or when they turn red. Dry hot peppers in sun; store for use in the winter.
Pests and diseases Slugs, aphids, whitefly, red spider mites.

TOMATOES

Tomatoes are a popular greenhouse crop, but can also be grown outside in most climates, and are ideal in deep beds. If you live in a cold area, choose early-maturing varieties, as the fruit on late-maturing plants will usually fail to ripen before the frosts (though it can make excellent green-tomato chutney, of a kind that cannot be bought in the shops). Tomatoes are obtainable as bush or upright (climbing) types. The fruit of bush types tends to be smaller. *Red Alert* is one of the best bush varieties, giving very early crops of small, tasty fruits; *Celebrity* is an excellent disease-resistant bush variety, with large fruits. Of the upright varieties, the best for cooler areas is *Gemini*. In warmer climates, the yellow variety *Golden Sunrise* is recommended for flavour. Suitable

Training tomatoes

Tie long piece of string to top of greenhouse. Dig hole directly underneath and flood with water. Loop string around root ball. Plant in hole, firming well. The root ball anchors the string.

Drying chilli peppers

Hot varieties can be dried outside on a raised wire frame, then stored in airtight jars or bottles.

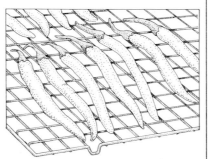

Peppers	SPRING Early Mid Late	SUMMER Early Mid Late	AUTUMN Early Mid Late	WINTER Early Mid Late
Sow inside				● ●
Plant out	● ●			
Sow outside				
Harvest		● ● ●		

varieties for the greenhouse are *Herald* and *Sonato,* which are both early and well-flavoured. The cherry-fruited *Gardener's Delight* and *Sweet 100* taste superb, but crop later and are not disease-resistant. For the greenhouse border, use a variety resistant to root rot, such as *Piranto* or *Celebrity.*

Soil and site Sun and well-manured soil retaining moisture and nutrients. pH 6.0. Plot A. Flood greenhouse borders with water two weeks before planting to flush out excess mineral salts from the soil: dig in well-rotted compost or manure, and one handful blood, fish, and bone meal per plant before planting.

Sowing and planting *Outside crops:* start seeds off inside mid spring in greenhouse or on windowsill, 2.5cm (1in) apart, in trays. Transfer to 8cm (3in) pots at seed-leaf stage. Harden off in cold frame late spring. Plant out early summer, 60cm (2ft) square (climbers against canes). *Deep beds:* plant 50cm (20in) apart. *Greenhouse:* sow mid winter onwards, depending on the heat available – in cold greenhouse, late winter at 21°C (70°F). When big enough to handle, transplant to 8cm (3in) pots. Grow on at a temperature of 10–12°C (50–55°F), spacing progressively so they are not crowded, to make short, bushy plants. Plant out in greenhouse border or growing bags 30cm (12in) apart mid spring in cold greenhouse. Water plants in initially; then leave for a week, so roots have to search for water and extensive root growth is thereby encouraged.

Maintenance Bush varieties need no staking or side-shooting; cover soil underneath plants with straw or bark to raise fruit off ground. Regularly tie climbing varieties in to canes, or to vertical strings in greenhouses. Remove side-shoots from each leaf joint while they are still small; take off bottom leaves when they turn

yellow. Pinch out tops after three clusters of fruit (four in warm climates); in greenhouses when reach top of house. Do not remove leaves above developing fruit cluster. Feed with liquid seaweed or animal-manure fertilizer, outside plants fortnightly from mid summer to early autumn, greenhouse plants with every watering from eight weeks after planting. *Greenhouse:* give each plant about 1 litre (2pts) of water a day, cherry tomatoes 1.5 litres (3pts) a week. At flowering, spray daily with water to provide humidity needed for good pollination. Shake strings to move pollen about.

Harvesting Pick fruits as soon as ripe for sweetest flavour and to encourage the production of more later in the season. At end of season, lay outside climbers flat on straw and cover with cloches or woven polypropylene to help ripen green fruit.

Pests and diseases Whitefly, aphids, leaf mould, red spider mites, potato blight, and virus.

Tomatoes	SPRING			SUMMER			AUTUMN			WINTER		
	Early	Mid	Late	Early	Mid	Late	Early	Mid	Late	Early	Mid	Late
Sow inside	●	●										
Plant out			●	●								
Sow outside												
Harvest					●	●	●	●	●			

Side-shooting
Remove side-shoots that develop from the angle between leaf stems and main stem.

Covering bush tomatoes
Protecting plants with a cloche at the end of the growing season helps to ripen green fruit.

Cultivating squash vegetables

Marrows, courgettes, melons, pumpkins, and cucumbers need slightly acid soil (pH about 6.0), enriched with compost or manure, and plenty of water to swell their pulpy fruits. If you are using the three-year crop rotation plan (*see page 128*), grow them in Plot A. Most need glass in temperate areas, but some can be grown outside after frosts have gone.

MARROWS AND COURGETTES

Courgettes are immature marrows, grown the same way. If space is short, grow a courgette variety, such as *Zebra Cross* or *Long Green Bush* marrows; towards the end of the season, allow a few fruits to grow into marrows. *Long Green Striped* is a fine trailing marrow; *Zucchini* and *Golden Zucchini* good courgettes.
Soil and site Plenty of compost or manure dug-in. pH 6.0. Plot A.
Sowing and planting Sow inside mid spring at 18°C (65°F), two seeds to each 8cm (3in) pot. Thin to one. Plant out 60cm (2ft) each way, in normal or deep beds. Or sow pairs of seeds outside two weeks before the last frosts.

Marrows, courgettes	SPRING			SUMMER			AUTUMN			WINTER		
	Early	Mid	Late	Early	Mid	Late	Early	Mid	Late	Early	Mid	Late
Sow inside		●	●									
Plant out			●	●								
Sow outside			●	●								
Harvest					●	●	●	●				

Protect with cut-off plastic bottles or cloches. In restricted space, grow up cane wigwams as for cucumbers (*see opposite*).
Maintenance Pinch out tops of plants when they reach the tops of the canes. Feed fortnightly from mid summer until harvesting with liquid seaweed or liquid manure fertilizer. Mulch with bark to control weeds and deter slugs.
Harvesting Cut courgettes when they are no more than 15cm (6in) long, to encourage further production. Cut marrows when they are large – up to 35cm (15in). Ripen at end of season and keep for short while in frost-free place.
Pests and diseases Slugs, aphids, mildew, cucumber mosaic virus.

PUMPKINS

True pumpkins are best suited to warm climates, but some of the related squashes can be grown for winter use in cooler climates. The largest pumpkins such as *Big Max* or *Mammoth Orange* are impractical for eating, unless your family is very large or you want to make jam. The smaller *Small Sugar* is good for general use in warmer areas. *Vegetable Spaghetti* is ideal for cooler climates and improves with keeping until mid winter. The apple squash *Gourmet Globe* is another small squash for either climate.
Soil and site Well-manured soil as required by all squashes: dig in plenty of compost or manure. pH 6.0. Plot A.
Sowing and planting *Outside crops:* sow inside mid spring at 18°C (65°F), two seeds in each 8cm (3in) pot. Thin to stronger seedling if necessary. Most winter squashes are trailing varieties and need plenty of room: plant at least 90cm (3ft) apart, late spring when frosts have gone. Or if sowing outside, do so about a fortnight earlier than that.
Maintenance Feed fortnightly mid summer/early autumn with liquid animal-manure fertilizer. Leave on male flowers. Pinch back trailing stems regularly.

Harvesting Leave winter squashes on plant as long as possible, while there is plenty of sunshine. At end of season, raise fruits off ground on wood or bricks to avoid rotting. When fruits start to fade, cut off, but leave in sun if possible to continue ripening: the harder the skins then, the better fruit will keep. Store in frost-free place, eat by mid winter.
Pests and diseases Slugs, aphids, mildew, cucumber mosaic virus.

Pumpkins, melons	SPRING			SUMMER			AUTUMN			WINTER		
	Early	Mid	Late	Early	Mid	Late	Early	Mid	Late	Early	Mid	Late
Sow inside	●	●	●									●
Plant out				●	●							
Sow outside				●	●							
Harvest						●	●	●				

MELONS

Because they can be grown without heat in summer and need only a little at the propagation stage, modern Cantaloupe and F1 hybrid varieties have replaced old-fashioned musk or sweet melons. In warm climates, these newer types are quite at home outside, and can be grown under cloches in cool climates. The small-fruited *Ogen* and *Sweetheart* varieties ripen quickly and are ideal for all areas. They and *Burpee Hybrid* are good for the greenhouse.

Soil and site Well-manured: dig in plenty of compost or manure. pH 6.0. Plot A.

Sowing and planting *Outside crops:* sow inside mid spring at 18°C (65°F), two seeds in each 8cm (3in) pot. Thin to one if necessary. Plant out late spring under cloches, 90cm (3ft) apart. *Greenhouse crops:* sow singly in 8cm (3in) pots early spring, at 21–24°C (70–75°F). Plant out 30–45cm (12–18in) apart in well-manured border or, ideally, hot bed; or in growing bags or pots (in these conditions plants need more careful watering). In cold greenhouse, plant mid spring.

Maintenance It is important to water regularly. *Outside crops:* pinch out growing point when plants have made three leaves. Plants will then make side-shoots: stop these after three leaves. When fruits form, pinch back to two leaves beyond fruit. *Greenhouse:* a week after planting, pinch out growing point to keep only two true leaves. Allow the two side-shoots that grow from this point to grow on the ground, or train them up wires. Stop these side-shoots after seven/ten leaves. Secondary leaves and flowers then appear. When embryo fruits appear, stop two leaves beyond fruit. Only allow about five fruits per plant. Place nets around maturing fruits for support and attach to overhead wires. Allow insects access to house for pollination. Spray leaves and damp paths and borders each morning, except when fruit is ripening; then leave atmosphere dry and ventilate freely. Feed with liquid fertilizer at each watering.

Harvesting Cut fruits when they feel soft at the ends.

Pests and diseases Slugs, aphids, mildew, cucumber mosaic virus.

CUCUMBERS

New varieties are well worth growing outside even in temperate climates; the greenhouse is only needed for the very earliest. *Sweet Success* produces long, almost seedless fruits. *Burpless Tasty Green* is said to be easier to digest! For greenhouses, *Fembaby* has small, superbly-flavoured fruit, *Uniflora D* is very heavy cropping, *Athene* ideal in slightly cooler houses. All these grow perfectly well in the same temperature and humidity as tomatoes, so they can share the same greenhouse.

Soil and site Well-manured soil: dig in plenty of compost or manure. pH 6.0. Plot A.

Sowing and planting *Outside crops:* sow inside mid spring at 18°C (65°F), two seeds to each 8cm (3in) pot. At germination, thin to stronger seedling. Plant out 60cm (2ft) apart late spring. Or sow pairs of seeds outside late spring at same spacings. Cover site with cut-off plastic bottle or cloches to protect against cold wind and slugs. Or grow up cane wigwam as on page 141, spacing four 3m (9ft) canes 60cm (2ft) apart, tied at top. Tie plants in as they grow to save space, and keep fruit away from slugs.

Deep beds: grow up canes 60cm (2ft) apart. *Greenhouse crops:* sow singly in 8cm (3in) pots of potting compost, from mid winter if house can be at 10°C (50°F), mid spring in cold house. Place pots in propagator at 24–27°C (75–80°F). At germination, move to light, airy place at 15–18°C (60–65°F). Plant and support in borders or growing bags as for tomatoes.

Maintenance Frequently tie in plants to canes or strings. Handle delicate plants carefully when twisting them round strings. Regularly trim side-shoots to two leaves for compact, bushy growth. Pinch out tops when plants reach tops of canes. Newer varieties mentioned here fruit mostly from main stem; older varieties on side-shoots, so remove any from main stem. Do not remove male flowers. Feed with liquid seaweed or animal-manure fertilizer, outside plants fortnightly from mid summer to harvesting, greenhouse plants after eight weeks at each watering.

Greenhouse: Never allow plants to dry out. Damp down paths and plants at least twice daily (morning and early afternoon). Ventilate to 18–24°C (65–75°F) during day; shut vents at night at least until early summer.

Harvesting Cut fruits regularly when young (with a bloom), to encourage more.

Pests and diseases Slugs, aphids, mildew, cucumber mosaic virus.

Cucumbers	SPRING Early Mid Late	SUMMER Early Mid Late	AUTUMN Early Mid Late	WINTER Early Mid Late
Sow inside	● ● ●			● ●
Plant out	●	●		
Sow outside	●			
Harvest		● ●	● ●	

Cultivating root vegetables

These staple and easily cultivated crops can not only be harvested and eaten fresh, but many of them, such as swedes, turnips, and beetroot, can be easily and conveniently stored to ensure a ready supply of fresh vegetables throughout the winter months. Many are a good source of minerals, vitamins, and dietary fibre.

JERUSALEM ARTICHOKES
All the flavour of globe artichokes, but much easier to grow. The plants can grow to 3m (9ft), making a useful windbreak. Generally just sold as Jerusalem artichokes – buy tubers from the greengrocer, choosing the least knobbly ones.
Soil and site Will grow practically anywhere, but a permanent, well-prepared site ensures bigger, smoother tubers. Dig trench 60cm (2ft) wide and a spade deep. Break up bottom; refill, working in as much well-rotted compost, manure or an alternative as possible. Acid soil (pH below 6.5).
Planting As early as soil conditions allow (usually late winter/early spring), set tubers 15cm (6in) deep, 30cm (12in) apart; make rows at least 1.5m (5ft) apart (but one row is usually all that is needed). In too shallow a drill, tubers may force their way to the surface and turn green.
Maintenance Weed and water. Mulch annually in early spring with well-rotted compost or manure. Handful of blood, fish, and bone meal per m/yd of row. In exposed areas, support plants with nylon string between two posts.
Harvesting Cut down stems mid autumn to leave 30cm (12in). Dig tubers as required. Leave some in ground for next year's crop.
Pests and diseases Trouble free.

Using Jerusalem artichokes as a windbreak
Position these vegetables to protect other plants from wind, but ensure they do not shade other crops.

Jerusalem artichokes	SPRING Early Mid Late	SUMMER Early Mid Late	AUTUMN Early Mid Late	WINTER Early Mid Late
Sow inside				
Plant out	•			•
Sow outside				
Harvest			• •	• • •

RADISHES
Radishes tolerate a wide range of soils and conditions, so can be grown almost anywhere you have room to spare, even as a "catch-crop" between rows of vegetables that mature more slowly, such as broad beans and parsnips. *French Breakfast* is the best variety, with long, mildly-flavoured, crisp roots. *Cherry Belle* is round and red, and a good fast developer.
Soil and site Will produce a reasonable crop in any soil, but better if enriched with well-rotted compost or manure. Ideally, give them shade and moisture in summer, full sun early spring and autumn. Plot C.
Sowing Scatter small amounts of seeds outside thinly in rows 15cm (6in) apart, late winter under cloches. After that, sow small amounts outside weekly until autumn. Thinning is not normally necessary. To improve yields, multiple sow early crops indoors and plant out under cloches. *Deep beds:* sow in wide, shallow bands, scattering the seeds thinly across the band.
Maintenance Water if soil is dry. Keep weed-free by hoeing.
Harvesting Pull regularly, to avoid the roots becoming hot and woody.
Pests and diseases Flea beetles.

Radishes	SPRING Early Mid Late	SUMMER Early Mid Late	AUTUMN Early Mid Late	WINTER Early Mid Late
Sow inside				
Plant out				
Sow outside	• • •	• • •	• •	•
Harvest	• •	• • •	• • •	•

CARROTS

It is possible to get a succession throughout the year. For multiple sowing, round types like *Kundulus* or *Paris Rondo* are essential. For early outdoor sowings, use fast-maturing varieties like *Amstel* or one of the *Nantes* strains. For maincrops, choose a larger type like *Autumn King* or *Chantenay Red Cored*.

Soil and site Best on light soil, with plenty of organic matter (well-rotted to prevent forking). On heavy soil, grow in raised deep beds. pH over 6.5. Plot A.

Sowing Multiple sow earliest crops late winter, six–seven seeds per cell. Plant out 23cm (9in) apart under cloches mid/late winter, in open ground mid spring. Or sow outside under cloches late winter – round varieties in wide bands; long types in drills 23cm (9in) apart, thinned when just big enough to eat. Thereafter, sow outside every three weeks, in drills 30cm (12in) apart. Thin to 8cm (3in). *Deep beds:* plant out multiple sowings in staggered rows 15cm (6in) apart. Or sow round varieties as above, long types throughout the growing season in drills 15cm (6in) apart. Thin to 8cm (3in).

Maintenance Hoe to keep weed free. Pull a little soil round swelling carrots to prevent "shoulders" going green and to deter carrot fly.

Harvesting Pull early and successional sowings while still young. Lift final sowing mid/late autumn; store in moist bark or compost. Left in ground too long, some may split, attracting slugs.

Pests and diseases Carrot fly, storage rot.

Carrots	SPRING			SUMMER			AUTUMN			WINTER		
	Early	Mid	Late	Early	Mid	Late	Early	Mid	Late	Early	Mid	Late
Sow inside											●	●
Plant out	●											●
Sow outside	●	●	●	●	●						●	●
Harvest		●	●	●	●	●	●	●	●			

SALSIFY AND SCORZONERA

These two gourmet vegetables are much alike in flavour and can be grown the same way. *Mammoth* and *Sandwich Island Mammoth* are good salsifies, *Habil* the best scorzonera.

Soil and site Very deep, well-manured soil. Plot A.

Sowing Sow outside mid spring in drills 2.5cm (1in) deep and 30cm (12in) apart. Thin to 15cm (6in).

Maintenance Hoe to keep weed free; better still, mulch in autumn with well-rotted compost.

Harvesting Lift roots late autumn and store in moist compost or bark in frost-free shed. Or leave some roots in ground, cover with soil to blanch leaves, harvest spring to use raw in salads. Or cook unblanched.

Pests and diseases Trouble free.

Salsify, scorzonera	SPRING			SUMMER			AUTUMN			WINTER		
	Early	Mid	Late	Early	Mid	Late	Early	Mid	Late	Early	Mid	Late
Sow inside												
Plant out												
Sow outside		●										
Harvest								●	●			

SWEDES

As a brassica, swede is sometimes prone to club root. New varieties are a great improvement on the old ones. Try *Purple Top Yellow* and *Marian*.

Soil and site To deter club root, well-drained soil is necessary, pH over 6.5. Plot C.

Sowing To guard against mildew, sow late spring/early summer, outside in shallow drills 45cm (18in) apart. Thin to 30cm (12in).

Maintenance Hoe to keep weed free. Water if necessary. Mulch with compost or manure.

Harvesting Roots can be left in soil in milder areas, but this may encourage disease. Better to lift mid autumn after frosts, twist off tops, store in moist bark or compost.

Pests and diseases Mildew, flea beetles, soft rot, club root.

Swedes	SPRING			SUMMER			AUTUMN			WINTER		
	Early	Mid	Late	Early	Mid	Late	Early	Mid	Late	Early	Mid	Late
Sow inside												
Plant out												
Sow outside		●		●								
Harvest								●	●			

CELERIAC

A superb vegetable with all the flavour of celery hearts. Try *Alabaster, Globus* and *Snow White*.
Soil and site Plenty of sun; water-retentive soil rich in organic matter. pH 6.0. Plot A.
Sowing and planting Sow inside in greenhouse or on windowsill at 18°C (65°F) mid spring (any earlier, and crop will run to seed). When first true leaves show, transplant to wider spacings. Harden off in cold frame. Plant out late spring – swelling at base of plant at soil level – 30cm (12in) apart, 35cm (15in) between rows. *Deep beds:* plant in blocks, 30cm (12in) between plants.
Maintenance Mulch with well-rotted manure. Keep well watered in dry weather. Draw soil around stems in early autumn to blanch.
Harvesting Lift regularly; store in boxes of moist bark or compost in frost-free shed.
Pests and diseases Trouble free.

TURNIPS

Very easy to grow. *Early Purple Top Milan* is best for first crops (especially multiple sown) and for successional sowing. *Tokyo Cross* stores well, as does *Golden Ball*.
Soil and site Grow earliest varieties in well-manured soil; maincrop and storage varieties with brassicas. pH above 6.5. Plot C.
Sowing and planting Multiple sow earliest crops late winter, six per block at 18°C (65°F). Harden off. Plant out late spring under cloches, 30cm (12in) apart. Or sow outside mid spring to mid summer, in shallow drills 30cm

Turnips	SPRING Early Mid Late			SUMMER Early Mid Late			AUTUMN Early Mid Late			WINTER Early Mid Late		
Sow inside												•
Plant out			•									
Sow outside		•	•	•	•							
Harvest			•	•	•	•	•	•				

(12in) apart. Thin to 15cm (6in).
Maintenance Keep meticulously weed free. Water if necessary. Mulch with well-rotted compost or manure to avoid tough roots.
Harvesting Pull first roots at golf-ball size, biggest at tennis-ball size. Mid autumn, lift maincrops, twist off tops and store in moist bark or compost.
Pests and diseases Flea beetles, soft rot.

BEETROOT

Try *Boltardy* or *Early Wonder* for earlies, *Cylindra* or *Burpees Golden* for successionals. Round types like *Boltardy* or *Detroit Dark Red* are good multiple sown.
Soil and site Deep, enriched soil. pH 6.5. Plot A.
Sowing Wash seeds in flour sieve to remove germination-inhibiting chemicals. Multiple sow two seed clusters per cell mid/late winter. Harden off early spring. Plant out under cloches mid spring, 30cm (12in) square. Or sow outside under cloches early spring, one/two clusters every 8cm (3in) in 2.5cm (1in) deep drills 30cm (12in) apart. Thin by pulling

Beetroot	SPRING Early Mid Late			SUMMER Early Mid Late			AUTUMN Early Mid Late			WINTER Early Mid Late		
Sow inside											•	•
Plant out												•
Sow outside	•	•	•	•	•							•
Harvest			•	•	•	•	•	•	•			

selectively at golf-ball size. Sow three-weekly until mid summer. Sow maincrops outside then. Thin to 8cm (3in). *Deep beds:* Sow earliest in wide bands; pull selectively. Sow successionally in staggered rows 8cm (3in) apart. Thin to 8cm (3in).
Maintenance Hoe regularly. Mulch with compost, manure, or wet newspaper.
Harvesting Pull earlies as "baby beet" at golf-ball size, maincrops at tennis-ball size. Lift mid/late autumn; store cool and frost-free.
Pests and diseases Mildew.

SWEET POTATOES

Only for warm climates. *Try Centennial* and *Porto Rico*.
Soil and site Sandy soil best; on heavy land, dig layer of compost or manure in bottom of deep furrows; ridge soil into mounds 25cm (10in) high. Plot A.
Planting A month after last frost, set bought plants 30cm (1ft) apart in rows.
Maintenance Weed until plants meet in rows. No need to water – plants thrive in hot, dry weather.
Harvesting Lift and store as potatoes, before the first frosts.
Pests and diseases Slugs, wireworms, cutworms, aphids.

POTATOES

Recommended European early varieties are *Maris Bard, Irish Peace* and *Arkula*. The numerous varieties perform differently in different areas: try a few tubers of a new type each year. In the USA, *White Cobbler* is excellent; *Arran Pilot* and *Cliff's Kidney* are good in Australasia.

Maincrop varieties are dug in autumn and stored for winter use. *Desiree* is a good, large European red, *Drayton* a fine white. In the USA, one of the best keepers is *Red Pontiac*; *Sebago* is highly thought of in Australasia.

Soil and site Water-retentive soil, with plenty of organic matter. Without enough well-rotted compost or manure for the whole plot, dig planting furrows deeply and put a layer in the bottom, setting the tubers directly on it. Acid soil (do not lime). Plot A.

Planting Buy seed potatoes as early as possible (small tubers with few sprouts, certified diseasefree). Put in boxes, or (if just a few) in egg cartons, in light place at 10°C (50°F) for good, short, bushy green sprouts. USA

seedsmen supply potato eyes rather than whole tubers. Pot these up and put in greenhouse or on windowsill until planting.

Earlies: plant late winter through black polythene under cloches (an ideal deep-bed method), or in rows 60cm (2ft) apart, tubers 30cm (12in) apart and 15cm (6in) deep, covered with woven polypropylene. Plant the first unprotected crop early/mid spring at same distances.

Maincrops: plant tubers at same time, but 35cm (15in) apart in rows 75cm (2ft 6in) apart. Set plants raised from eyes at same spacings late spring after last frost.

Maintenance If shoots emerge before all frost has gone, cover with a little soil. At 15–20cm

(6–8in), handful of blood, fish, and bone meal per m/yd of row. Earth up by pulling soil between rows up to shoots: leave a few centimetres showing. Repeat three weeks later if plants in rows have not met.

Harvesting *Earlies:* lift for immediate needs when flowering begins, leaving rest to grow on. *Maincrops:* dig mid autumn. Cut and compost foliage (burning any diseased leaves). Dig from sides of ridges to avoid tuber damage. Dry in heap for few hours. Store perfect tubers in paper or hessian sacks in frost-free place. Use blemished tubers at once.

Pests and diseases Slugs, wireworm, potato cyst eelworm, potato blight, scab, potato blackleg, spraing, wart disease.

Potatoes	SPRING			SUMMER			AUTUMN			WINTER		
	Early	Mid	Late	Early	Mid	Late	Early	Mid	Late	Early	Mid	Late
Sow inside												
Plant out	●	●	●									●
Sow outside												
Harvest				●	●	●	●	●	●			

PARSNIPS AND HAMBURG PARSLEY

The distinctive sweet taste of parsnips makes them popular winter roots. *Hollow Crown* forms long, tapering roots. The smaller *Avonresister* has longer roots and a marked resistance to canker disease. Hamburg parsley is grown the same way as parsnips.

Soil and site Tolerate fairly poor conditions, but best with plenty of dug-in compost or manure. pH 6.5. In stony soil, make holes with crowbar at 15cm (6in) intervals, 45cm (18in) deep and 8cm (3in) diameter. Fill with good soil or organic matter. Plot A.

Sowing Little point in sowing too early – germinate very slowly below 12°C (45°F). In cold areas, sow outside in stale seed bed mid

spring, in warmer areas, early autumn: two/three seeds 15cm (6in) apart in shallow drills 30cm (12in) apart; sow a few radishes in the drill to mark it for hoeing. Or pre-germinate seeds and fluid sow. On heavy soil, sow two/three seeds per pre-made hole. Thin to one. *Deep beds:* sow in blocks 15cm (6in) apart.

Maintenance Keep weed free.

Water fairly constantly to prevent roots cracking.

Harvesting In cool climates, lift after first frosts (these improve flavour and kill off top growth). Store in frost-free shed in boxes between layers of moist bark or compost. In warm areas, parsnips can be left in ground.

Pests and diseases Carrot root fly, parsnip canker.

Parsnips, Hamburg parsley	SPRING			SUMMER			AUTUMN			WINTER		
	Early	Mid	Late	Early	Mid	Late	Early	Mid	Late	Early	Mid	Late
Sow inside												
Plant out												
Sow outside	●						●					
Harvest									●			

Cultivating leaf vegetables

Most leaf vegetables are brassicas and therefore prone to club-root disease so crop rotation and careful soil preparation are essential. As for soil and site requirements for brassicas, lime soil if necessary to raise the pH to 6.5–7.0. Dig in any spare compost or manure. Add two handfuls of blood, fish, and bone meal per square metre/yard. The soil should be well-firmed, so there is no need to dig after the last crop is lifted, except for summer cabbages (planted in spring). With three-year crop rotation, grow brassicas in Plot C (*see page 128*).

BRUSSELS SPROUTS

Improved greatly by a touch of frost. Brussels sprouts can be interplanted with fast-maturing crops like lettuces and radishes. To ensure a long harvesting period, grow the more expensive F1 hybrids that stand for a long time without deteriorating. You will only need two seasonal crops: the early *Peer Gynt* is ready in early autumn and holds on the plant until mid winter; *Fortress* or *Citadel* takes over until spring.
Soil and site See above.
Sowing and planting Need longer growing period than other brassicas, so sow thinly outside in seed bed early/mid spring, in shallow drills 15cm (6in) apart. Net against birds. Plant out when 5–8cm (2–3in) tall, spaced 1m (3ft) square for eating fresh, but 50cm (20in) square for smaller sprouts to freeze. Use a dibber and firm in well. Water, then leave for at least a week before watering again.

Deep beds: growing this way does not increase yield, but sprouts grow perfectly well, at same distances as above, with other crops between rows. No need to firm. Support in winter.
Maintenance Water and weed. Either grow "catch crops" between plants or cover soil with compost, paper, or black polythene to control weeds and reduce watering. Do not add too much fertilizer for "catch-crops", or sprouts will become "soft"; on fertile, organic soil, "catch-crops" should thrive without added fertilizer. Compost yellowing leaves in autumn. Net against birds. Stake tall types with a post at each end of row, nylon twine stretched either side of plants.
Harvesting Start early autumn, or when bottom sprouts are firm; continue until early spring. Pick from bottom upwards, removing and composting yellowing leaves to prevent fungus disease. Dig out stripped plants, pulverize or shred before composting.
Pests and diseases Cabbage butterfly, cabbage moth, cabbage root fly, club root.

Brussels sprouts	SPRING Early Mid Late			SUMMER Early Mid Late			AUTUMN Early Mid Late			WINTER Early Mid Late		
Sow inside												
Plant out												
Sow outside	•	•										
Harvest	•						•	•	•	•	•	•

KALE

Perhaps not the most flavoursome of brassicas, but hardy and useful in hard winters. Newer varieties are greatly improved. There are curly and smooth-leaved types. *Cottagers* stands most winters, but does not taste as well as *Dwarf Green Curled* or *Hungry Gap*.
Soil and site See above.
Sowing and planting Sow outside in seed bed mid/late spring in shallow drills 15cm (6in) apart. Plant out 45cm (18in) apart. *Deep beds:* plant 35cm (15in) apart.
Maintenance Water regularly. Hoe and mulch to keep weed free. Support on exposed site.
Harvesting Pull a few leaves from centre of each plant while still young and tender. When harvesting is complete, pull rest of plant to deter club root.
Pests and diseases Cabbage butterflies, cabbage moth, cabbage root fly, club root.

Kale	SPRING Early Mid Late			SUMMER Early Mid Late			AUTUMN Early Mid Late			WINTER Early Mid Late		
Sow inside												
Plant out												
Sow outside		•	•									
Harvest	•								•	•	•	•

SPINACH

No garden should be without spinach. Try *Bloomsdale* and *Melody*. Amaranth spinach ("Timpala" or "Hinn Choy") withstands high temperatures in hot areas, as does the spinach substitute New Zealand spinach.
Soil and site Rich, moisture-retentive soil: add organic matter. pH above 6.5 (lime if necessary). Some shade (runs to seed in sun). Plot B.
Sowing Sow first crops inside in greenhouse or on windowsill late winter at 18°C (65°F), pairs of seeds in polystyrene cells or small pots. Thin to stronger seedling. Plant out under cloches early spring, 15cm (6in) apart in rows

30cm (12in) apart, New Zealand spinach mid spring 60cm (2ft) apart. Sow monthly outside until mid summer in shallow drills 30cm (12in) apart. Thin to 15cm (6in). Sow amaranth spinach outside late spring after frosts, in shallow rows 20cm (8in) apart. Thin to 15cm (8in). *Deep beds:* plant out or sow

in blocks, 20cm (8in) each way.
Maintenance Water and weed.
Harvesting Take a few leaves for continual growth. Pick amaranth spinach regularly, 5–8cm (2–3in) shoots of New Zealand spinach from mid summer to first frosts.
Pests and diseases Aphids, downy mildew, mosaic virus.

Spinach	SPRING Early Mid Late			SUMMER Early Mid Late			AUTUMN Early Mid Late			WINTER Early Mid Late		
Sow inside											•	
Plant out	•											
Sow outside	•	•	•	•	•							
Harvest			•	•	•	•	•	•	•	•		

SPINACH BEET

Usually just sold as *Spinach Beet* or *Perpetual Spinach*.
Soil and site Rich, moisture-retentive soil. pH above 6.5. Shade if possible. Plot B.
Sowing Sow outside in 2.5cm (1in) drills in spring for summer picking, in summer for winter, two seeds every 30cm (12in), 30cm (12in) between rows. Thin to single seedling. *Deep beds:* seeds in staggered rows 23cm (9in) apart.

Maintenance Water copiously in dry weather. Hoe out weeds.
Harvesting Pick outer leaves when still young and crisp. Never strip plants, so leaves regrow.
Pests and diseases Slugs, birds.

Spinach beet	SPRING Early Mid Late			SUMMER Early Mid Late			AUTUMN Early Mid Late			WINTER Early Mid Late		
Sow inside												
Plant out												
Sow outside	•	•			•	•						
Harvest	•	•	•	•	•	•	•	•	•	•	•	•

SWISS CHARD

Regarded as a "spinach substitute", but with quite a different flavour and considered a delicacy in some parts of the world. It is generally just offered as *Swiss Chard, Seakale Beet,* or *Silver Beet. Ruby Chard* has no advantage in flavour, but its distinctive red stems make it attractive in the flower borders.
Soil and site. Rich, moisture-retentive soil best: add any spare organic matter. pH above 6.5 (lime generally required). Plot B.
Sowing Mid spring, sow groups of two/three seeds outside 30cm (12in) apart in shallow drills 35cm (15in) apart. Thin clusters to strongest seedlings. Sow again

mid summer for winter use. In very cold areas, sow where crop can be covered with cloches. *Deep beds:* sow at same time. Thin to 23cm (9in) in staggered rows.
Maintenance Water and weed. Cover rows with cloches in very cold winters.
Harvesting Mid summer, pull

leaves off plant as with rhubarb: cutting causes bleeding. Take just a few leaves from outside of plant, leaving remainder to grow on. Fleshy mid-ribs considered a delicacy and sometimes cooked separately. Can withstand frost, so harvest throughout winter.
Pests and diseases Slugs.

Swiss chard	SPRING Early Mid Late			SUMMER Early Mid Late			AUTUMN Early Mid Late			WINTER Early Mid Late		
Sow inside												
Plant out												
Sow outside		•		•								
Harvest					•	•	•	•	•	•	•	•

CAULIFLOWERS

The most difficult of the brassicas to cultivate, but well worth it on land free of club root. The three types mature in summer, autumn, and winter/spring. Among the summer types, *Snow King* grows fast, with a good flavour; *Snow Crown* is also recommended. Of the autumn types, *All the Year Round* lives up to its name, but best late summer to early autumn. *Dok Elgon* is superb, maturing in 16 weeks and going on to late autumn. *Veitch's Self Protecting* matures late autumn, and stands until mid winter. Available in many countries, the Australian *Barrier Reef*, *Canberra* and *Snowcap* give a good succession.

Of winter/spring cauliflowers, *Newton Seale* produces large, white heads in mid/late winter, standing very low temperatures. The reliably hardy *Purple Cape* crops early spring, its purple curds turning green when cooked. *St. George's* very large curds are ready mid spring; *Asmer Juno* goes on through late spring, into early summer in some areas.

Soil and site See Introduction (*page 152*). Few plants react to signs of nutrient deficiencies (*see right*). If lime levels are correct and symptoms still occur, hoe in two handfuls of seaweed meal per sq. m/yd to replace trace elements.

Sowing and planting *Summer types:* make first sowing inside mid winter, in heated greenhouse or on windowsill. When big enough to handle, transfer to wider spacings in a larger seed tray. Plant out late winter when no more than 5cm (2in) high, 50cm (20in) square under cloches. Check each plant has a growing point and is not "blind". Ensure plants never stay too long in trays. Sow second crop inside the same way late winter. Plant out in open ground early spring. Continue sowing outside in seed bed in shallow drills 15cm (6in) apart, every three weeks from early to late spring. Before 8cm (3in) high, transplant at same distances. Water before and after transplanting. *Autumn types:* sow outside mid spring in seed bed in shallow drills 15cm (6in) apart. Plant out early/mid summer, 60cm (2ft) apart, at same depths. *Winter/spring types:* sow outside mid/late spring in seed bed. Before 8cm (3in) high, plant out 75cm (2ft 6in) square. *Deep beds:* plant summer types in staggered rows, 45cm (18in) apart each way; other types 60cm (2ft) apart, at same time as normal beds.

Maintenance Keep weed free. Plants must never go short of water. Mulch with organic matter, polythene, or paper; hand water in dry weather. Firm autumn types in ground late summer. Bend winter/spring types over to face north late autumn.

Harvesting *Summer types:* cut curds. If too many mature simultaneously, lift and store for few weeks in cool shed. Remove and compost stumps. *Other types:* break a few leaves over mature curds; cut as needed. Remove rest of plant. No need to lift as they will not run to seed.

Pests and diseases Cabbage butterflies, cabbage moth, cabbage root fly, club root. Shortage of molybdenum may cause "whiptail" (thin and deformed leaves); lack of boron makes small, bitter curds, and stems and leaves turn brown; shortage of magnesium may turn leaves yellow, reddish or purple.

Cauliflowers	SPRING Early Mid Late			SUMMER Early Mid Late			AUTUMN Early Mid Late			WINTER Early Mid Late		
Sow inside										•	•	
Plant out	•											•
Sow outside	•	•	•									
Harvest	•	•	•	•	•	•	•	•	•	•	•	•

CHINESE CABBAGE

Tip Top and *Two Seasons Hybrid* are both good, resisting bolting (flower and produce seed).

Soil and site. See Introduction (*page 152*). Grow in shade, alongside other brassicas, but in a special bed with plenty of compost or manure.

Sowing Sow outside late spring to mid summer in shallow drills 30cm (12in) apart, two seeds every 23cm (9in). Thin to stronger seedling. As they will not store, sow fortnightly for a succession. *Deep beds:* sow in blocks, 23cm (9in) apart. Thin to 23cm (9in).

Maintenance Always keep soil moist. Hoe regularly to weed.

Harvesting Eight to ten weeks after sowing.

Pests and diseases Club root, flea beetles, slugs, millipedes.

Chinese cabbage	SPRING Early Mid Late			SUMMER Early Mid Late			AUTUMN Early Mid Late			WINTER Early Mid Late		
Sow inside												
Plant out												
Sow outside			•	•	•							
Harvest					•	•	•	•				

CALABRESE AND BROCCOLI

Calabrese is simply broccoli that matures in summer. *Green Comet* produces succulent green heads 40 days after planting. *Romanesco* makes creamy yellow heads of superb flavour in late summer and autumn. *Early Purple Sprouting* and *White Sprouting* give spears from mid winter to late spring.
Soil and site See Introduction (*page 152*).
Sowing and planting Sow outside in shallow drills 15cm (6in) apart in seed bed: calabrese mid spring, broccoli late spring. Plant out calabrese 15cm (6in) apart, broccoli at least 60cm (2ft) apart, 30cm (12in) between rows.

Calabrese, broccoli	SPRING Early Mid Late	SUMMER Early Mid Late	AUTUMN Early Mid Late	WINTER Early Mid Late
Sow inside				
Plant out				
Sow outside	• •	•		
Harvest	• • •	• •	• •	•

Maintenance Water regularly. Mulch against weeds by covering soil with organic matter or black polythene.
Harvesting Cut central shoot first, while it is still green, to encourage the production of side-shoots. Broccoli continues to produce side-shoots over a considerable period if they are removed regularly. Prevent broccoli from flowering by pinching out the buds.
Pests and diseases Cabbage butterfly, cabbage moth, cabbage root fly, club root.

CABBAGES

To harvest cabbages all year, plant three different types: spring, summer, and autumn/winter cabbages. The spring *April* is very resistant to running to seed. *Durham Early* stands a long time. *Hispi* is probably the most popular summer cabbage, with hard, crisp hearts; its leaves make fine collards ("spring greens"). *Hornspi* is even earlier. For a succession of autumn/winter cabbages, you need two varieties. For early autumn, use *Minicole* or *Celtic*. Good winter varieties are the savoys *January King* and *Savoy Ace Hybrid*. Of the red cabbages, *Ruby Ball* is excellent. Cabbages grow satisfactorily in deep beds.
Soil and site See Introduction (*page 152*).
Sowing and planting *Spring types:* sow outside in seed bed mid/late summer in shallow drills 15cm (6in) apart. Only a very short row is needed – no more than 45cm (18in) long produces 50–100 plants. Plant out in 45cm (18in) squares early/mid autumn. *Summer types:* sow earliest crop inside late winter, on windowsill or in greenhouse. When large enough to handle, transplant to wider spacing in seed tray. Harden off.

Plant out under cloches early spring, 45cm (18in) squares. At same time, plant out hardened-off plants in open ground for later harvesting. Sow outside mid spring in seed bed. Transplant late spring/early summer to 45cm (18in) apart when large enough. *Autumn/winter and red types:* sow outside in seed bed mid/late spring in shallow drills 15cm (6in) apart. Transplant mid summer to 45cm (18in) squares.

Deep beds: Spring types: plant out in blocks, plants staggered 15cm (6in) each way. *Summer and autumn/winter types:* timings the same as normal bed, but space 35cm (15in) apart.
Maintenance *Spring types:* weed. Water freely when young. One handful of dried blood per four plants late winter. *Summer and autumn/winter types:* keep weed free and watered.

Harvesting *Spring types:* harvest first pickings as "spring greens" selectively to leave final spacings 30cm (12in) each way. Leave other plants to harvest early spring to early summer. *Summer types:* cut when hearts feel firm. Cut a cross in top of remaining stem, and a couple of new small cabbages will grow. Or dig up the root to discourage pests and diseases. *Autumn/winter types:* harvest when heads are firm and solid. Pull *Minicole* late autumn; hang upside down, stalk attached, in cold shed to keep for two months. Savoys stand any amount of frost, so can be left in ground until needed. Cut red cabbages when heads are firm and solid. Late autumn, pull and hang in cool shed for winter.
Pests and diseases Cabbage butterflies, cabbage moth, cabbage root fly, club root.

Cabbages	SPRING Early Mid Late	SUMMER Early Mid Late	AUTUMN Early Mid Late	WINTER Early Mid Late
Sow inside				• •
Plant out	•			•
Sow outside	• • •	• •		
Harvest	• • •	• • •	• • •	• • •

Growing
Organic
Fruit

This chapter gives advice on growing fruit trees and bushes. Look at pages 44–57 for ideas on the range of fruit available. All fences and walls can be utilized for growing fan-trained fruit. A warm, south-facing wall is particularly valuable, especially in temperate regions for the more tender types, such as peaches, nectarines, and figs. Pears and apples can be grown on east- and west-facing walls, and morello cherries and quinces on walls facing north. Vines also look good scrambling up walls and will give a good crop of wine berries. Redcurrants and gooseberries can be grown as decorative double or triple cordons against walls or fences.

Grow strawberries, gooseberries, redcurrants, and blackcurrants in the ornamental borders and consider a cherry, mulberry, orange, lemon, peach, plum, apple, or pear tree as a lawn specimen. If you need a hedge to divide one part of the garden from another, try cordon apples and pears or single-tier espaliers, or stepovers, only 30cm (12in) high, as a decorative and productive edging to a fruit plot.

All-time favourites
One of the most luscious soft fruits and really needing no introduction, strawberries are easy to grow in the organic garden.

Selecting fruit trees and bushes

Many local features, such as slopes, which may cause frost pockets, altitude, and wind protection, will affect the fruit in your garden. There are several simple measures you can take to prevent any adverse effects.

Frost is one of the main problems. If your garden is in a frost pocket, you may be limited to varieties that flower late and so escape spring frosts: recommendations are given in the cultivation sections (*see pages 164–75*).

Strong winds can also be a problem, since they desiccate foliage, damage flowers, and discourage vital pollinating insects. If your site is exposed, it is worth protecting fruit: initially by erecting a temporary plastic windbreak, then by planting a hedge nearby to take over from the windbreak when it has grown high enough. To avoid creating an artificial frost pocket in your garden by cutting off the escape route of cold air, raise the foot of the windbreak 30cm (12in) off the ground and keep the bottom of the hedge free of vegetation and rubbish. The cultivation details (*see pages 164–75*) give the best site for each fruit.

Soil preparation

Soil preferences and optimum pH are also given for each plant in the cultivation details. Before planting fruit, it is essential to prepare the soil well. Some plants have specific requirements, dealt with in the relevant sections, but, for most, the normal organic methods of soil care will ensure healthy trees and bushes and so produce bigger yields.

Choosing fruit

There are several important points to bear in mind when choosing varieties. Pollination is the first essential. Some varieties are self-fertile, while others need to be fertilized with pollen from a plant of a different variety, and you need to grow at least two varieties.

The size of the tree is important (*see opposite*). Take into account, too, the keeping qualities of the fruit: early apples, though wonderful when eaten straight from the tree, will not keep as well as late-maturing varieties.

Buying fruit trees and bushes

Firstly, always buy your plants from a specialist grower. If you can visit the nursery, you will have the opportunity of choosing the best-shaped trees and bushes – look for a uniform shape and a good root system.

Secondly, buy young plants; the old wives' tale that trees take seven years to come into bearing, so the older the tree you buy the better, is untrue. In fact, the reverse is the case. Young trees establish very quickly and will crop earlier than those that have languished in a pot or a field for several years.

Thirdly, buy fruit trees and bushes as bare-rooted plants, and plant in winter when they are dormant. Bare-rooted plants tend to be better quality and cheaper than those in containers.

Finally, in most countries fruit is covered by a Government health scheme. If the nursery cannot guarantee that their stock is certified free from disease, go elsewhere.

POLLINATION	ROOTSTOCKS
Choose self-fertile trees or grow two that can pollinate each other; "triploids" cannot pollinate other trees but need pollinating so you need three trees. Greenhouse and early flowering plants have to be pollinated by hand. This can be done by gently dabbing the centre of each flower with a camel-hair brush.	A rootstock is a selected root system on to which is grafted a variety. It controls the growth rate and size of tree; the grafted variety decides the type of fruit that will be produced.  **Planting a grafted root stock** *The grafting point must be 10cm (4in) above the soil to prevent the variety rooting.*

TREE SHAPES

The ultimate size and shape of a tree are important considerations. When you are choosing, keep in mind that most trees will cast some shade and this could very easily affect nearby plants. Always check the eventual height and spread of a tree as shown. If you have a large garden, a standard or bush tree can be very attractive. However, if your garden is small, many of the larger trees can be grown on "dwarfing rootstocks" to keep them small, or trained to a space-saving shape. Training details are given on pages 162–63, 165, and 167.

Standard tree
Grown on a tall stem, makes a fine specimen tree but difficult to pick and prune without a ladder. Only need prune dead, diseased or crossing branches. Height 6–9m (20–30ft).

Bush tree
Exactly the same as a standard tree, except that it is grown on a stem about 1.2m (4ft) shorter. Can still grow too large to pick and prune from the ground. Height 5–8m (15–25ft).

Cordon
Usually a single stem, at 45° to the ground, supported on post-and-wires to make a hedge. Takes up very little room and is decorative. Maximum height 1.8m (6ft), spread 75cm (2ft 6in). Plant trees 75cm (2ft 6in) apart.

Espalier
Takes up very little room. Makes a decorative wall feature, with branches coming horizontally from the stem at 30cm (12in) intervals. Maximum height 2.5m (8ft), spread 4.5m (15ft). Plant trees at least 3.6m (12ft) apart.

Festooned tree
Branches are bent down and tied to the main stem or the branch below in a series of hoops. An attractive small tree that can carry heavy crops. Height 1.8m (6ft), spread 90cm (3ft). Plant trees 1.5m (5ft) apart.

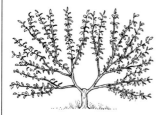

Fan
Normally pruned so that two opposite shoots grow from the main stem. Shoots from these form the fan shape. Maximum height 2.5m (8ft), spread 3.5m (12ft).

Dwarf pyramid
An attractive free-standing tree grown to a pyramidal shape, lower branches longer than the upper. Easy to prune and pick. Height 2.5m (8ft), spread 1.5m (5ft). Plant 1.5m (5ft) apart.

Stepover
A foreshortened espalier with only one branch on either side. Can be used as a productive edging round the vegetable garden or along paths. Maximum height 30cm (12in).

Cultivating fruit trees and bushes

F ruit trees and bushes are generally planted in the same way as the ornamentals (*see pages 90–91 and 110*). Most fruit plants are best planted in early winter, although container-grown ones can be planted at any time of year. However, if plants arrive when the soil is frozen, do not plant in their permanent positions but heel them in.

If planting against a wall, position the tree or bush so that its base is at least 30cm (12in) away from the wall. This area is likely to be the driest spot in the garden protected by overhanging eaves, so ensure the plant has plenty of water immediately after planting. Later, the roots will spread away from the wall and find their own water.

It is often not necessary to stake one-year-old trees unless container-grown or on a very dwarfing rootstock, when they should be staked with a short stake as recommended for ornamental trees (*see page 90*). If it is a fruit tree, it requires a post-and-wire support; erect this first to avoid root disturbance (*see page 116* for different types of support).

The detailed cultivation techniques vary somewhat and are given for each fruit on pages 164–75. There are, however, some cultivation points common to all fruit.

Feeding
In early spring apply two handfuls of blood, fish, and bone meal per square metre/yard around the plants. The feeding roots are at the tips of the plant's main root system rather than near the stem, so apply fertilizer in a wide band round it. Mulch around the stem with well-rotted

Applying fertilizer
Feeding roots are towards the tree's outer limits, so apply fertilizer below the tree, roughly from the furthest extent of the branches to halfway back to the trunk.

compost or manure, to inhibit weed growth, conserve water, and supply necessary trace elements. In the unlikely event of deficiency symptoms becoming apparent (*see pages 66–67*), spray immediately with liquid seaweed fertilizer and apply seaweed meal to the soil.

Watering
Applying water at the right time can greatly increase the weight of a fruit crop. For best results, water when fruit is swelling. Stop when the fruits colour up or you could encourage fungus disease. It is a mistake to put just a little water on the soil since this brings the roots nearer the surface and greater danger of drying out. If possible, apply water through a hose and sprinkler, which must be left on for at least an hour at a time in dry weather.

Thinning
Most people are quite happy to grow fruit smaller than that in the shops, but for bigger fruit, thin the clusters as they develop. Trees and bushes will drop fruits naturally if carrying more than they can support. This normally happens in mid summer so delay thinning until then. Remove the central fruit from each cluster: it will probably be badly shaped. How much you thin depends on the variety, but thinning will not reduce the total weight; there will be fewer fruits but each will be bigger.

TIPS FOR PLANTING

- Use one- or two-year-old trees or bushes.
- Buy and plant in winter.
- Prepare as large an area as possible. Dig deeply and incorporate plenty of well-rotted compost or manure throughout all levels.
- Once the tree is planted, mulch around the stem with well-rotted compost or manure.

Encourage bud growth (far left)
To encourage growth of a particular bud on a barren length of shoot, take a notch out of the bark above the bud you want to encourage.

Thinning fruit (left)
If the developing fruits are growing in a crowded cluster, remove the central fruit known as the "crown" fruit.

Encouraging growth

Sometimes fruit trees of all types will fail to produce shoots along one part of the stem. For some reason the buds simply do not grow out. This can be corrected by manipulating nature. So that the top of the tree grows more strongly, nature sends a growth-retarding hormone down the tree to retard all the other buds. The transport channels are just below the bark so, to prevent the retarding hormone reaching the bud you wish to encourage, simply take out a tiny notch in the bark above it. The hormone then flows round the bud without affecting it. Conversely, to ensure that a bud does not grow, nick underneath it to concentrate the hormone.

Weed control

Competition from weeds must be reduced. Many fruit plants are shallow-rooted so hoe lightly. Mulching with compost, manure, or black plastic (*see pages 216–17*) is better.

Pests and diseases

The most troublesome pests of fruit are our allies, the birds. We do not want to frighten them away because of the other good work they do, but they cannot be ignored. If you have room, a fruit cage is a good investment. If not, net small bushes and trees, or protect individual fruits with transparent, perforated polythene bags. For other pests and diseases, *see pages 196–209*.

PROTECTING FRUIT FROM BIRDS

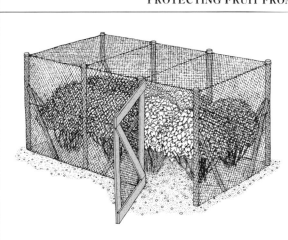

If you have space build a fruit cage. Alternatively, cover bushes with netting or enclose individual fruit such as apples or pears in a perforated polythene bag when nearly ripe, to prevent attack by birds or insects.

Making a fruit cage

One large enough to walk inside is worth the extra effort. Mark out the shape, then drive stout wooden posts into the ground and stretch wires between them. Fix special, heavy-duty fruit-cage netting between the posts, using the wires as a support. Leave an access "flap" or door in one corner.

PRUNING AND TRAINING FRUIT TREES AND BUSHES

Pruning is the deliberate cutting back of plants, usually applied to trees and shrubs. It is a method of controlling size, training to shape and encouraging flower or fruit buds to form. Commonly used pruning terms are below.

The leading shoot is the main stem of the plant. A side-shoot grows from the main stem; a secondary shoot grows from the side-shoot. A fruiting spur is the group of shoots that produce fruit (made by pruning secondary shoots and side-shoots hard back). A downward-facing bud refers to the bud's angle on the shoot.

Tips and techniques
- If you remove a branch, cut back to 1cm (½in) beyond where it meets the main stem.
- A bud will grow in the direction it faces: always cut to an outward-facing bud.
- Summer pruning restricts growth and encourages fruiting buds instead.
- Always use a sharp pair of secateurs that will make a clean cut. Angle cut away from bud.
- Always prune to a point just above a bud: any stub of shoot left will die back and may introduce disease. Never prune too close.

Secondary shoot   *Side-shoot*

Too close   *Too far away*   *Wrong angle   Correct*

Training cordons
Grow cordons against a post-and-wire support or wires strung at 60cm (2ft) intervals. Before planting, tie canes onto wires to prevent stems chafing against wires. Plant trees 75cm (2ft 6in) apart so that the arms will be 12in apart. Multiple bush cordons grow less vigorously so do not need to be grown at an angle.

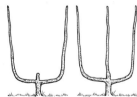

Double cordon   Triple cordon

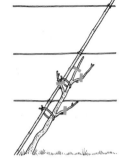

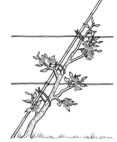

1 *At planting, cut leading shoot back to two-thirds of that year's growth. Cut side-shoots to downward-facing bud, leaving each shoot 7cm (3in) long.*

2 *The first summer, prune back side-shoots on the main stem to 7cm (3in), secondary shoots to 2.5cm (1in). In the second winter, prune leading shoot to two-thirds of that year's growth.*

3 *Each summer, prune like this until the top of cane is reached. Lower cane for more room. When tree is right length, prune leading shoot in summer to 7cm (3in) and side-shoots to 2.5cm (1in).*

Training a dwarf pyramid

1 *At planting, prune leading shoot to 60cm (2ft) above ground. Next winter, prune five or six evenly spaced lower branches to downward- or outward-facing buds to leave 25cm (10in) long.*

2 *The same winter, prune all other branches to 15cm (6in) above top branch to form a second tier. Prune leading shoot to 30cm (12in) above top branch.*

3 *Every summer, prune main shoots to 15cm (6in) of current year's growth, side shoots to 10cm (4in), and secondaries to 5cm (2in). Every winter, prune leading shoot to 20cm (8in).*

Training a festoon

1 *At end of first summer, pull leading shoot down and tie it to the base of tree with soft string, forming a "hoop". Second summer, prune shoots at the top of the curve as for cordons (see right).*

2 *The same summer, bend more shoots into hoops and tie. Prune any unwanted branches (see far right). In following summers, prune fruiting spurs as for cordons.*

Training an espalier

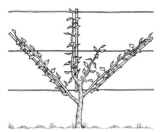 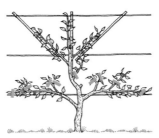 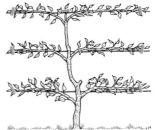

1 *At planting, prune to 5cm (2in) above first wire, leave three good buds. In spring, train side-shoots to canes fixed to wires at 45°. In summer, prune branches on leading shoot to 7cm (3in).*

2 *In winter, tie two branches to lower wire; prune leading shoot to 5cm (2in) above second wire. In summer (see above), prune side-shoots to 7cm (3in), secondaries to 2.5cm (1in).*

3 *Treat second tier as first the previous summer. Each summer, repeat until required height is reached. Train two buds for final tier. Then, every summer, prune each arm as for cordon.*

Cultivating tree fruit

One or two fruit trees in your organic garden add year-round height to the planting, decorative and insect-attracting flowers in spring, and luscious fruit in autumn, which you will know has not been drenched with insecticide or coated with arsenic to improve its shelf-life. You may have to put up with the odd blemish from the birds that were ridding your garden of aphids, but the organically grown crop is usually large enough to withstand a few bird attacks. There are, however, some hints on dealing with fruit pests and diseases on pages 206–9 and with general problems on pages 196–201.

The following pages give details of how to grow specific fruit trees, such as apples or plums; for general cultivation and pruning details, refer to pages 158–63.

CHERRIES

Stella is the only self-fertile sweet cherry, hence suitable for the small garden. With more room, grow a self-fertile, acid *Morello* cherry, and a sweet cherry such as *Bigarreau* that flowers at the same time, since the acid varieties pollinate the sweet ones. *Colt* rootstock reduces tree size by a third and induces earlier cropping. **Tree shapes** Sweet cherries grow very large as standard and bush trees: to avoid excessive shade and protect from birds, grow as fans on south-facing walls. Only grow as bush trees on the very dwarfing rootstock *G.M.9.*

Acid cherries are less vigorous: grow as fans on north-facing walls. **Soil and site** Deep, well-drained loams are best. Dig deeply, adding organic matter. pH 6.0–7.0. Sweet cherries grow in sun, acid cherries in shade. **Planting** In winter, set standards 4.5–6m (15–20ft) apart, bush trees 3–4.5m (10–15ft) apart, fans 5.5m (18ft) against wired wall. **Maintenance** Feed with annual mulch of well-rotted compost or manure. Excess lime sometimes causes magnesium deficiency: dress with seaweed meal. Prune standards and bushes very little. After a few years, every mid

summer prune dead, diseased, and crossing branches back to main stem. Prune fan-trained sweet cherries as plums (*see opposite*), acid cherries as peaches (*see page 167*). **Protection** Net sweet cherries against birds. **Harvesting** Crops from 4–5 years. Leave fruit on tree as long as possible; pick before they split. Eat sweet cherries immediately; cook and eat acid cherries no more than few days after picking, or bottle, or make into jam. **Pests and diseases** Blackfly, winter moth, bacterial canker, silver-leaf.

APRICOTS

Apricots are grown in the same way as plums (*see opposite*), but need plenty of sun. All varieties are self-fertile, so only one tree is necessary. In colder areas you may have to hand pollinate, as they flower early. Choose *Farmindale, Moor Park,* or *Blenheim.*

Tree shapes Fans against south-facing wall in temperate climates; dwarf pyramids in warmer areas. **Soil and site** Soil not too rich, but well-drained: unless very light, prepare area 1m × 3m (3ft × 10ft), two spades deep, with rubble in bottom. Refill with soil liberally mixed with organic matter. pH 6.0. Very sunny, sheltered site.

Planting Bare-rooted trees in autumn: fans 4.5m (15ft) apart; dwarf pyramids 1.5m (5ft) apart. **Maintenance** Thin if necessary. **Harvesting** Crops from 2–3 years. Pick and eat when soft. To dry, pick and split when still firm. **Pests and diseases** Birds, aphids, red spider mite, sawfly, rust, silver-leaf, bacterial canker.

MULBERRIES

These very decorative trees bear fruit for 40 years or more. Mulberries are self-fertile: only one tree is needed. There are three types – red (*Morus rubra*), white (*M. alba*), and black (*M. nigra*), which produces the best fruit; try the *Large Black* and *Downing* varieties.

Tree shapes Bush or standard. **Soil and site** Any deep, fertile soil. pH 6.0–6.5. Warmth and sun. **Planting** Generally grown singly, but, if you are planting more than one, set at least 9m (30ft) apart. Best container-grown as the very brittle roots are easily damaged. Keep tree area grass-free until tree starts to fruit.

Maintenance Prune overcrowded shoots to 10cm (4in) late summer. **Harvesting** Crops from 10 years. Fruit can be picked or shaken onto sheets laid on grass in late summer. Juice stains skin and clothes. Mulberries do not store well unless bottled. **Pests and diseases** No specific pests and diseases.

PLUMS

Plums are relatively easy to grow and can bear very heavy crops. However, they may not be worth growing in areas that get very late frosts. Damsons are related to plums and are grown in exactly the same way. The following varieties are self-fertile: plums – *Dennistons Superb, Czar, Iroquois, Victoria, Italian Prune, Marjories Seedling*; damsons – *Merryweather, Shropshire, King of the Damsons*. Trees grow very large unless on dwarfing rootstocks – *St. Julien A* (semi-dwarfing rootstock for dwarf pyramids and fans), or *Pixy* (for small trees to be trained against a strong support).

Tree shapes Standards, dwarf pyramids, festoons, or fans.

Soil and site Plums prefer deep, well-drained loam or clay, but damsons will tolerate shallower topsoil. pH 6.0–6.5. Fans grow best on south- or west-facing walls: on north-facing walls fruit will be produced later in the year.

Planting Plant bare-rooted trees autumn (*see page 91*): standards 3m (10ft) apart, dwarf pyramids on *St. Julien A* at the same distance, and on *Pixy* 1.8m (6ft) apart; fans 3.5m (12ft) apart on wall or post-and-wires; festoons 1.8m (6ft) apart. When tying the plum tree to its support, use a proprietary tree tie with collar to prevent chafing, as the pernicious silver-leaf disease enters through wounds caused by wires.

Maintenance Feed the plant as shown on page 160. Never prune in winter: wounds will not heal quickly and silver-leaf disease may enter. Heavy crops may break branches: wait for natural mid summer drop before thinning fruits to 7cm (3in) apart. Support heavily laden branches with forked prop covered in sacking to prevent chafing, or tie the branch up to main stem (*see page 168*).

Harvesting Crops from 3–5 years. Fruit is ripe when comes off the tree easily. Pick for cooking or bottling when bloom appears on skin. For eating, leave fruit on tree until fully ripe (feels soft).

Pests and diseases Aphids, birds, wasps, plum sawfly, red spider mite, rust, silver-leaf, bacterial canker.

FAN-TRAINING PLUMS

Fan-trained plums grow best on south- or west-facing walls. On north-facing walls, they produce fruit later in the year. Plums, damsons, apricots, sweet cherries, and quinces should be fan-trained as below. Grow against wires fixed to the wall at 23in (9in) intervals with vine eyes (*see page 116*).

1 *In winter, plant a one-year-old tree against wall. The first spring, cut back to 45cm (18in) high.*

2 *In summer, select three strong shoots to grow on; pinch back other shoots to two leaves.*

3 *The following spring, prune two main side-branches to 45cm (18in). Tie to first horizontal wire. Remove central shoot.*

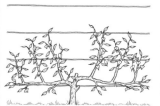

4 *Every spring and summer, tie upward-growing shoots from side branches on to wires, using soft string, to make a fan shape.*

5 *Later in summer, pinch out any shoots growing into or away from wall. Pinch out any other shoots not required for the fan shape.*

6 *When fruit has been picked, cut out any dead wood and shorten the shoots you have pinched out by half.*

FIGS

The darker-skinned *Brown Turkey* and *Brunswick* are the hardiest. *Mission, Celeste,* and *Verdone* are for warmer areas. The cultivation details below apply to figs grown outside and in the greenhouse.
Tree shapes Bush trees or fans. No special training for fans: tie branches to wires 23cm (9in) apart.
Soil and site Any well-drained but moisture-retentive soil. pH 6.5–7.0. South-facing wall to give plenty of sun. Also to encourage fruiting, essential to restrict root growth: dig hole 1m × 1.5m (3ft × 5ft), two spades deep. Cover with rubble and contain sides with corrugated iron or bricks. Refill with equal mix of topsoil and well-rotted compost or manure.
Planting Free-standing bushes 3m (10ft) apart; plant fans 4.5m (15ft) apart.
Maintenance Hand water first year. Cut out old wood in winter; thin in summer, so sun ripens fruits. Protect from frost by wrapping plant in straw, secured with hessian.
Harvesting Crops from 3–4 years. Eat figs straight from tree when they change colour (dark-skinned ones turn deep purple; light ones turn yellow). Will store only if dried or frozen.
Pests and diseases Botrytis, birds, canker.

OLIVES

Olives will grow in areas with cold winters and hot summers, hence they are extensively cultivated in Mediterranean countries. African olives bear beautiful flowers, but inedible fruit. European olives take five or six years to produce fruit, but are extremely long-lived. Try the self-fertile varieties *Mission, Sevillano,* and *Verdale.*
Tree shapes Always standards.
Soil and site Any well-drained soil; like grapes, a useful crop for poor or stony soil. Full sun.
Planting Plant container-grown, grafted trees 7.5–12m (25–36ft) apart at any time of year, but best planted in autumn when wetter weather can be expected.
Maintenance Need plenty of nitrogen, so mulch annually with well-rotted compost or manure. If growth is slow, two handfuls of hoof and horn fertilizer per sq. m/yd in spring. Prune overcrowded or crossing branches to allow plenty of sunlight for maximum fruit production.
Harvesting Crops from 5–6 years. Pick by hand to avoid bruising, either green fruit in autumn for pickling, or black fruit in winter to press for oil.
Pests and diseases No specific pests and diseases.

QUINCES

Quinces flower later than their pear relatives, so are in little danger of frost damage. Only one tree is needed as they are self-fertile. Choose from *Meeches Prolific, Vranja, Champion, Fuller,* or *Apple-shaped.*
Tree shapes Bush; in temperate climates, fans on south-facing walls.
Soil and site All well-drained, deep soils. pH 6.0–6.5 (lime only if below 6.0). Sunny site.
Planting Bare-rooted plants early winter, bush trees 6m (20ft) apart, fans 4.5m (15ft).
Maintenance Feed and water as page 160. Prune fans the same way as plums (*see page 165*).
Harvesting Crops from 2–3 years. Quinces are ripe when they become yellow and give off strong aroma. Make jelly immediately after harvesting, or store the fruits on shelves or in boxes, in a cool, moist, frost-free shed for up to three months.
Pests and diseases Greenfly, mildew, wasps, winter moth, woolly aphid, codling moth, sawfly, canker, fireblight, bitter pit, brown rot, scab.

PEACHES AND NECTARINES

Peaches and nectarines are identical in cultivation. Ideal for warmer climates or greenhouses, both will grow in temperate regions if fan-trained on a south-facing wall. Peaches are a better choice for this, being slightly hardier. Both fruit for 30 years. The only difference in greenhouse cultivation is that the better conditions may make it necessary to check growth and fruiting.

Peaches and nectarines are self-fertile, so you need only one tree. *Duke of York, Peregrine* and *Rochester* are good peaches; *Golden Jubilee* or *Reliance* for colder areas. Grow *Early Rivers* or *Golden State* nectarines. Dwarfing rootstocks are not necessary, but *Pixy* is used for small trees in tubs. For fans, use *St. Julien A* or *Brompton.*
Tree shapes In warm areas, where frost will not damage flowers, grow free-standing bush trees. In temperate climates, grow as fans.
Soil and site Good drainage essential; prepare well (*see pages 90–91* for standards and bushes). For fans, dig trench 60–90cm (2–3ft) wide, 3m (10ft) long and a spade deep. Dig rubble or broken bricks into bottom; cover with compost or manure. Work in more organic matter while refilling. Peaches prefer medium loam, nectarines not too rich a soil. Both will grow on sandy soils with plenty of added organic matter. pH 6.5–7.0. Sunny position, not in a frost pocket.
Planting *Outside:* in winter, set standards or bushes 4.5m (15ft) apart as pages 90–91; one-year-old fan-trained trees 3.6m (12ft) apart against wires spaced 23cm (9in). *Greenhouse:* plant in same way against wall or post-and-wires.
Maintenance Before old enough to fruit, feed as page 160. When they come into bearing, mulch annually with well-rotted compost or manure. Reinstate feeding programme if deficiency

symptoms appear (*see pages 66–67*). Prune free-standing trees in spring, removing all dead, diseased, and crossing branches. Prune fan-trained trees as recommended below. When frost is forecast, protect blossoms with woven polypropylene or fine netting (old net curtains are fine). *Greenhouse:* keep as cold as possible in winter to keep tree dormant. In spring/summer, let temperature reach 10°C (50°F) before ventilating. Spray daily with clear water in spring/ summer except at flowering. Mulch early spring with well-rotted compost or manure, then feed weekly during growing season with liquid seaweed fertilizer. Flowers are early, so may have to be hand-pollinated as there will be few insects. Do not let too many fruits develop – 15 per sq.m/yd.
Harvesting Crops from 4 years. Fruit is ripe when comes off easily if gently lifted and twisted: bruises very easily. Peaches and nectarines will not store for more than few days unless bottled.
Pests and diseases Peach-leaf curl, red spider mite, scale insects, mildew.

FAN-TRAINING PEACHES AND NECTARINES

Fan-training is a pruning method which produces trees that grow flat against the wall. The reflected and stored heat allows otherwise tender fruits to be grown successfully in temperate climates. Grow the trees against wires fixed to a wall, 23cm (9in) apart, with vine eyes (*see page 116*).

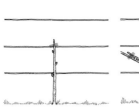

1 *Immediately after planting, cut back to a strong bud, making sure there are two buds beneath this. Leave tree about 45cm (18in) high. In spring, three shoots will grow.*

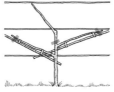

2 *The second winter, remove central shoot. Prune two remaining shoots to 45cm (18in) long. Tie them to canes fixed to wires about 20° above the horizontal.*

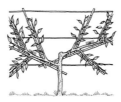

3 *The following summer, select four shoots from these side-branches; two from the top, one underneath, and one of the side branch itself. Tie in; rub off any other buds.*

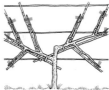

4 *In the third winter, cut back the selected shoots, leaving them about 45cm (18in) long.*

5 *The following summer, tie in branches as they grow. Select side-shoots 10cm (4in) apart as fruit-bearing shoots. Rub off any unwanted buds that appear.*

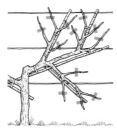

6 *The fourth winter, reduce growth from main framework branches by about half. From now on, pruning aims at producing fruit.*

7 *The following summer, allow side-shoots to grow four/six leaves and form a new shoot at their base. Pinch out any other new growth.*

8 *Once fruit has been picked, prune out fruited shoot. Tie replacement shoot into its place. Repeat process every year.*

APPLES

Apples grow fairly easily in most parts of the world. They fruit for about 30 years. To crop fully, they must be pollinated by a different variety: choose at least two trees that flower at the same time. Some early-flowering dessert apples are *Discovery, Willie Sharp, James Grieve, Jupiter, Early McIntosh, Red Gravenstein, Spartan, Kent, Crispin, Idared*; cooking apples *Bramley's Seedling, Grenadier.* In an area with late frosts, try the dessert apples *Merton Charm, Orleans Reinette, Ashmeads Kernel, Golden Delicious, Red Delicious, Suntan, Jonathan, Granny Smith,* and cooking apples *Howgate Wonder, Lanes Prince Albert.*

M106 is the standard rootstock for most trees. Use the dwarfing *M9* for cordons or dwarf pyramids (but only if soil is very fertile, and trees will always need staking). The very dwarf *M27* rootstock is suitable only for trees in tubs, on very fertile soil, or for those trained as stepovers.

Tree shapes All.

Soil and site Any deep, well-drained soil prepared and managed properly. Try to get preparation work done in advance of planting,

and on wet soil work from boards. pH 6.0–6.5 (lime only if below 6.0). Sun and shelter preferable.

Planting Bare-rooted early winter – standards and bushes 6m (20ft) apart, dwarf pyramids and festoons 1.5m (5ft), fans, espaliers and stepovers 4.5m (15ft), cordons 75cm (2ft 6in).

Maintenance Feed and water as page 160. For pruning the various shapes, see pages 162–63.

Harvesting On modern rootstocks, crops from 2 years (depending on variety, rootstock and conditions). Fruit is fully ripe when it comes off easily if lifted slightly and gently twisted, without pulling. Always pick carefully, placing fruit in basket lined with soft cloth to avoid bruising; this is especially important if you are going to store the apples. Pick early varieties in summer, just before fully ripe and leave a couple of days before eating; if left on tree to ripen fully, they will go slightly soft and mealy. Pick late varieties autumn/early winter when fully ripe. To store, look over fruit carefully, rejecting any that are damaged or diseased – these will affect healthy fruit. Pack one variety at a time in polythene bags; seal with twist tie.

Supporting a laden branch
Tie a length of string around the centre of branch, fixing the other end to main trunk of the tree.

Never mix varieties in a bag. Make pinholes in bag for fruit to breathe. Store in cool, frost-free place. Check them regularly, removing any that show signs of disease or rotting.

Pests and diseases Greenfly, mildew, wasps, winter moth, woolly aphid, codling moth, apple sawfly, canker, fireblight, bitter pit, brown rot, apple scab.

PEARS

Pears flower early and may be damaged by frosts in temperate climates. Fruiting continues for 25–30 years. Pears have to be pollinated with a different variety, so choose trees that flower at the same time. Early-flowering types are *Conference, Williams Bon Chrétian (Bartlett), Beth, Merton Pride.* Some late-flowerers include *Gorham, Onward, Doyenne du Comice, Beurre d'Anjou.*

There are only two rootstocks in common use. *Quince A* should be used on poorer soils. *Quince C* produces smaller trees which fruit earlier in their lives and should be used when growing pears as cordons on very fertile soils.

Tree shapes All.

Soil and site All well-drained, deep soils. pH 6.0–6.5 (lime only if below 6.0). Shelter and sun. Try to get preparation work done in advance of planting, working from boards on wet soil.

Planting The best time to plant is early winter, using bare-rooted trees – standards and bushes 6m (20ft) apart, dwarf pyramids and festoons 1.5m (5ft) apart, fans, espaliers, and stepovers 4.5m (15ft) apart, and cordons 75cm (2ft 6in) apart.

Maintenance Feed and water as page 160. For pruning the various shapes, see pages 162–63.

Harvesting Crops from 2 years, depending on conditions. Pears

are ripe when they part easily from tree if gently lifted and twisted. Pick early varieties before they are ripe (when still hard and green). Will keep for two weeks: put on shelf in cool shed. A few days before you want to eat them, bring indoors for final ripening. If kept for too long, pears become mushy and metallic-tasting. Leave late-maturing varieties on tree until they come off easily. Store the same way. To keep longer than two weeks, bottle or dry before too ripe.

Pests and diseases Greenfly, mildew, wasps, winter moth, woolly aphids, codling moth, fireblight, sawfly, canker, bitter pit, brown rot, scab.

Cultivating citrus fruit

In temperate climates, grow citrus trees in a greenhouse, or varieties recommended for outdoor use in tubs of diameter at least 45cm (18in), with soil-based potting compost at 7°C (45°F) or more. Water well during growing season, but allow to dry out between each watering. In summer, spray foliage every morning until flowering; keep plants drier in winter. Feed weekly during growing season with liquid seaweed fertilizer. Thin out crossing, overcrowded, dead, or diseased branches, and fruited shoots after harvesting.

KUMQUATS
Can be grown outdoors in warmer areas. In temperate zones, grow in pots or tubs in a heated greenhouse. Try *Marumi* and *Nagami*.
Tree shapes Always bush.
Soil and site Medium heavy, well-drained loam ideal, working in organic matter for water-retention. Raise heavier soils. pH 6.0–6.5. Open, sunny site.
Planting Plant container-grown or balled trees at any time, 4.5m (15ft) apart.
Maintenance Mulch with compost or manure. Water well while fruit swelling. After harvest prune current season's growth.
Harvesting Crops from 7–8 years. Pick when orange. Eat raw, or make into marmalade.
Pests and diseases Gall wasp, little leaf, lemon scab, red spider mite, aphids, scale insects.

LEMONS AND LIMES
Usually need frost-free areas; with shelter the *Meyer* hybrid lemon tolerates −9°C (15°F). Other lemons are *Lisbon* and *Eureka*. Try *Mexican* and *Tahitian* limes.
Tree shapes Bush.
Soil and site Slightly heavy soils are best, beds raised at least 45cm (18in). Enrich with compost or manure. Prefer slightly acid conditions: pH 6.0–6.5. Outside, need very sunny, sheltered site.
Planting Plant container-grown or balled trees at any time of year; if outside, spring or autumn are best. For most light, space 4.5m (15ft) apart.
Maintenance Young roots are easily scorched by excess fertilizer: feed only manure mulches, or one handful blood, fish, and bone meal per sq. m/yd early spring; repeat summer, watering in well. Roots need plenty of water, especially the first few years. Prune lemons to keep compact, removing inward-pointing, straggling shoots, and those that have borne fruit. Thin lime trees, removing dead, diseased, or crossing wood.
Harvesting Both fruits crop from 7–8 years and fruit all year. Cut with secateurs when ripe; store in cool place in paper-lined crates, covering the fruit with dry sand.
Pests and diseases Gall wasp, little leaf, lemon scab, red spider mite, aphids, scale insects.

Storing lemons
Store in layters of dry sand in a wooden crate or paper-lined box in a cool place. Lemons will keep this way for up to two months.

ORANGES
In temperate areas, oranges must be grown inside. Sweet eating oranges are *Jaffa, Parramatta, Late Valencia, Washington Navel*. *Seville* is a sour orange for marmalade-making.
Tree shapes Bush.
Soil and site Light and sandy soil: oranges abhor bad drainage. On heavier soils raise planting area at least 45cm (18in). Enrich with plenty of well-rotted compost or manure. Prefer slightly acid conditions: pH 6.0–6.5. As sunny and sheltered a site as possible (with a windbreak if necessary).
Planting As lemons and limes, but spaced 7.5m (25ft) apart.
Maintenance As lemons.
Harvesting Crops from 7–8 years. Leave fruits on tree – they can stay for up to six months until ready to use. Pick when well coloured. Store as lemons.
Pests and diseases As lemons.

GRAPEFRUIT
Try *Marsh's Seedless, Redblush,* and *Wheeny*.
Tree shapes Bush trees.
Soil and site Sun, shelter, and good drainage: dig deeply; add compost or manure. Raise heavy soil 45cm (18in). pH 6.0–6.5.
Planting As lemons, but spaced at least 9m (30ft) apart.
Maintenance As lemons.
Harvesting As oranges.
Pests and diseases As lemons.

Cultivating soft fruit

Soft fruits range from briars and shrubs to herbaceous perennials, and cultivation techniques vary accordingly. Cane and briar fruits need support, but are well worth growing if space is available. Bush fruits are generally grown as free-standing shrubs. Strawberries are the only herbaceous perennials in the group. They take up little room.

RASPBERRIES

Raspberries respond well to organic methods, and their very heavy crops handsomely repay the space they occupy. They are self-fertile. Recommended are *Malling Promise, Glen Cova, Malling Jewel, Malling Leo,* and *Latham.* For autumn fruit, grow *Heritage* or *Autumn Bliss.*

Bush shapes Grown as canes tied in to post-and-wires; autumn-fruiting types free-standing.

Soil and site Heavy, rich, well-prepared, deep soil, with plenty of moisture. pH 6.0 or a little below. Above 7.0, iron deficiency may occur. Tolerate a little shade.

Planting Bare-rooted canes autumn/early winter. Dig trench a spade deep, at least 60cm (2ft) wide. Break up bottom and add 10cm (4in) layer of well-rotted compost or manure. Refill with mix of organic matter and soil. Dress with bone meal (one handful per sq. m/yd run of trench). Set plants 45cm (18in) apart, a little deeper than nursery level, 1.8m (6ft) between rows. Prune canes to within 15cm (6in) of ground.

Supporting and training Erect post-and-wires as for cordons, wires 10cm (4in) apart. Tie in

Pruning raspberry canes

1 *When fruit has been picked, cut all fruited canes, and any weak ones, down to ground level.*

2 *Space new shoots at 10cm (4in) intervals. Cut out excess canes. Pull out unwanted suckers.*

canes as they grow. Cut off tips when 7cm (3in) above top wire. *Autumn-fruiting types:* on windy site, run lengths of nylon twine either side of row to stop canes blowing about.

Maintenance Mulch late winter with well-rotted compost or manure. Yellowing between leaf veins means iron deficiency: spray with liquid seaweed and dress with seaweed meal (one handful per sq. m/yd). Canes fruit only on one-year-old wood: after picking, cut old canes to ground level, and

tie in new ones instead. Pull out any unwanted suckers. Autumn-fruiting canes bear fruit on one-year-old wood: cut to ground level late winter. Net canes before fruit colours to prevent bird attack.

Harvesting Crops at one year. Pick berries for cooking a little before fully ripe. Leave "plug" (centre core) on canes. Will not store unless frozen or bottled.

Pests and diseases Birds, aphids, botrytis, virus diseases, raspberry beetle, spur blight, and cane spot.

BLUEBERRIES

The best edible blueberries are the High Bush type (slow to bear fruit, but then cropping very heavily for many years). Recommended varieties are *Bluecrop, Michigan, Earliblue, Blue Ray,* and *Berkeley.* They are not self-fertile, so two or more varieties are needed.

Bush shapes Free-standing.

Soil and site Acid soil (pH 5.0–5.5 ideal). In alkaline soil, grow in raised bed, in sunny spot.

Planting Autumn/early winter, 1.8m (6ft) apart, slightly deeper than nursery level. Two handfuls bone meal per sq. m/yd. Mulch thickly with compost or manure.

Maintenance Mulch annually with well-rotted compost or manure; two handfuls of blood,

fish, and bone meal per sq. m/yd late winter. As bush grows, prune out old or weak shoots. Ensure free passage of light and air by removing branches less than 15cm (6in) apart. Net ripening fruit against bird damage.

Harvesting Crops from 3–8 years. Fully ripe ten days after turn blue. Does not store well.

Pests and diseases Birds.

REDCURRANTS AND WHITECURRANTS

These do best in temperate climates, but flower early, so may need frost protection in very cold areas. *Red Lake* is the most popular redcurrant; the most grown whitecurrant is *White Versailles*. Both kinds of currants are self-fertile.

Bush shapes Grown on a short stem called a "leg": free-standing, or as single, double or triple cordons against fence, wall, or post-and-wire support.

Soil and site Heavy, moisture-retentive soil. Two handfuls bone meal per sq. m/yd. pH 6.5. Sun.

Planting Plant container-grown bushes at any time of year, but best in autumn/early winter. Remove suckers. Plant free-standing bushes at level they grew in the nursery, 1.5m (5ft) apart, 1.8m (6ft) between rows. Plant cordons with "arms" 30cm (1ft) apart – single cordons spaced 30cm (1ft) apart, double cordons 60cm (2ft) apart, and triples 90cm (3ft) apart. After planting, tie arms at right angles to wires. Mulch thickly round bushes with well-rotted compost or manure.

Supporting and training *Free-standing bushes:* the first three winters, to produce strong, cup-shaped bush with open centre, prune main branches to half that year's wood, side-shoots to 7cm (3in). Remove broken, dead, diseased, overcrowded, or crossing branches. After three years, summer prune immediately after harvesting; reduce side-shoots to five leaves. Do the same to main branches when they reach desired length. *Cordons:* Train upwards rather than at an angle. Winter prune main arms to leave two-thirds of the previous season's growth. After harvesting, summer prune side-shoots to 7cm (3in), secondary shoots to 2.5cm (1in).

Maintenance Need extra feeding: in spring one handful rock potash per sq. m/yd. Browning of leaf edges means potash deficiency: spray with liquid seaweed and feed with rock

Growing on a leg
Buy bushes with a good stem beneath branches. Pull off any suckers at root level. Plant bush at level it grew in the nursery.

potash. If frost threatens while flowering, cover with woven polypropylene or fine meshed netting. Birds like currant buds, so net bushes as soon as buds appear; leave nets until harvest.

Harvesting Crops from 1–2 years. Pick sprigs, removing individual currants later with kitchen fork. Will not store fresh, but can be frozen or bottled.

Pests and diseases Aphids, birds, mildew, sawfly, leaf spot.

BLACKCURRANTS

Blackcurrants are a rich source of Vitamin C, well worth the space they occupy. Two popular old varieties are *Carter's Black Champion* and *Black Naples*. New varieties more resistant to disease and yielding well are *Ben More* and *Ben Lomond*. Blackcurrants are self-fertile.

Bush shapes Free-standing bushes, pruned to form "stools" with shoots coming from ground level or below. Not really suitable as cordons.

Soil and site Heavy, rich soil preferred: blackcurrants are gross feeders and repay good soil preparation. pH 6.5. Will grow in partial shade, but fruits much better in sun.

Planting Autumn/early winter, plant bare-rooted bushes 1.5m (5ft) apart, 1.8m (6ft) between rows. To create a "stooled" plant, set 5cm (2in) lower than nursery level, pruning all shoots to ground.

Supporting and training Nothing special.

Maintenance Needs high nitrogen: two handfuls blood, fish, and bone meal per sq. m/yd early spring. Mulch with well-rotted compost or manure. If growth still poor, give similar fertilizer early summer. Most fruit made on previous year's wood, so no pruning and little fruit in first year. Second and subsequent years, cut fruited shoots to ground late summer, or with fruit still attached mid summer. As bushes get older, they may produce fewer shoots from below ground: prune out fruited wood as low as possible, just above a new young shoot; take a few older shoots back to ground level, even if this means cutting out some new wood.

Harvesting Crops from 2 years. Harvest as suggested while pruning, or pick sprigs, removing individual fruits with kitchen fork. Eat immediately, or bottle or freeze to store.

Pests and diseases Aphids, birds, sawfly, big bud mite, leaf spot, mildew, reversion disease.

Stooling a blackcurrant bush
Plant bush 5cm (2in) lower than it grew at the nursery. Cut all shoots back to ground level.

STRAWBERRIES

In the organic garden, strawberries can be grown with relative ease. They grow best in cool, moist climates, but suitable varieties such as *Redgauntlet, Sunburst, Earlibelle, Midland,* and *Guardian* will grow in warmer climates. The varieties offered are constantly changing as further research into this profitable crop takes place. In temperate areas, try *Pangruella, Hapil, Aromel,* and *Totem* (freezes well). All are self-fertile.

Soil and site Well-drained, but moisture-retentive soil: raise growing area to form 1.2m (4ft) wide beds. Two handfuls bone meal per sq. m/yd. Sunny site; to discourage mildew, avoid areas with little airflow.

Planting Buy plants guaranteed disease-free from a reputable grower. Plant late summer (any later, and they will not crop the following year): 60cm (2ft) apart, 45cm (18in) between rows; in 1.2m (4ft) raised beds, plant first row 15cm (6in) from edge to give three rows 45cm (18in) apart. Set crown (where leaves join roots) at soil level: too high and plant may lift out of ground; too low and the crown will rot. Water well. Can also be planted through black plastic to prevent water evaporation, suppress weeds and prevent new plantlets on stems ("runners") shooting into soil. Traditional "strawberry pots" give mixed results, top plants doing well but others less so. Shallow containers are better.

Maintenance Little fertilizer necessary: after picking, handful of rock potash per m/yd row. Mulch with straw when fruits swell to protect against slugs or mud splashes. Propagate by pinning new "runners" into pots sunk in soil. Once runner roots, separate from parent plant and force in greenhouse. (Do not use to restock beds: virus disease could spread.) Net ripening fruit against birds; cover autumn-fruiting varieties with cloches to protect against frost.

Harvesting Crops at ¾–1 year. Pick fruit when red all over, "plug" (central core) as well. Store only a few days, or make into jam. After

Growing in traditional strawberry barrels
So water reaches plants at the bottom of pots, put two stones into bottom and rest a length of drainpipe on them. Surround pipe with small stones, as you fill the pot with compost. Water the top and fill the pipe.

harvesting, cut plant to within 2.5cm (1in) of crown with shears or rotary grass cutter. Compost undiseased leaves and straw.

Pests and diseases Aphids, slugs, botrytis, mildew, virus diseases, red spider mite, birds.

Propagating from runners
Pin plantlet, still attached to its runner, into pot of compost buried near parent plant. Secure with a piece of wire bent like a hairpin.

Planting through black plastic
Cover raised bed with sheet of black plastic. Cut slits for planting 45cm (18cm) apart. The raised bed will protect against soil-borne diseases; the plastic suppresses weeds.

Protecting strawberries
Surround developing fruits with straw to raise off ground, away from slugs and mud splashes. Tuck the straw under the plants.

BRIAR FRUITS

These include blackberries, loganberries, and hybrid berries such as Tayberry, Boysenberry, and Youngberry. Their great value lies in their late harvesting period, following on from raspberries. Some hybrid berries will grow in warmer climates if winters are suitably cool. All varieties are self-fertile, so only one need be grown. *Blackberry Aston Cross* tastes most like the wild blackberry. *Variety L654* is the recommended loganberry to grow.

Bush shapes Trained on wires.

Soil and site Any deep, well-prepared and well-drained soil that holds plenty of moisture. pH 6.0 or a little below; above 7.0, iron deficiency may occur. Will grow in shade. Some of the hybrid berries will grow in warmer climates with cool winters.

Planting Best in early winter, though container-grown plants can be planted at any time of year. Dig a trench and fertilize as for raspberries (*see page 170*). Plant 3m (10ft) apart; cut down to 15cm (6in).

Supporting and training Support briars on wires on 1.8m (6ft) posts. Start wires 1m (3ft) from ground, and continue every 30cm (12in) to top of posts. Train in briars as they grow, or they become inextricably intertwined. Fruiting takes place on one-year-old wood, so keep this and new wood separate as shown below.

Maintenance Mulch late winter with well-rotted compost or manure. Yellowing between leaf veins is iron deficiency – treat as for raspberries. After picking, cut fruited briars to ground level. Net bushes before harvest to protect from birds.

Harvesting Crops from 1–2 years. Twist slightly when picking to leave "plug" in. Will not store unless frozen or bottled.

Pests and diseases As raspberries (*see page 170*).

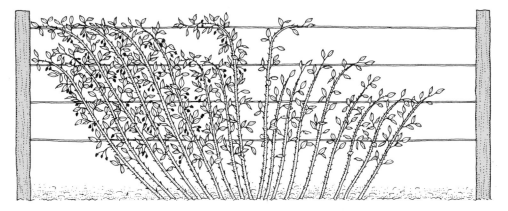

Training briar fruits
Do not leave briars sprawling on the ground as this will create irrevocable damage to the training process. The first year, train all shoots to one side of the support. As the new shoots grow, train to the other side. This will keep the one-year-old fruiting shoots away from the new wood.

GOOSEBERRIES

All are self-fertile. One of the best is *Jubilee*, which is resistant to mildew, as is the slightly later *Invicta*. *Welcome* and *Oregon Champion* are American varieties less susceptible to mildew.

Bush shapes Free-standing, or can be grown as single, double, or triple cordons against a fence, wall, or post-and-wire support, when they take up only 15cm (6in) of garden room. The bushes are grown on a "leg", a short stem below the branches.

Soil and site Heavy, moisture-retentive soil. pH 6.5. Prefer sun. Frost-protection in cold areas.

Planting Best planted bare-rooted autumn/early winter, though container-grown plants can be planted at any time of year. Before planting, remove any suckers that may be present. Two handfuls bone meal per sq. m/yd before planting. Plant free-standing bushes at the level they grew in the nursery, 1.5m (5ft) apart, 1.8m (6ft) between rows. Plant cordons with "arms" 30cm (1ft) apart – space single cordons 30cm (1ft) apart, doubles 60cm (2ft) and triples 90cm (3ft). Mulch thickly with compost or manure.

Supporting and training As redcurrants (*see page 171*).

Maintenance Need plenty of potassium or potash, so give extra feeding as redcurrants. Browning of leaf margins indicates potash deficiency: treat as redcurrants (*see page 171*). Immediately after

harvesting, reduce side-shoots of free-standing bushes to five leaves; when main branches are long enough, cut back the same way, also removing dead, diseased, or overcrowded branches. Prune side-shoots of cordons to 7cm (3in), secondary shoots to 2.5cm (1in). Thin a heavy crop by starting to pick before fully ripe, so other berries swell to proper size. Cook unripe berries. If frost threatens, cover with woven polypropylene or fine netting.
Harvesting Crops from 1–2 years. Pick for cooking before fully ripe. Store frozen or bottled.
Pests and diseases Aphids, birds, mildew, sawfly, leaf spot.

Harvesting gooseberries
This painful business is made easier if the bushes are grown as upright cordons.

GRAPES
Only in Mediterranean and semi-tropical countries will grapes grown outside produce dessert-quality fruit: varieties include *Golden Muscat, Concord, Fredonia, Delaware,* and *Niagara.* Dessert grapes for the greenhouse include *Muscat of Alexandria* (which needs some heat) and *Black Hamburgh* (can be grown in an unheated house). In temperate regions, fruit grown outside is usually only suitable for wine-making: suggestions are *Madeline Angevine, Müller Thurgau, Siergerrebe, Seyve-Villard,* and *Brandt.*
Soil and site. Grape vines thrive on poor soil, provided it is well drained and contains plenty of organic matter. pH 6.5–7.0. Sunny site essential.
Bush shapes Grown outside as vines on post-and-wires or south-facing wall; in greenhouse, on wall or along wires set 30cm (12in) away from glass to prevent scorching of plants.
Planting *Outside:* autumn/early winter 1.5m (5ft) apart. Mulch with well-rotted compost or manure. *Greenhouse:* late autumn dig wide, deep hole; put in 30cm (12in) layer of gravel and cover

with turf. Plant vine on top; if you are planting more than one, space them 1m (3ft) apart.
Supporting and training
Outside: against a wall, simply train shoots to decorative shape. On post-and-wires, prune out fruited shoots as shown.
Greenhouse: train shoots horizontally along a wall, 1m (3ft) from ground. Train the fruit-bearing shoots that spring from these arms upwards. Alternatively, train shoots against wires that are set 30cm (12in) away from the glass of the greenhouse and run up to the ridge. After planting, remove one-third of previous year's growth. The first year, pinch back side-shoots to five leaves. After leaf-fall, prune main shoot to half of the previous year's wood, and all side-shoots to three buds to form fruiting spurs. Subsequent summers, allow only two shoots to grow from each spur, stopping the weaker after three leaves. When an embryo bunch of grapes forms on the stronger shoot, allow it to make three more leaves, then pinch out tip. Repeat the winter pruning exercise as soon as possible after leaf-fall.
Maintenance *Outside:* mulch

annually with well-rotted compost or manure. If growth is poor, two handfuls blood, fish, and bone meal per sq. m/yd. Thin dessert grapes using nail-scissors or special grape-thinning scissors. Remove misshapen or diseased berries, allowing the remaining fruits to become pea-sized. Then begin to remove berries judiciously to enable rest to swell. Thinning is unnecessary if your grapes are for wine-making. *Greenhouse:* in early winter, untie vines and lay on border to prevent top spurs growing faster than lower ones. When growth starts in spring, put vines back on wires. Keep temperature at 20°C (70°F). Spray to increase humidity. When the vines flower, stop spraying and tap wires to dislodge pollen. Water and feed weekly. Thin dessert grapes as described above for outdoor crops.
Harvesting Crops from 2 years. When stems turn brown, the fruit is ready for picking. Cut off bunches carefully using secateurs. To store grapes, lay bunches on tray in cool, shady place – they will keep for about a month.
Pests and diseases Wasps, birds, mildew, botrytis, red spider mite, vine weevils, scale insects.

TRAINING A GRAPE VINE OUTSIDE

To grow a vine against a wall, space out shoots to a decorative shape. Before planting the vines, make a post-and-wire support for them by erecting a row of 1.2m (4ft) posts. Run wires between them, top wire 1.2m (4ft) from ground, bottom one 45cm (18in) from ground, with a wire strung in between them. Put a 1.8m (6ft) post at each planting point.

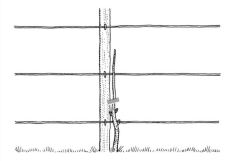

1 *Immediately after planting the vine, cut main shoot back to leave three strong buds.*

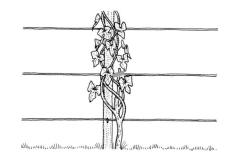

2 *In the first summer, three shoots will grow up. Tie these on to the stake. In autumn, pinch back the growing point of the main stem.*

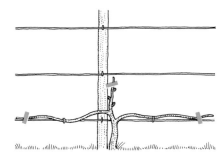

3 *In the second winter, tie two strongest shoots to bottom wire, one either side of stake; prune back to 75cm (2ft 6in). Prune central shoot back to leave three buds.*

4 *In the second summer, central shoot will again produce three shoots; tie these to the stake. Pinch back any side-shoots to three leaves. Over the summer, shoots tied in horizontally will produce side-shoots. These will bear the fruit; tie to wire above. As they grow longer, tie them in to top wire and pinch off tips. Pinch back any secondary shoots to one leaf. The first fruiting year, allow only four bunches of fruit to develop. In subsequent years, allow one bunch per shoot to grow. Cut out fruited shoots after harvesting.*

5 *The following season (left), tie two shoots from central stake to wires, cut back the middle shoot and start the process again.*

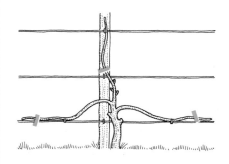

CHAPTER NINE

TOOLS AND TECHNIQUES

The basic techniques of practical organic gardening draw much from traditional methods. The spade, with us since Roman times, remains the very best tool for digging; gardeners have been controlling weeds with the hoe ever since people started to cultivate the soil, and it is still the most effective and beneficial method of garden weed control.

It would, however, be foolish to ignore some of the results of modern research and technology. It may be manufactured, and it is certainly not organic in origin, but polythene sheeting is immensely useful in the garden. And nylon twine lasts much longer than old-fashioned hemp string. So, the organic techniques of today should combine the best of modern technology with tried and tested traditional methods, without sacrificing organic standards.

Gardening is like many other types of activity, in that you need to have a basic core of information, perhaps gleaned from more experienced "old hands" or from books such as this; and, of course, the correct tools for particular tasks.

Storing pots
If you do not have a shed, keep all your old pots and other materials in a spare corner of the garden.

Choosing the right tools

If you are new to gardening, you might easily spend hundreds of pounds on a complete set of tools. Alternatively, by choosing the bare essentials, you can buy just what you need for relatively little money. Bear in mind, however, that it is a false economy to buy anything but the best. Cheap tools just do not last and, far worse, they make work more difficult. So, if your budget is tight, buy slowly, one tool at a time, but the best quality you can afford. And, with all tools, but the fork and the spade in particular, do not buy anything too large for you. You can do a lot more, much quicker, with a smaller fork that does not tire you out than with a larger one that you find difficult or awkward to use. Some of the more common tools are listed below. Beware of "gimmicks" claimed to be indispensable: you can usually manage just as well without them.

Power tools can be a great boon, saving many hours of repetitious, exhausting work, but they are expensive. If machinery, such as a lawn mower or hedge trimmer, will be used regularly, its purchase is easily justified. If, however, you have only an occasional need for machinery such as a rotary cultivator, then, unless you have an enormous garden, it is better to hire it. When hiring machinery check it comes with full instructions, with all safety features fitted, and is fully operational.

THE BASICS

Fork
The digging fork is second only to the spade in usefulness in the garden, and invaluable for loosening the soil without inverting it. It is listed first because, if you have no equipment at all, you can use a fork in place of the spade for most digging jobs (and it will double as a rake, too). Buy a fork of forged steel, fitted with a wooden or metal handle. Never buy a pressed-steel fork: it will bend and distort as soon as you put it under pressure.

Spade
You will probably use a spade more than any other tool, so it is worth buying a really good one. Stainless-steel spades are undoubtedly the best: soil, however sticky, simply falls off the polished surface, making digging much easier. A stainless-steel spade should last a lifetime. If you cannot afford stainless steel, buy a strong, forged-steel spade and always keep it clean. Once this type is worked in (the blade being sharp and corners rounded) digging is much easier.

Hand fork
A small hand fork is not as useful as a trowel, but many gardeners use one for weeding and for tickling over the border soil.

Trowel
Trowels are used extensively in the ornamental garden for planting and, to a lesser extent, in the vegetable garden. As with spades, stainless-steel are undoubtedly best.

Buckets
Plastic rather than metal buckets are best: they are lighter to carry when full and last longer. All the "bucketful" measurements given in this book are based on a 9-litre (2-gallon) bucket.

Wheelbarrow
The best type is a builder's wheelbarrow – often cheaper to buy from a builder's merchant than from a garden centre. Choose the type with a pneumatic tyre: much easier to wheel over rough ground when heavily laden. If you ever use it for concreting, wash off every speck of cement afterwards.

Rakes
Forged-steel rakes are the best. Those consisting of a metal strip with "nails" driven through tend to be awkward to use, as do rakes with more than about 12 teeth unless you are very strong.

A spring-tine, or lawn, rake is useful for removing dead leaves from lawns.

Hollow-tined fork
A useful tool for conditioning the lawn in the spring. It has a frame, attached to which are two or more tubes. When pushed into the lawn, its hollow tubes remove cores of soil. Fill these holes with grit, sand, or compost to improve drainage.

Shovel
A shovel is not simply a large spade. A shovel's blade is angled quite differently from a spade's to make shovelling much quicker and easier. Use for mixing compost or shifting a lot of soil in a new garden. Buy a builder's shovel with a metal handle and, if you ever use it for concreting, take great care to wash off every speck of cement.

CUTTING TOOLS

Knives
A pocket knife is just about the most used tool in the garden. Buy one that fits comfortably into your pocket and make sure that you keep it sharp on a small carborbundum sharpening stone. For budding, you need a special knife with a notch at the bottom of the blade.

Pruning saw
A useful tool for cutting branches too large for secateurs or pruners to handle. The saw is slightly curved with a narrow blade to allow you to cut in restricted spaces.

Edging knife
A half-moon-shaped tool for cutting out lawn edges. If you are the type of gardener who demands absolute precision, it is essential. Otherwise, a spade will do this job well enough.

Secateurs
Both the anvil type and the "parrot-bill" type are perfectly good for most pruning jobs and choice is largely a matter of personal preference. Use them on the size of wood they are designed for.

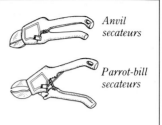

Anvil secateurs

Parrot-bill secateurs

Shears
A short-handled pair will cut hedges and a long-handled pair trim the lawn edges. It is worth buying expensive shears that will hold a good, sharp edge.

LARGE TOOLS

Spring-tine rake

Hollow-tined fork

Onion hoe   *Dutch hoe*   *Draw hoe*

Hoes
Ideally, you should have two hoes – a Dutch, or push, hoe and a swan-necked, or draw, hoe. When choosing a hoe, make sure its handle is long enough for you to work almost upright without straining your back.

Push the Dutch hoe backwards and forwards while walking backwards, thus avoiding treading the weeds back into the soil. Walking forwards will push the weeds back into the soil, thus effectively transplanting them. Walking backwards leaves them sitting on the surface, a prey to drying winds and the sun. Use the swan-necked hoe for hoeing weeds too large to hoe any other way, for earthing-up vegetables, and for making drills for sowing seeds.

A small "onion" hoe is ideal for working between closely planted subjects and particularly useful on deep beds. A wheel hoe is a great time saver, and invaluable on larger vegetable plots, though you must space your plants to allow for its width. It is a hand-pushed tool with a simple wheel in front of a cutting blade.

WATERING EQUIPMENT

Watering can
Buy the largest you can carry easily, but remember that it will be much heavier full. To water at the back of the greenhouse staging, it needs a long handle and spout. A fine rose for seedlings is essential.

Hose
Essential for thorough watering. Types that do not kink are expensive, but worth the extra. Hoses are best stored on a reel. A seep hose slowly drips water along its length and can be left permanently under polythene mulches, and turned on wherever needed.

Sprinkler
You will never put on enough water if you have to stand and hold a hose. Choose a sprinkler with a fine spray, the head mounted on a tall stand.

Sprayer
Organic gardeners think spraying the last resort, though it is sometimes needed. Buy a sprayer that deposits the solution evenly in small droplets.

HOMEMADE TOOLS

Sieve

A sieve with a 1.5mm (1/16 in) mesh is necessary for sprinkling a fine layer of compost over sown seeds. Nail a piece of plastic mesh on to a frame.

Planting board

A planting board is invaluable for the accurate spacing of plants. Make it 3m (10ft) long, made from 8×2.5cm (3×1in) wood with a sawcut every 8cm (3in). Mark each 30cm (12in) division with nails. For deep beds, make a 1.25m (4ft) board, with 15cm (6in) divisions.

Garden line

Two sticks, or pegs, and some thick nylon string used to mark lines for drawing seed drills and to mark off areas of soil for digging. Make at least two lines.

Dibber

Used to transplant seedlings. Cut a broken spade or fork handle to 30cm (12in) and shave the end to a point.

Tool cleaner

Cut a piece of wood to a spade shape and use regularly when digging, to remove any dirt sticking to the blade. Use it to clean all your tools before putting them away.

Firming board

A firming board is a 1cm (1/2in) thick piece of wood cut slightly smaller than your seed trays with a handle screwed to one side. It is invaluable for levelling off compost when filling the trays and for firming down compost evenly prior to sowing. Make one to fit each tray size.

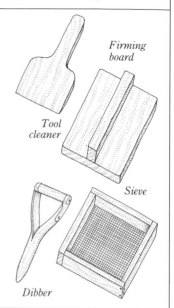

Firming board

Tool cleaner

Sieve

Dibber

GARDENING MACHINERY

Mowers

There are two main types of mower: a cylinder mower and a rotary grass cutter, the former generally producing a better finish. Choose one with as many blades on the cylinder as possible.

Rotary mowers come into their own in areas of tall grass. You can use them on closer-cut lawns but they will not give a very fine finish.

You can buy petrol- or electric-powered mowers. With the latter, fit a device that instantly cuts off the current if you accidentally cut through the cable or if there is any other kind of electrical fault.

Rotary cultivator

A rotary cultivator is invaluable in a very large garden: you can make a very fine seed bed in half the time it takes to dig by hand, and it is extremely useful for

incorporating green manure, compost and other organic matter into the soil. However, you must hand dig at least part of your garden every year because constant rotary cultivating can "glaze" the soil, creating an impermeable layer; most machines cultivate down to about 15cm (6in) and rarely deeper than about 23cm (9in). The types with blades at the rear are easiest to use.

Strimmer

A short length of strong nylon line turns at speed and cuts grass without any danger of anything more substantial being damaged. This enables you to use a strimmer right up to walls or trees.

Shredder

This machine shreds woody material extremely finely, taking all the prunings that would

otherwise only be burned. The resulting material is excellent for mulching and a cheap alternative to chipped or composted bark.

Hedge trimmer

Useful for a large area of hedging. Once you are accustomed to it, it can do almost as good a job as hand shears – but not quite.

Hedge trimmer

Shredder

Cultivation techniques

Any gardening involves a certain amount of physical work. Knowing how to cultivate the soil with the least amount of effort for the greatest effect is invaluable, so that the labour will be a pleasure rather than a chore.

Digging

Hand digging is the main method of cultivating the soil: it breaks up compacted land, introduces air and allows water to drain away and roots to penetrate. It also enables you to work organic matter into the lower levels, increasing the depth of the topsoil. Prepare all new ground by double digging (*see page 182*), then single dig every year, in autumn for heavy soils and in spring for light soils.

Digging heavy soils

It is best to dig heavy soils in autumn, before the worst of the winter rains makes cultivation difficult. Choose your moment carefully, when the soil is neither too dry and hard nor too wet and sticky. If necessary, cover an area of soil with polythene to keep it dry. When digging

---

BASIC RULES OF DIGGING

Digging can cause severe back strain or it can be a healthy, invigorating, and enjoyable exercise – it all depends on using your common sense.

- Never dig when the soil is wet enough to stick to your boots – you risk spoiling its structure.
- Use a spade and fork the correct size for you. You gain nothing by using oversized tools, which tire you quickly and slow you down.
- Never take spadefuls too big to handle comfortably. By taking smaller amounts, and not straining yourself, you can dig more for longer.
- Always take your time: there is no point in rushing. Adopt a rhythmic and methodical approach, conscious all the time of avoiding strain. As soon as you feel you have had enough or you begin to find it difficult to straighten up – stop! It is now that you are likely to do damage to yourself. Above all, do not try to do all the digging at once. Leave plenty of time so that you can do it in stages.
- Finally, keep your tools in good, clean condition. Carry a scraper in your pocket and use it regularly to clean soil from your tools. When you finish, clean the tools thoroughly and rub them over with an oily cloth to prevent rust.

SINGLE DIGGING

With single digging it is only necessary to dig one spade deep and incorporate one layer of manure, and so there is no need to mark out trenches as carefully as for double digging (*see overleaf*).

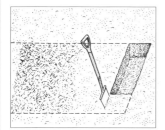  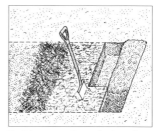

1 *Mark out the plot as for double digging (see page 182). Dig out the first trench one spade deep. Throw all the soil behind you, spreading it out more or less evenly over the surface of the bed.*

2 *Spread a layer of manure over the soil about 1 metre/yard behind you: enough to fill up to three trenches with a 5–8cm (2–3in) layer of manure. Scrape some into the bottom of the first trench.*

3 *Dig a second trench, throwing the soil forward to cover the organic matter in the first trench until all the organic matter has been dug in. Spread another layer further down the plot and carry on.*

heavy soils in winter, throw the spadefuls forwards, leaving them rough and unbroken for the winter. This leaves the maximum amount of soil surface exposed. By spring, drying winds and frosts will have broken the surface down to a fine tilth that you need only rake before sowing. Leaving soil rough allows heavy rains and frost to kill weeds and pests, and makes them more accessible to predators.

Digging light soils

Sandy and chalky soils (*see page 65*) will crumble to a fine tilth more readily than heavy soils. The problem with light soils is that they drain easily, causing leaching of the nutrients. To minimize this, keep the ground covered for the winter by sowing a green-manure crop in autumn and digging it in a short time before sowing your main crop in the spring.

DOUBLE DIGGING

You should double dig all new ornamental borders before planting, to work organic matter to the lower levels of soil. The vegetable plot will also benefit from initial double digging; subsequently, double dig at intervals of about five years, depending on soil type. The best way to achieve this is to dig at least one-fifth of your land each year, on a rotation basis.

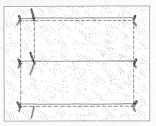

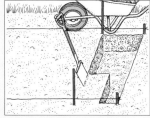

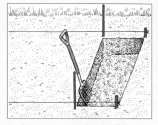

1 *Mark out the plot with lines down either side; divide a wide plot down the middle as well. Cut two 60cm (2ft) canes to mark the trench width, each exactly the same size so you refill each one with the same amount of soil as you have taken out.*

2 *Mark out the first 60cm (2ft) trench with the canes and dig out all the soil to the depth of the spade, putting it in a wheelbarrow. Barrow it to the other end of the plot. With a wide plot divided into two halves, put the soil at the start of the other half.*

3 *Clean out crumbs of soil from the bottom of the trench and "fork" the soil to the depth of the fork. This is the subsoil and should not be inverted. Simply loosen it by digging it up and throwing it back as it came out.*

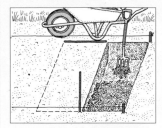

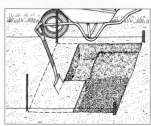

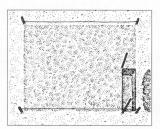

4 *Put a 5–8cm (2–3in) layer of organic matter in the bottom of the trench. Then, leaving one cane in the corner of the trench you have dug out, mark out the second trench, to the same size, with the other cane.*

5 *Start digging out the new trench to the same depth, but throw the soil forward to cover the organic matter in the first trench. Spread another layer of organic matter in the first trench and cover it with the soil from the second trench to raise the bed.*

6 *Carry on working down the plot: when you get to the last trench, refill it with the soil you removed from the first trench. Cover the entire area with another layer of organic matter. The rain will soon wash it into the bed.*

Removing weeds

Whenever you are digging, put any perennial weeds in a bucket and burn or throw them away. Annual weeds can go in the bottom of the trenches to add to the organic content of the soil. It is sometimes suggested that you can scrape annual weeds off the soil surface with a spade before starting to dig. However, there are usually a few perennials mixed with them, difficult to recognize without their foliage, so remove them by hand as you dig.

Raking

Rake the soil level before you sow. Choose a rake that suits your size; a large-headed rake is difficult to control by a small person.

Try not to lunge forward with the rake, pulling back soil from some way away; it will result in a wavy, uneven surface. Instead, reach forward no more than about 30cm (12in) and keep the head of the rake nearly parallel to the surface of the soil. Step back now and then, squat down and squint across the soil surface, looking for any high and low spots.

Hoeing

This is the principal organic method of weed control, and there really is no need to resort to chemicals (see pages 179 and 216–17).

Watering

All plants require adequate supplies of water and there are always occasions when it is necessary to water artificially. However, simply pouring water on to the soil can, in fact, do more harm than good.

First, never add water in small amounts. You must apply enough to get right down to the root zone, or roots will come to the surface in search of water, and be even more vulnerable to the effects of heat and lack of moisture.

Second, although large quantities of water are required, you must apply it carefully. Water applied as large droplets or with great force will cause the soil "crumbs" to break down and

form a hard surface crust. This prevents further water entering the soil and also inhibits the free interchange of air and gases, with disastrous effects – even stopping seedlings pushing through. Apply water through a sprinkler with a fine spray pattern of small droplets. When watering seed trays, use a can fitted with a fine rose. Start pouring the water to one side of the tray or pot, then pass the can over the seedlings, keeping the angle of the rose constant throughout. When you have finished, do not raise the can until it is clear of the tray or pot.

When to water

It is not necessary to keep the soil moist all the time – water when the soil is dry, but before the plants begin to suffer – and, provided you use a fine sprinkler, you can water at any time of day. However, timing is important. For example, watering when fruits or vegetables are swelling will greatly increase their overall weight. Once fruits, in particular, begin to colour, though, extra water could invite a fungus attack.

How much water to give

It is, of course, not difficult to overwater, especially with plants in pots. Try to strike a balance between an aerated soil or compost and one with sufficient moisture. A cold, wet, airless compost will not do anything to encourage plant growth. In the ornamental or vegetable garden, leave the sprinkler on for at least an hour.

Watering new plants

When you have just planted a plant, encourage it to search for water, thus increasing its root system. Water it thoroughly immediately after planting, then leave it to its own devices for a while, almost allowing the soil to dry out, before watering the plant again.

Mulching

This is a technique that involves covering the surface of the soil – either with organic matter to condition the soil (see pages 68–9), or with paper or polythene to inhibit weeds (see page 217).

Propagation techniques

The modern trend is towards "convenience gardening", and a whole industry has developed to service this market. We are encouraged to buy young plants from garden centres or nurseries. For the organic gardener, this "convenience" method is not good enough. First, you probably want to do the whole thing from start to finish. Second, it can be difficult to find plants raised organically without the "benefit" of chemical sprays or fertilizers. So you have no alternative but to raise all your plants yourself. Growing from seed is the most common method of propagation. Some plants will not produce exact replicas from seed and require alternative, vegetative techniques of propagation. Division is the simplest method, but, for plants that you cannot divide, layering, cuttings, budding, and grafting will ensure that the new plants are exactly the same as the parent.

Growing from seed

Sow directly into your garden or start seeds in the greenhouse. Prepare the soil well for sowing outside and use a good compost in containers (*see page 101*).

SOWING OUTSIDE

The cheapest method of raising plants is by sowing seeds directly into prepared soil – the method used for most vegetables, hardy annuals, and many herbaceous perennials.

Rake the soil down level and sprinkle on fertilizer. Compress the soil by walking over the surface with your weight on your heels. Next, rake it down to a fine tilth, but never when wet enough to stick to your boots. Never tread on deep beds, but leave for three or four weeks after digging for the soil to settle.

The correct time to sow varies from one plant to another. There is, however, no point in sowing too early: seeds in soil below 7°C (45°F) will not usually germinate until the soil warms up. You can start earlier under cloches placed in position two weeks before sowing.

DRAWING SEED DRILLS

Both narrow and wide seed drills should be as shallow as possible and of uniform depth. Rake your soil to a fine tilth and tread down firmly. Set up a tight planting line, and make a furrow as shown.

Drawing a narrow drill
This is the most commonly used seed drill. Put one corner of a draw hoe in the ground and pull it towards you gently. Alternatively, if you prefer, draw a regular drill using a short stick.

Making a narrow seed drill with a broom or rake handle
If you find it difficult to draw a drill using a hoe, place a broom handle or rake handle along the planting line and press it into the soil with your foot.

Drawing a wide band
Put your hoe flat on the ground and pull it towards you, making a furrow of a uniform depth. Use wide bands in deep-bed cultivation when sowing vegetable crops that are thinned selectively.

Some seeds with extremely hard coats can germinate more successfully if soaked overnight in water. File very hard seeds with a nail file to assist the entry of water into the seed coat. Other seeds, such as beetroot, have a natural inhibitor within the seed coat to prevent premature germination. Wash the seeds under the cold tap or soak overnight.

The main cause of seeds failing to germinate is being sown too deeply. If the seed's food reserve runs out before the shoot reaches the surface, the seedling will never appear. It is, of course, impossible to be that accurate when sowing seeds 6mm (¼in) deep or less: simply make a "shallow" drill (which means making a furrow as shallow as you can).

Space seeds and drills correctly to avoid overcrowding. Some seeds can be thinned and transplanted later; others, such as root crops, will "fork" if transplanted.

Sowing techniques

Always sow seed thinly. With the vast majority of seed varieties, between 80 and 90 per cent will germinate; if seedlings come up too thickly, they will compete for available light, becoming thin and straggly. Instead of sowing straight from the packet, often it is more accurate to hold the seeds in the palm of the hand and sow a pinch at a time.

Some large seeds can be sown singly or in "stations" (groups of two or three at the required distances, thinned if more than one germinates). With deep beds adopt a block-sowing technique (see pages 132–3).

If your soil is very dry, water the drills before sowing. Use a can, more or less fill up the drill and allow the water to drain, then sow as directed. Never water after sowing; this leads to "capping", where the soil forms a crust

THE STALE SEED BED
Cultivate the seed bed a few weeks before you need it. Let dormant weed seeds germinate, then hoe them out immediately before sowing. This way weeds that appear later will not only be fewer in number but, lagging behind the cultivated varieties you have sown, they will be easy to recognize.

on top that can prevent the entry of further water or even prevent young seedlings from breaking through to the light.

Cover all seeds by running the back of your rake down the centre of the row. Lightly tap down the soil with the back of the rake, so that the seed is in close contact with the soil.

Always use a proprietary plant label to mark the row clearly with the plant's name. A seed packet stuck on a cane always seems to blow away or becomes unreadable after heavy rain.

Sometimes it is an advantage to pre-germinate seeds such as parsnips and lettuce inside and sow them outside only after they have started to grow (see page 130).

SOWING INSIDE

By sowing seeds inside in trays or pots you can start much earlier in the year. Vegetables can be sown in mid winter and planted out under cloches in early spring. This way, they will give you your first crop in late spring. A greenhouse is ideal for this purpose, because it is easier to control the environment to give the seeds the best possible start, but you could put them on a windowsill indoors. Check the recommended sowing temperature and ensure that you can provide it by starting the seeds off in a heated propagator in the greenhouse, or, if you do not have one, in the airing cupboard.

SAVING SEED
Seed can be expensive to buy, so save it, if you can, from season to season. Always open seed packets in a dry place and take out only as much as you need. Reseal the packets, put them into a dry, airtight container, and keep in a cool but frost-free place. You can "harvest" your own seeds from many plants, but not F1 hybrids because they will not grow true to type. Allow seeds to ripen on the plants and remove the pods just before they fall. With a little practice, this soon becomes quite easy. If it is difficult, when the pods are almost mature, place a paper bag over them to catch seeds as they ripen. Alternatively, cut the whole flowering stem and hang it in an airy shed upside down over a sheet or bowl to catch the seeds as they fall.

POTS AND CONTAINERS

Wood and clay are the traditional materials used for raising and growing on plants, but plastic and polystyrene containers are much cheaper and, in some respects, better. Polystyrene is easily damaged, but retains warmth. You can buy polystyrene blocks divided into the small cells. Holes in the cells match pegs on a special polystyrene presser board, so seedlings and compost can be pushed out together, without root disturbance. Use clay pots and soil-based compost for plants like alpines that need good drainage; plastic pots and soil-less compost for most other plants. Seed trays are shallow containers, usually 5–7cm (2–3in) deep and either 35×20cm (15×9in) or 15×10cm (7×4in). Wooden trays can harbour disease, but plastic ones can be sterilized with boiling water.

You can also use any shallow container for sowing seed, from polystyrene meat trays to margarine tubs or even the foil containers used for take-away food. Plastic yogurt containers, polystyrene coffee cups, and cut-off plastic bottles make ideal pots for sowing large seeds or for cuttings. Remember, they must be thoroughly cleaned and have adequate drainage holes.

SOWING IN SEED TRAYS

1 *Fill tray with moist sowing compost. Remove excess by running the side of a firming board across the top. Press compost into the tray's edges with your fingers. Consolidate by pressing it lightly with the firming board.*

2 *Pour seed into your palm and cup the hand slightly to form a channel. Tap hand with your finger to move seeds. Sow seeds around edge of tray, then work into centre. Cover seeds with own depth of compost.*

Sowing tiny seeds
Put a small amount of silver sand in the seed packet as a spreading agent. Put the resulting mixture into your hand and sow.

Sowing large seeds
Sow two to a pot. Make holes in the compost using a small stick, or dibber, and put the seeds in on their sides. If both seeds germinate, thin the weaker carefully.

Fill a pot or tray with moist seed compost (*see page 101*) and firm lightly. Soil-less composts need little firming: push your fingers into the compost. Level with a firming board if using a tray, or with the bottom of another pot.

It is important to moisten the compost thoroughly before sowing: spread it on to your work bench, make a well in the centre and pour in some water. Gradually work the water into the compost by rubbing it through your hand. Fill the container, then water again, since watering after sowing tends to wash the seeds into one spot, or even right out of the pot! Let it drain for a few minutes before sowing.

Cover all except very small seeds with their own depth of compost. Then cover the pot or tray with opaque polythene and put in a warm place. The airing cupboard is useful, but check the temperature: the shelf directly above the hot water cylinder may be too hot. Check the seeds every day; when the first germinates, remove the container to a light place, but not direct sunlight; cover the seedlings with newspaper if the sun may scorch them.

On a windowsill, light always coming from only one direction may make seedlings long and spindly. Reduce this to a minimum by making a "light-box" out of an orange box, lined with kitchen foil to reflect available light all around the plants. In winter, bring the light box into the warmth of the centre of the room at night. Cover with polythene, then remove in the morning.

THINNING AND TRANSPLANTING SEEDLINGS

When seedlings are large enough to handle, thin them to prevent overcrowding. Seedlings sown outside can be transplanted and thinned at the same time. However, root crops will probably fork if transplanted, but most ornamentals and leaf vegetables can be moved.

Seedlings grown outside

Before either thinning out or transplanting, water the rows well. To thin, simply pull up unwanted seedlings, leaving the others at the required distance from one another. Remove the thinnings to the compost heap. Left on the ground, the bruised stems attract pests.

If you need thinnings for transplanting, handle by the leaves only: stems bruise easily and could succumb to fungus attack. Thin to one row of seedlings at the required spacing, then transplant the rest in new rows.

Container-grown seedlings

Container-sown seedlings need to be thinned, or transplanted, into a larger seed tray or pot when large enough to handle. Transplanting from seed trays or pots into another container is known as "pricking out". Before they are planted out, seedlings grown in the greenhouse must be acclimatized to the colder conditions by being placed first in a closed, unheated cold frame. Gradually open up the frame a little during the day and, later, a little at night, until it is completely open.

Thinning pot-grown seedlings
Remove the weaker of the two seedlings when 5–7cm (2–3in). Firm down roots of the stronger one.

TRANSPLANTING AND PRICKING OUT

Transplanting outside
1 *Water seedlings the day before. Firm soil round plants by straddling stems with your fingers (far left). Place fingers under seedlings; lift carefully with as much root as possible.*
2 *Transplant seedlings to new rows, spacing with a planting board (left). Water using a watering can with a fine rose.*

Pricking out
1 *Fill a larger seed tray with soil-less compost. Water seedlings well. Push small dibber under roots and lift carefully, handling leaves, never stems (far left).*
2 *Make holes in new compost with a dibber. Plant seedlings and firm compost. Water well and place in light place but out of direct sunlight (left).*

Division

Division is used to increase perennials. It is perhaps the simplest and most effective method of propagation and produces good, sizeable plants very quickly. Indeed, many perennials which form spreading clumps begin to lose vigour after a few years and benefit greatly from being divided to perpetrate the existing stocks.

For most perennials, division should be done in autumn. Cut back the old flower stems and lift the whole clump from the border using a fork. Divide in half, small clumps by hand or with a trowel; larger or very old clumps may have to be prised apart with two garden forks stuck back to back into the centre of the clump and used to force it apart. Remove the young shoots from the outside of the clump by breaking or cutting them off. Discard the centre of the clump (the older, less vigorous part of the plant). Cut the leaves back to 2.5cm (1in) and replant.

Dividing plants with fleshy roots

Some plants, such as plantain lilies (*Hosta* sp.), have fleshy roots and should be treated differently. These are best lifted for division in spring. You will be able to see new buds and thus have an idea of where to cut. Each new piece should have at least one good bud. Cut through the root with a sharp spade or a large knife and replant the parts as soon as possible.

Taking cuttings

Most plants can be propagated without too much difficulty by cuttings. There are many different types of cuttings recommended for various plants, but an easy rule is to take "hardwood" cuttings in autumn, when the wood is ripe, and "softwood" cuttings in summer, when the shoot is still growing. Half-hardy perennials require slight modification of the basic technique. They are best taken in late summer or in early spring when the tubers produce new shoots. They root more readily than shrubs, but need a temperature of 13–15°C (55–60°F) at the roots.

Softwood cuttings

This method can be used to increase any shrubs at any time during summer, but early in the season is best. The small amount of equipment, should cost next to nothing, and the success rate should be about 80 per cent.

Some gardeners use hormone rooting powder to encourage cuttings to root quickly. It can be argued that this is not entirely organic because the hormones have been chemically synthesized, In fact, the hormones are synthesized in the same way as they would be in the plant, so rooting powder can be used with confidence in an organic garden provided it contains no additives. Take cuttings of soft, new plant growth, selecting shoots about 10cm

TAKING SOFTWOOD CUTTINGS

1 *Fill tray with coir. Take cutting 10cm (4in) long from healthy shoot. Trim cutting by half, just below leaf joint. Trim away all side leaves, then dip in copper fungicide solution.*

2 *If using hormone rooting powder, dip end of cutting into powder and shake off excess powder. Put cuttings in tray of compost. Space cuttings in rows 2.5cm (1in) apart each way.*

3 *Water with a copper fungicide solution. Wrap tray in light polythene so that the sheeting touches tops of cuttings and is sealed under tray. Place tray in softwood cuttings frame.*

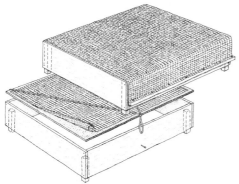

Making a softwood cuttings box
*Make two wooden frames about 15cm (6in) deep,
exactly the same size. Make a lid for the first box from a
sheet of corrugated plastic and use netting as shading.
Hold in place with a thick rubber band, nailed on to
one side and hooked to a nail on the other side. As the
plants grow, the other frame can be set on top, and a
new lid of netting, weighted down at the front with a
batten and nailed to the back, can be hung over the top.*

(4in) long, a method suitable for most shrubs.
Use the same method for conifer cuttings, tear
the leaves away from the shoots to bruise the
stems so that they will root.

Once the cuttings are potted up and placed in
a cold frame or homemade softwood cuttings
box, providing the right amount of light is a
vital ingredient. The cuttings will be feeding
through their leaves, so they need some
sunshine, but not too much, so adjust the
amount of shading matching accordingly.

TAKING HARDWOOD CUTTINGS

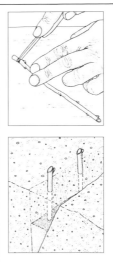

1 *Cut off a length of
stem about 20–23cm
(8–9in) long. Trim
below the lowest bud.
Cut off soft top growth
just above a bud.
Make narrow trench
and line bottom with
sharp sand.*

2 *Place cuttings in
trench, 7.5cm (3in) of
the tops out of the
ground. Refill trench,
firm in and leave one
year. Next winter,
plant out 15–23cm
(6–9in) apart in rows.
Leave for year, before
final planting.*

Hardwood cuttings

This method is used to increase deciduous
fruiting shrubs such as blackcurrants, and is
worth trying with most deciduous shrubs. It is
simple and cheap and the plants will not suffer
from the small amount of pruning required.

Hardwood cuttings should be taken in the
autumn, just after the plants have lost their
leaves, although some, such as gooseberries,
can be taken earlier. Hardwood cuttings take
some time to establish, but are worth the effort.

TAKING CUTTINGS OF HALF-HARDY PERENNIALS

1 *Take cutting with a new shoot
and at least three leaves.
Carefully cut away all the lower
leaves. Trim stem of cutting just
below lowest leaf joint. Dip in
rooting powder; tap off excess.*

2 *Fill pot with soil-less compost.
Make hole with small dibber;
insert cutting, and firm by
pushing the dibber into compost
and pressing sideways towards
the cutting.*

3 *Bend a piece of wire to form
arch over cutting and place in pot.
Cover with polythene bag; or place
whole pot in polythene bag, blow
up the bag with air and seal
the top.*

Layering

This method of increasing plants involves putting part of the plant into the ground and leaving it attached to the parent until it has developed a root system sufficient to support itself. The three different methods are: tip, normal and serpentine layering.

Tip layering
Used mainly for plants that root readily, particularly briar fruits such as blackberries. In late summer, pull down the shoots you need and make a hole in the soil where the tip of each shoot rests. Place the tip in the hole and pin it in position with a forked stick. Cover with soil and leave until the leaves of the parent plant fall. Cut the layer from the parent, lift and transplant to its permanent position.

Normal layering
This method involves burying part of the shoot with the tip exposed, and leaving it to root. Layering is usually carried out in early spring for shrubs and early summer for climbers, on plants that root less readily, such as abelia, magnolia, camellia, and azalea. You may be able to cut the layer away from the parent by the following autumn, but some plants need longer to root: rhododendrons can take two, even three years. You can tell when the layer has rooted by its more vigorous appearance.

Serpentine layering
This method of propagation is suitable for certain types of climber, particularly clematis. Follow the instructions for normal layering, but alternately bury and expose parts of each stem, making many more plants. Wound the stem by slitting it underneath and place that part underground. Repeat the process further along the stem, checking there is at least one bud between the layers to provide the new shoot. The layers will produce shoots along the stem and, when these show signs of growing, separate them from the parent and split them up to provide several new plants.

Grafting and budding

These are two similar techniques used to put new varieties on to existing plants, particularly fruit trees, and certain ornamental plants. Grafting is generally used to change a variety of an apple or pear tree completely, or to put a pollinator on to an existing tree. With the latter, if the new variety is less vigorous, the first tree may dominate.

Cleft grafting is normally used to graft a new variety on to an existing tree; use the whip-and-tongue method to graft a variety on to a rootstock, or to graft varieties on to ornamental plants that do not respond to budding.

Grafting is done in late winter or early spring, just as the tree is beginning its new growth, but prepare the "limb" in mid winter.

Budding is a modified form of grafting and slightly easier. It is most commonly used to put new varieties on to rootstocks. It involves making cuts in the bark of the tree or rootstock and inserting one or more buds from another variety into them. It should be done in early to mid summer, when the sap is running well and the bark will separate freely from the tree. It is generally possible to buy bare-rooted rootstocks from any nursery where they do their own budding. Plant them the winter

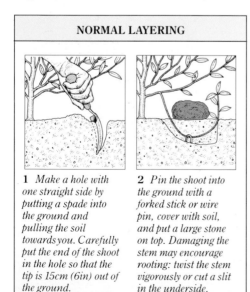

NORMAL LAYERING

1 *Make a hole with one straight side by putting a spade into the ground and pulling the soil towards you. Carefully put the end of the shoot in the hole so that the tip is 15cm (6in) out of the ground.*

2 *Pin the shoot into the ground with a forked stick or wire pin, cover with soil, and put a large stone on top. Damaging the stem may encourage rooting: twist the stem vigorously or cut a slit in the underside.*

CLEFT GRAFTING

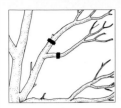   

1 *In mid winter, prepare the limb graft site by cutting back two branches just above a fork.*

2 *At end of winter/early spring, split each of the cut ends by hammering in a bill hook.*

3 *From the variety, cut four 10–15cm (4–6in) lengths of one-year-old stem (scions), cutting each base to a wedge shape.*

4 *Insert and tie scions into each cut, matching cambium layers just beneath the bark. Cover with grafting wax.*

WHIP-AND-TONGUE GRAFTING

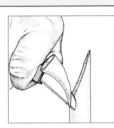  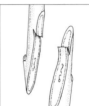 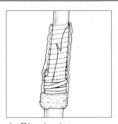

1 *Trim the rootstock back and, with a sharp knife, make a long slanting wedge-like cut in the top part of the stem.*

2 *Using a one-year-old scion as above, cut the end to form another corresponding wedge to the rootstock's wedge.*

3 *Cut two fitting tongues (upwards in the rootstock and downwards in the scion).*

4 *Fit scion into rootstock, so that the cambium layers correspond. Tie with raffia and cover with grafting wax.*

BUDDING ON TO A ROOTSTOCK

   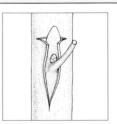

1 *In summer, cut a length of stem from variety to be budded. Remove leaves, leaving leaf stalks on. (Remove rose thorns first.) Immerse in water.*

2 *Cut a T-shaped slit in bark of rootstock and peel back slightly. See picture 4. Remove a bud from the prepared stem by pulling it upwards.*

3 *Remove the sliver of wood in the bud's centre with your fingernail. Slide bud into the T-shaped slit using leaf stalk as a handle.*

4 *Cut away excess bark to fit. Tie bud to tree with rubber tie or raffia. In autumn, prune off growth above new shoots. Tie shoot.*

· CHAPTER TEN ·

PESTS AND DISEASES

Nowhere is the mimicry of the professional grower more evident than in the field of pest and disease control. As soon as a new chemical is produced for commercial use, a slightly diluted version appears in garden centres, accompanied by seductive claims of its effectiveness.

The plain fact is that, by cultivating a natural organic garden, you simply will not come across the problems that can face the mono-culture grower. Where large acreages of one crop are grown every year, a rapid build-up of pests and diseases occurs because of plentiful food and lack of competition. In the organic garden with a great diversity of planting, you will attract the complete spectrum of wildlife to create a natural balance. The hover-flies and ladybirds eat the greenfly, the birds eat the caterpillars, and so on – no insect pest, fungus disease, or bacterium will ever have it all its own way. However, do not think that all insects are friendly and all fungi benign. Pests and diseases will rear their heads in the organic garden just as surely as anywhere else. Prevention is the best approach and there are many ways of doing this.

Attracting insects

*A varied insect population is vital in the organic garden. Butterflies and hover-flies are attracted to the ice plant (*Sedum spectabile*) by its brightly coloured, nectar-filled flowers.*

Maintaining a healthy garden

The very first rule to pest control is good cultivation practices. The organic approach – feeding the soil instead of the plant – produces much stronger growth that is, firstly, not so attractive to pests and diseases as the soft lushness of a force-fed plant and, secondly, able to cope with an attack if it does occur.

Keep the garden as clean and tidy as possible. Never leave rubbish lying around: put weeds on the compost heap straightaway. This is even more important with thinned seedlings, because insect pests are often attracted by the smell of bruised stems.

Put only healthy plant waste on the compost heap. If there is any sign of disease, burn the plant. Never compost the top growth of maincrop potatoes because of the spores of potato blight. Burn prunings from fruit trees, quite likely to be infected with mildew. You can, however, use the ash as a fertilizer.

Use only pots and seed trays that have been thoroughly cleaned and, if possible, sterilized with boiling water or steam. Keep your greenhouse clean too and pick off a pest or a fungus on a leaf straightaway and get rid of it, preferably by burning.

Daily vigilance

Make a habit, especially in the summer, when pests and diseases are most likely to appear, of walking round the garden at least once a day. Remove errant weeds with a hoe, but above all keep an eye open for the first signs of attack from pests and diseases. If you see signs of mildew or find a caterpillar – pick it off immediately, put it into a plastic bag and later into the dustbin. The first attack of greenfly can often be removed by simply rubbing the stem of the attacked plants with your finger to squash them.

Buying healthy plants

Bought plants must be healthy. It is only too easy to buy in a load of trouble (virus or fungus diseases or even pests or their eggs). Some plants are covered by a certificate of health from the Government. In many countries it is possible to ask for a certification number to show that the plant you are buying is free from disease.

In some cases consider replacing your stock with new plants after a few years. Strawberries, for example, will lose their vigour after a while, often a sign of virus diseases. Potatoes too can become infected with virus diseases spread by aphids.

Different varieties of the same plants may have varying degrees of resistance to pests and disease. Some varieties of potato, for example, are less susceptible to slug damage; others show resistance to potato eelworm. Plant breeders are constantly trying to breed pest- and disease-resistant plants, so check the current position on new varieties before buying anything notoriously disease-prone.

Raising healthy plants

You should also employ the same safeguards with plants you have raised yourself, though it is much more difficult to be ruthless about weeding out weaklings. Remember a young plant infected with a disease or attacked by a pest is at a disadvantage from the start.

Use plastic seed trays and pots because they are easier to sterilize. Time your spring sowing so that plants do not have to remain in the greenhouse getting leggy and pot-bound because the weather is too cold to plant them out. The real secret is to get plants growing away and then to keep them growing steadily. Make sure they never go short of water and food: often all you need to control even the most virulent and damaging of diseases.

One final point: F1 hybrid varieties (the result of a first-generation cross between two selected parents) have much more vigour than those raised from open-pollinated seed.

Companion planting

This is a technique practised by many organic gardeners. The theory behind companion planting is that plants have specific likes and dislikes concerning their close companions. Similarly, by planting a particular species you can reduce the number of weeds or attract certain pest predators.

Many recommendations for companion planting are based on folklore and, as with many of these tales, there is some truth in them. Some are not proved, like the well-known theory that, because carrot-fly are attracted by smell, they can be prevented by planting carrots between rows of onions, so the smell of the carrots is disguised. On the other hand, the cabbage white butterfly is attracted to its host plant by smell and can be fooled by planting the highly aromatic French marigold (*Tagetes*) between rows of cabbages. Many gardeners have also reported similar results with eelworms, soil pests that attack potatoes, where French marigolds are grown. Scientific research has confirmed that this is indeed due to a secretion from the roots of the marigolds. French marigolds are also said to help kill couch grass (*Agropyron repens*).

Reducing aphids

There is no doubt that marigolds (*Tagetes* and *Calendula*), planted near tomatoes or roses, for example, greatly reduce the frequency of attack by aphids because they attract hover-flies whose larvae devour greenfly by the thousand. Hover-flies are the most valuable pest predators in the garden. The female lays eggs on colonies of aphids so that the larvae have a readily available source of food. The hover-fly has a short feeding tube, so needs to feed from an open-structured flower where pollen is easily accessible. So plant marigolds (*Tagetes* and *Calendula*), poppies (*Papaver* sp.), nasturtiums (*Tropaeolum*) or dwarf morning glory (*Convolvulus tricolor*) between plants, to minimize aphids. So far, garlic grown under rose bushes as a control for greenfly, and savory next to beans for the same purpose, have not yet been proved to be effective.

Encouraging other predators

It is more difficult to attract some of the other predators because they do not necessarily feed on flowers. Some, such as ladybirds, lacewings, and several species of wasps that feed on and lay their eggs inside aphids and other soft-bellied pests, including caterpillars, can be encouraged by providing a varied collection of plant life. Also provide a small area of water. By doing all this you will build up a varied colony of useful insects and birds and thus keep problems to a minimum.

It has also been found that some pests are attracted to their host plants by sight. By mixing ornamental plants and vegetables in an ornamental border, you can camouflage the host plants which deters the pests. There is also evidence that weed-infested vegetable plots suffer less than clean ones. However, the yields are also lower because the weeds compete for the light, nutrients, and water.

A source of water
A pond, however small, will attract all kinds of insects and small mammals.

Controlling birds and animals

The most destructive pests in gardens are the larger ones – birds, deer, rabbits, moles, mice, and so on, although birds are as much friend as foe, because they act as pest controllers and are aesthetically pleasing as well. There is no doubt that the most effective control is to prevent them reaching the crops by physical means.

Birds

There is no really effective bird deterrent available. Scarecrows are reasonably effective for a day or two, but then the birds get used to them and take no notice. The same happens with the more elaborate electric scarecrows that have waving arms, flashing lights, and screaming sirens or blazing shot-guns. If moved around constantly, they have some effect but they are more likely to frighten your neighbours than the birds! If a scarecrow is combined with regular shooting it will be more effective, but you will also disturb the natural balance and that is like biting the hand that feeds you.

The only really effective control for birds in the productive garden is netting, not nearly as expensive as it may seem. Plastic netting is relatively cheap and will last a very long time if used carefully (see below).

The ideal is to build yourself a fruit cage to cover the entire productive garden (see page 161). If you do not wish to go to that extreme, cover only the rows of vulnerable crops. You can place a row of small wire hoops along the beds of low plants and drape nets over the top. Alternatively, with crops such as strawberries or rows of fruit bushes, simply drape the netting over the row. If the plants may grow through the netting, as with peas, for example, support the net on stakes to be higher than the plants. Otherwise, you will damage the plant when you remove the netting. The netting must be firmly fixed at ground level, or birds or hedgehogs may still get underneath and could be injured trying to get out.

Unlike most of the insect pests, birds generally cause most damage during the winter, when there is little else around for them to eat. They will attack the fattening buds of fruit – particularly blackcurrants. The

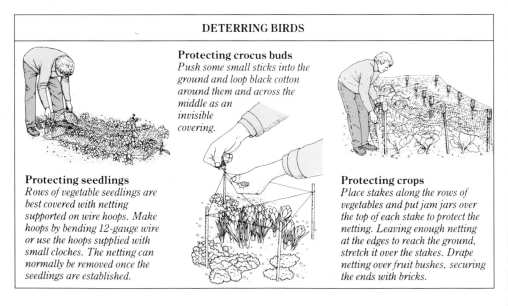

DETERRING BIRDS

Protecting crocus buds
Push some small sticks into the ground and loop black cotton around them and across the middle as an invisible covering.

Protecting seedlings
Rows of vegetable seedlings are best covered with netting supported on wire hoops. Make hoops by bending 12-gauge wire or use the hoops supplied with small cloches. The netting can normally be removed once the seedlings are established.

Protecting crops
Place stakes along the rows of vegetables and put jam jars over the top of each stake to protect the netting. Leaving enough netting at the edges to reach the ground, stretch it over the stakes. Drape netting over fruit bushes, securing the ends with bricks.

cabbage (*Brassica*) family are also at risk, because they are often the only edible plants visible in snow.

Protecting the ornamental garden is rather more difficult because plastic netting will do nothing for the appearance of the flower borders. And some birds are particularly keen to remove buds from all kinds of plants, particularly crocuses in the spring. They seem to go mainly for the yellow ones so avoid these if birds are a problem. Protect the rest by stringing black cotton over the top. Birds do not see the cotton strands and, if they touch them, they will panic and fly off.

New grass seed is extremely vulnerable to attack by birds. Obviously it is impossible to rake in all the seed, but birds can be deterred by black cotton, though this is not practical over large areas. A more effective method is to cover the seeded area with perforated polythene sold at garden centres as "floating cloches". It keeps the birds away and also encourages germination by warming the soil.

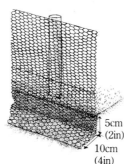

Erecting rabbit fencing
Hammer fencing posts into the ground. String two strands of wire between, one a third of the way up the posts, the other near the top. Fix wire netting to the strands, burying the bottom 15–20cm (6–8in) in a trench, curving away from the fence base.

5cm (2in)
10cm (4in)

Animals

Animals such as hedgehogs, frogs, and toads should be encouraged in any garden because they feed on pests. Other animals such as deer, rabbits, moles or mice, must be kept out because they feed on the plants or undermine them. Good fencing will deter deer and rabbits, but the only solution to mice and moles is trap them.

Deer
If you live in the country near woodland, deer can be quite a problem because they eat most vegetation and strip bark from trees in winter. They can jump a 3m (10ft) fence, so building one tall enough is expensive. An alternative is an electric fence powered by a car battery or through a transformer run from your mains electricity. It is important to get an expert to install this fencing safely, so seek the advice of an agricultural merchant.

Rabbits
Rabbits are a problem in many rural gardens because they eat almost anything. There is only one way to control them effectively. No

amount of shooting, trapping, or ferreting will keep their numbers down; they have to be fenced out with wire netting (*see above*). It is important to use 2.5cm (1in) mesh netting and bury it at least 15cm (6in), with 75cm (2ft 6in) above the ground.

Mice
Mice are not usually a serious problem, but if entire rows of larger seeds such as peas or beans disappear, suspect mice. They dig them out and carry them away, and rarely leave a visible trace. You can either trap them with a conventional mousetrap or acquire a cat.

Moles
These animals can be a particular problem because not only does their burrowing damage plant roots – sometimes even leaving the roots suspended in mid-air – but they also eat large numbers of worms. They undermine lawns and borders as well, leaving large mounds of earth and uneven soil sinkage.

Moles are almost impossible to keep out of the garden. Smoke seems to drive them off only temporarily, and the trick of making their tunnels uncomfortable by filling them with holly leaves simply makes them dig elsewhere.

If all else fails, the only reasonably effective method is to trap them, though it goes against the grain because they are very attractive creatures indeed. Barrel traps are the most effective and at least the moles are killed instantly. The position of the traps must be marked with a stick or coloured marker so you do not forget where they are, and the traps themselves must be checked every day.

Controlling soil pests and insects

Soil pests and insects have always proved a great headache for organic gardeners because there is no suitable organic chemical with which to treat them. Three soil pests that cause great problems, are wireworms, cutworms and leatherjackets. One way of reducing all soil pests is to hoe between plants regularly, bringing them to the surface, where the birds will find them.

There are, however, some very effective physical controls for some of the most troublesome. Natural predators can be encouraged to help get rid of pests (*see also page 200*). Insects can also be controlled without resorting to chemicals. Many insects are specific to certain plants and are dealt with on pages 202–9. Those discussed here attack a wide range of plants.

PHYSICAL TREATMENT

Caterpillars
Larvae of moths and butterflies are common garden pests. Some live in the soil and feed on roots, others attack stems or fruit, but the majority live on leaves. The most seriously affected plants are those of the cabbage (*Brassica*) family.

What to do
If you can spot the small clusters of tiny eggs, simply remove them. Pick caterpillars off and drop into a jar of paraffin.

Leatherjackets
Unmistakable, being white, fat, and very ugly, these larvae of the crane fly can be found just below the surface of the soil, nibbling away at the roots of just about anything. They sometimes surface on a warm night.

What to do
You generally find leatherjackets when digging or hoeing. They are easy to see and squash: normally all that is needed for control. Ground beetles eat them so encourage these with ground-cover plants.

Wireworms
These larvae of the click beetle are thin, shiny worms with yellowish skins. They make small holes in potatoes and carrots, which can be mistaken for damage caused by slugs. Wireworms attack any plant, but particularly those with fleshy roots.

What to do

In the first year or two of cultivating newly turned soil, grow a row of wheat between the crops. The wireworms will be attracted to the wheat, which can be dug up and put on the bonfire. You can also use old potatoes or carrots to trap the wireworms. These can be spitted on a stick and buried, so that you know where the trap is and can easily remove it for burning. Alternatively, trap wireworms by splitting an old cabbage stalk and pushing it 5–7cm (2–3in) into the ground near affected plants. Lift potatoes periodically, and remove and destroy the wireworms.

Cutworms
Perhaps even more troublesome than the tiresome wireworms or leatherjackets, cutworms live just below the surface. They feed at the base of plants during the day, cutting them off at soil level.

What to do
If plants have keeled over, search the soil just below the surface. Hoe an area up to about one metre/yard away from the affected plant to expose the grubs; destroy them by squashing, burning, or drowning in paraffin. Again, attract ground beetles.

Ants
Ants rarely harm growing plants directly, but carry aphids from plant to plant, so protecting them against ladybirds and hover-fly larvae. This is because the ants feed on the sticky honey-dew excreted by feeding aphids.

What to do
It is often enough to control aphids (see opposite). If ants are a real nuisance, put down a mixture of equal parts icing sugar and borax, on a piece of wood or stone, near to ant activity, and cover to protect from rain. Ants love sweet things and will devour the bait. The poison will be carried into the nest. As ants eat their droppings, soon the entire colony will be destroyed.

Slugs
Very large slugs live on fungi and dead organic matter and will not harm plants. The ones to worry about are the small brown or black slugs, some of which live underground and are difficult to catch. They come to the surface only in mid summer, the time to attack them.

What to do

Go into the garden at night and drop the slugs into a jar of paraffin. Or surround the most vulnerable plants with lime, soot, or pine bark (avoid spreading lime around acid-loving plants). In early spring surround seedlings or shoots with plastic bottles cut off at the bottom. Protect large plants by removing the top and bottom of a plastic can and placing it over them. Attract hedgehogs to the garden, since they eat hundreds of slugs. Birds, frogs, and toads should also be encouraged.

Earwigs

Earwigs crawl to budding plants and nibble the embryo flower, especially of dahlias and chrysanthemums; they also attack leaves. The damage distorts the flower.

What to do

Put a flower pot upside down on the top of a cane near the flower heads. Fill with dried grass or leaves and the earwigs will crawl into it to avoid daylight. Once a week, remove the pot and burn the grass. If they are still a problem, smear grease on stems just below the blooms.

Aphids

These are amongst the most common and troublesome of garden and greenhouse pests, and include those species known as greenfly and blackfly. All suck the sap of plants, causing distortion and particularly attacking young growing tips. Aphids excrete sticky honeydew on which sooty mould can grow, and transmit virus diseases.

What to do

A number of predators, such as ladybirds and hover-flies, eat aphids by the thousand. Attract these by planting French marigolds (Tagetes). Also rub the insects off with your fingers or hose them off with a powerful spray of water. Spray badly infested plants with insecticidal soap (see page 200).

Whiteflies

These tiny insects, often found on the underside of leaves, suck the sap of many greenhouse and outdoor plants; those which affect brassicas are especially persistent and resilient.

What to do

Whitefly are strongly attracted to anything yellow, so hang up a yellow card or square of plastic, coated with thin grease, in the greenhouse. The whitefly will stick to the grease. The flies can be controlled with the parasitic wasp Encarsia formosa *(see page 200). As a last resort, spray three times with derris (see page 200) at five-day intervals, but not at the same time as* Encarsia.

The cabbage whitefly can survive outdoors over winter, so make sure that there is no garden debris left around for it to eat.

Flea beetles

These tiny beetles make hundreds of small "shot-holes" in the leaves of seedlings, and particularly in those of the cabbage (Brassica) family. Sometimes, in good growing weather conditions, seedlings will overcome it and suffer only a minor setback. In a

bad growing year, when the weather is cold and constantly wet, the damage that is caused by the beetle can set the plants back many weeks and may even kill them completely, so it is always best to control them.

What to do

These insects jump sharply into the air when approached, just like a flea. Use a piece of wood 30×15cm (12in×6in). Coat one side with heavy grease – old engine grease is ideal. Holding the board grease-side down, pass it along the row of seedlings about 2.5–5cm (1–2in) above them. The beetles jump up and stick to the grease.

Other pests

Woodlice do much damage to seedlings and young plants, coming out at night to nibble on roots, stems and leaves.
Millipedes are small black insects with short legs. They usually remain beneath the surface, feeding on roots and aggravating slug damage.
Snails pose similar problems to slugs, eating seedlings and all parts of mature plants.

What to do

In each case these pests hide and breed under stones or garden debris during the day, coming out at night to feed, so keep the garden as tidy as possible. Regular and thorough cultivation of the soil will expose millipedes and woodlice to birds, hedgehogs, and ground beetles. Watch out for the snails' slime trails. Drop snails into a jar of paraffin, or use one of the methods described for controlling slugs (left).

Natural control

A natural balance in the organic garden will ensure predators to feed on the garden pests. A simple rule for distinguishing between "friend" and "foe" is that pests are usually slow-moving and predators tend to be faster and more agile. Attracting helpful creatures often eradicates or lessens the need for other forms of pest control. Biological control (research into nature's own techniques for combating one organism like whitefly or red spider mite with another such as a parasitic wasp or a predatory mite) is making advances.

ENCOURAGING NATURAL PREDATORS

Predator	Prey	Encourage with
Birds	Grubs, caterpillars, slugs, aphids	Food tables, bird baths, nest boxes
Ground beetles	Eelworms, cutworms, insect eggs, leatherjackets, other larvae	Ground cover (leaf cover, deep beds, green manure)
Centipedes	Many insects, slugs	Ground cover
Frogs and toads	Slugs, woodlice, small insects	Pond
Hedgehogs	Slugs, cutworms, woodlice, millipedes, wireworms	Difficult to attract, but encourage to stay with food and water
Hoverfly larvae	Aphids	Marigolds and nasturtiums
Lace-wings and ladybirds	Aphids	Varied planting

SOME PERMITTED PESTICIDES AND FUNGICIDES

Organic chemicals

When physical pest control is not practicable, you may have to use chemical control. Several organic pesticides will not harm you or your garden "friends" if used with care. Such pesticides are non-persistent (active for only a day). Organic fungicides are not really organically derived, though non-persistent. Those chemicals permitted are noted here.

Pesticide/fungicide	Controls
Insecticidal soap (persists only one day)	Aphids, whitefly, red spider mite, scale insects, mealy bugs
Soft soap (less effective than above)	Aphids, red spider mite
Quassia (harmless to birds and ladybirds)	Aphids, some caterpillars, sawfly, leaf miners
Derris (not selective, use as last resort)	Caterpillars and similar pests
Pyrethrum and rotenone (not selective)	Most insects, especially aphids
Copper fungicide (Bordeaux and Burgundy mixture)	Mildew and blights
Dispersible sulphur	Most fungi, rust

Using pesticides and fungicides

- Keep in a safe place away from children or pets.
- Always leave chemicals in their own bottles.
- Dilute as specified on bottle.
- Avoid spraying beneficial insects with non-selective chemicals.
- Use a good sprayer; wash out thoroughly after use. Pour leftover solution down the drain.
- Spray only on a windless day and in late evening, when "good" insects are asleep.
- Never spray any open flowers for fear of harming bees.

Garden and greenhouse diseases

Some common diseases which occur on the whole range of garden and greenhouse plants are described below. They can build up rapidly in a greenhouse because of the warmth and humidity. Prevent attacks by vigilance and cleanliness. For aphids and whiteflies, see page 199; for red spider mite, see page 206; for virus diseases, see page 204.

Botrytis (grey mould)
Probably the commonest disease, of both greenhouse and outdoor plants. Brown spotting or blotching, followed by furry grey mould; thrives in cold, damp conditions and poor circulation.
What to do
Handle seedlings carefully and give good air circulation. Fertilize sparingly; avoid overwatering, wet mulches and planting in low, shady areas. Burn infected shoots.

Mildews
Mealy, pale grey coating on buds, leaves, flowers, and young shoots of plants in garden and greenhouse, resulting in yellowing and a general loss of vigour. Downy mildew gets right inside the plant and can eventually kill; powdery mildew stays on the surface. Most common on herbaceous plants and roses, worst when roots are dry.
What to do
Thrives in cool, damp, and humid conditions. Treat downy mildew as botrytis. Burn leaves with powdery mildew. In greenhouses, make sure plants never go short of water. Spray severe cases with copper fungicide or dispersible sulphur.

Sooty mould
A superficial black fungus, the sticky secretions of pests such as aphids. Restricts plant yields.
What to do
Control aphids (see page 199) and mould will disappear.

Fungus leaf spot
Leaf spotting can affect the foliage of most plants, especially in wet and high humidity. The black spot disease of roses is a common strain. Leaves may wither and die.
What to do
Crop rotation and air circulation help prevent disease. Burn infected plants or leaves. Spray with dispersible sulphur. Hard prune roses in autumn; burn prunings.

Rust
Many different types of rust affect plants. Leaves and young stems develop yellow, red, brown or black raised pustules. Leaves may then wither and fall or whole plants can become stunted and even die.
What to do
Burn leaves with rust spots. Spray with dispersible sulphur. In greenhouses, ensure humidity is not too high and avoid wetting foliage.

GREENHOUSE PESTS

Vine weevils
Small grubs, with white bodies and brown heads, invade potting compost and eat roots of many plants. Badly affected plants will keel over.
What to do
Make up a solution of derris and immerse pots in it completely.

Leaf miners
This pest burrows into leaves, making characteristic yellow tunnels that are clearly visible.
What to do
Destroy affected leaves as soon as seen, or squash the grubs by squeezing the leaf.

Scale insects
Small, disc-like insects that cling to leaves and stems, sucking sap and secreting honeydew. Affected plants turn yellow, and their leaves drop.
What to do
Scrape off with a piece of wood.

Damping off
A greenhouse disease affecting seedlings, shows as a blackened area at the base of the stem. Affected plants will topple over and die.
What to do
Sow more thinly, water less, increase greenhouse temperature. Sometimes, the disease is carried in the soil; sterilize by heating to kill it. Water with copper fungicide.

Blight
Brown marks on leaves, and sometimes fruit. The marks can later turn black.
What to do
Remove infected leaves immediately; if persists, spray with copper fungicide.

Leaf mould
Yellow spots and brown mould on leaves, thrives in poor ventilation and overcrowded conditions.
What to do
Space plants to give more air and adjust greenhouse ventilation.

Vegetable pests and diseases

Most vegetables are susceptible to a range of specific pests and diseases in addition to those that may attack all garden plants (*see pages 198–201*). Correct soil management techniques and crop rotation should prevent mineral deficiencies (*see pages 66–67*), but it is important that the more serious problems are identified quickly and treated correctly.

LEAF VEGETABLES

Brassicas are especially prone to problems; prevent with correct soil management and cultivation. Boron deficiency causes brown heart (*see pages 66–67*).

Caterpillars

Several butterflies lay their eggs on leaf crops and the caterpillars make round holes in the leaves from mid summer until autumn. The worst offender is the cabbage-white butterfly.

What to do
Pick off caterpillars regularly and drop into a jar of paraffin. Rub eggs off by hand or spray with the bacterium Bacillus thuringiensis or with derris (see page 200).

Mealy cabbage aphid

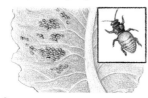

Dense colonies gather on leaf undersides and suck sap. Rare in organic gardens.

What to do
Encourage hover-flies and lady-birds (see page 200). Spraying with insecticidal soap will control an aphid build-up.

Cabbage root fly

Perhaps the worst of all brassica pests, causing complete collapse of young plants. The adult fly lays her eggs in the soil right next to the stem. When the larvae hatch out, they immediately burrow into the root and begin to feed. Symptoms are wilting and collapse of the plant, by which time it is too late to save.

What to do
The organic answer – and the only one that is completely successful – is to surround the stem at planting time at soil level with foam-rubber carpet underlay. Cut the underlay into 15cm (6in) squares, make a slit into the centre of each and a small cross-slit at the end. Slip the underlay around the base of the plant, ensuring a tight fit.

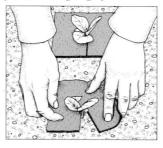

Club root

The most debilitating disease of the cabbage family, caused by a soil-borne fungus which distorts and thickens the root and causes stunting or failure to develop at all. Worse on badly drained soil and in acid conditions.

What to do
There is no cure and club root will live in the soil indefinitely. Give plants a healthy start by raising them in pots before planting outside. Seedlings will be partially affected by the disease, but crops will be satisfactory – though cauliflowers must be abandoned. Rotate crops regularly.

Mosaic virus

Sometimes known as "spinach blight", this shows as a yellowing of the leaves.

What to do
No cure, but prevent the disease by controlling the aphids that spread it and by using resistant varieties.

SHOOT VEGETABLES

Mineral deficiencies cause black heart or brown heart in celery.

Asparagus beetle

Adult beetles and their grubs feed on the shoots and foliage of asparagus. A severe attack can strip the foliage completely or girdle stems, causing death of the plant.
What to do
Dust with derris as soon as attack seen, usually in summer.

Celery fly

Damage usually seen first in late spring: leaves turn pale green, then brown and shrivelled.
What to do
Burn affected leaves.

Asparagus rust

Reddish pustules on stems and foliage in summer.
What to do
As soon as the first signs are seen, remove affected shoots. Spray the

crop every two weeks with a copper fungicide until early autumn.

Celery leaf spot

Brown spots on leaves and stems, turning into black pustules. The fungicide used to treat seed by seedmen is not organic.
What to do
Remove affected leaves. Spray rest of crop with Bordeaux mixture every fortnight until two weeks before harvest.

BULB VEGETABLES

All bulbs are prone to a range of disorders, but onions are more likely to suffer.

Onion fly

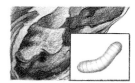

Plants begin to yellow and die in early or mid summer. White maggots can be found round roots.
What to do
Hoe regularly to expose grubs to birds. The female fly is attracted by onion scent, grow from sets or multi-sown blocks.

Onion eelworm

These microscopic, soil-borne creatures get inside the bulbs, causing swelling and distortion.

What to do
Grow brassicas and lettuce on the area for two, or ideally four, years to remove a host for the eelworms.

White rot

A mouldy growth near the neck of stored onions which then become soft and rotten.
What to do
Remove affected bulbs. Do not overfeed. Only store fully ripe bulbs. Never bend the tops over to ripen.

Neck rot

A white, fluffy fungal growth on the roots. Diseased plants turn yellow and eventually die.
What to do
Treat with Bordeaux mixture. Do not resow for at least two years.

Storage rot

There are several different fungi that can make bulbs in store go soft and slimy.
What to do
Ensure that stored bulbs are completely ripe and have plenty of air circulating around them. Inspect regularly, and remove any affected straightaway.

SQUASH VEGETABLES

Only one major disease affects outdoor crops. (*See also page 201* for greenhouse pests.)

Cucumber mosaic virus

Attacks all squash vegetables. Leaves pucker and turn mottled and yellow, growth is stunted.
What to do
Guard against aphids which carry the disease. No cure: destroy affected plants.

POD AND SEED VEGETABLES

Birds can be a major pest with pea crops, and broad beans are sometimes attacked by black bean aphid (*see page 199*).

Pea moth

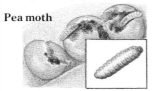

This moth is responsible for the small maggots that make peas inedible. It lays eggs on plants in flower. Difficult to control: spray also kills beneficial insects.

What to do
If attacks are severe, you can use derris, but it is better to protect the plants physically by draping woven polypropylene over them. Pheromone traps are not yet available to non-commercial growers. These sticky pads use a chemical naturally secreted by the female pea moth to attract males away from the females.

Pea and bean weevil

A greyish-brown beetle that makes U-shaped notches in leaves of peas and broad beans.

What to do
This is not a great problem unless young seedlings are being attacked. Dust lightly with derris.

Halo blight

Angular spots on leaves surrounded by lighter-coloured halo, turning reddish-brown and can ooze white.

What to do
The disease is seed-borne, so use only reputable seed.

Chocolate spot

Brown spots or streaks on leaves and stems of broad beans, sometimes joining up and blackening, leading to plant death.

What to do
Avoid by good cultivation methods (see page 140), especially adequate feeding and manuring. If signs seen, spray whole crop with a copper fungicide. Pull up and burn affected plants.

Failure to set

French and runner bean flowers may drop off having failed to set, usually because of dry roots or lack of insect pollination.

What to do
Protect plants from cold winds to encourage insects. In dry weather, water to prevent flowers wilting and closing, so bees reach the pollen.

FRUITING VEGETABLES

(See also page 201 for greenhouse pests and diseases).

Red spider mite

Only a problem in very dry years, the tiny mites cannot be seen with the naked eye, but form visible webs. Leaves have a charactcristic mottled and yellowed appearance.

What to do
The mites like dry conditions, so spray with water regularly. Spray small infestations with derris, or use parasitic mite Phytoseiulus persimilis *as a biological control.*

Potato blight

Black or brown spots on leaves.

What to do
Spray with Bordeaux mixture fortnightly when signs appear.

Leaf mould

Yellow patches on the upper surface of leaves and brown patches beneath are typical symptoms of leaf mould.

What to do
Most modern varieties are resistant. Spray once with copper fungicide to control any outbreak that does occur.

Virus

Stunting of plant, yellowing and mottling of leaves.

What to do
There is no cure. The disease is carried by aphids, so try to control them as a preventative measure. Grow tomatoes in growing bags the following year, or use plants on KNVF rootstock.

ROOT VEGETABLES

The root crops include several members of the *Brassica* family, prone to the same disorders as cabbages (*see page 202*). Boron deficiency may cause corkiness in some roots (*see pages 66–67*).

Carrot fly

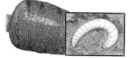

Female flies lay eggs at the base of carrots, parsnips, parsley, and celery. Grubs burrow into roots, causing brown marks and tunnels.
What to do
Surround carrots with a polythene barrier supported by short posts. These pests fly a few centimetres above the ground: when they meet the barrier, they fly upwards and miss the crop.

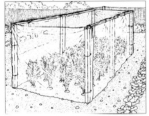

Potato cyst eel-worm
A microscopic pest that causes premature death of the plants and results in undersized tubers.
What to do
Grow resistant varieties only and rotate crops annually.

Potato blight

This fungus causes brown patches on leaves, especially in warm, wet weather. These spread and become black and the foliage dies. The spores can also cause tubers to turn black inside and rot.
What to do
Spray with Bordeaux mixture in mid summer and fortnightly thereafter until harvesting.

Scab

A disease which causes ugly corky marks on the outside of tubers.
What to do
Avoid trouble by incorporating plenty of organic matter into the soil and watering during dry spells. Use resistant varieties.

Gangrene

A fungus disease attacking damaged or wet potatoes in storage, causing the insides to rot.
What to do
Lift and store as described on page 151. Burn infected tubers.

Potato blackleg

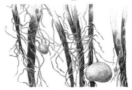

A bacterial disease that causes the base of the stems to blacken and die. Tubers too can be affected and transmit the disease, so only buy seed certified disease-free.
What to do
Remove and burn affected plants as soon as symptoms are seen.

Spraing

Red-brown lesions on the tubers. If you cut one in half, you will find wavy, semi-circular marks.
What to do
There is no cure, so grow resistant varieties only.

Soft rot

A bacterial disease of swedes and turnips, showing as a white or grey mushy rot, worse on badly drained, unrotated soil.
What to do
Grow swedes and turnips on raised deep beds if your soil is heavy.

Parsnip canker

Reddish brown marks on top of the root that often spread.
What to do
Good cultivation methods (see page 151) and resistant varieties.

Fruit pests and diseases

Fruit is attacked by a number of general garden pests and diseases such as aphids, birds, botrytis and mildew; and also some more specialized pests which attack only certain species of fruit. Advice on how to deal with general pests and diseases can be found on pages 198–201, although any details specific to fruit are given below.

GENERAL PESTS AND DISEASES

Some pests and diseases will affect any plant, wherever it grows in the garden. Many will be kept under control by organic measures, such as companion planting. Control measures for problems specific to fruit, however, are given below and on pages 207–209.

Birds

One of the most troublesome pests of the fruit garden, birds are most fond of soft fruits, although they do peck holes in hard fruits, which are attacked by wasps. They eat fruit buds, greatly reducing the crop.

What to do
The only real protection from bird attack is to use netting, since birds soon get used to any other deterrent. Cover fruit with netting, individual plastic bags or, better still, build a fruit cage.

Wasps

These insects attack ripening fruit, and will damage both tree and soft fruits as they eat their way into the fruit. As they tend to attack at an initial blemish, like a bird peck, try to protect the fruit from damage in the first place (*see above and on page 161*).

What to do

Waylay wasps before they get to the fruit, by setting a beer trap. Half fill a jar with stale beer, cider or anything else sweet. Cover the top with a piece of paper or polythene with a smallish hole in it. The wasps get into the jar, attracted by the smell, but once inside, cannot get out and drown.

Red spider mite

A problem in very dry years, tiny mites cannot be seen with the naked eye, but the webs they form are visible. They suck the plant's sap, and affected leaves take on a characteristic mottled and yellowed appearance, eventually falling.

What to do
Only a problem in a dry atmosphere, so increase humidity. If it persists, use the parasitic mite Phytoseiulus persimilis. *Deal with small infestations by spraying with derris three times at six-day intervals (not with* Phytoseiulus).

CITRUS FRUIT

The pests and diseases below attack fruit grown outside. Greenhouse fruit may be affected by general ailments such as red spider mite, scale insects and moulds (*see left and page 201*).

Little leaf
Caused by zinc deficiency. Leaves become mottled and crinkled and the fruit may be deformed.
What to do
Ensure that the soil contains all the trace elements by applying a dressing of seaweed meal to the soil, or mulching round the tree with well-rotted compost.

Lemon scab
A fungus disease that causes distortion of the fruits, making irregular ridges on the skin.
What to do
Spray with copper fungicide when half the petals have fallen.

Citrus gall wasp

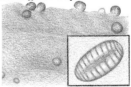

This wasp burrows into new spring growth to lay eggs. The larvae burrow within the shoot, causing round swellings, or galls.
What to do
No effective control but cut out visible galls in summer and burn.

SOFT TREE FRUIT

This group contains all the tree fruits that have soft flesh surrounding a central stone, or pit. They are easily damaged by birds and wasps and are very prone to fungus diseases.

Plum sawfly

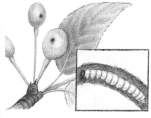

The caterpillars of this pest make holes in the fruit, rendering them inedible and causing them to drop.

What to do

As the pupae live in soil beneath the tree, regular hoeing exposes them to birds. If necessary, spray with derris after petal fall.

Blackfly

This aphid attacks cherries in particular (*see page 199*).

Bacterial canker

Bacterial canker is a very serious and widespread disease of plums.

The first signs are brown marks on the leaves. Subsequently, the leaf tissue begins to fall away, leaving what looks like holes of caterpillar damage on the leaves. The branches then start to exude a sticky substance. The following spring, buds on infected branches fail to open or, if they open, produce only small, yellow leaves.

What to do

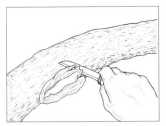

Cut away and burn all infected wood. Spray the leaves with copper fungicide (see page 200) in mid summer and then twice more, each time after a month gap.

Peach-leaf curl

A fungus disease that attacks all the *Prunus* species. It causes red blisters on the leaves which swell up and then turn white. The leaves fall early and the vigour of the tree is affected.

What to do

Remove infected leaves, but expect an infestation every year. Spray with copper fungicide in mid winter and repeat every two weeks for at least four days. Spray again in autumn before leaf fall. Protect fan-trained trees from rain, which carries the spores.

Silver-leaf

Many fruit trees suffer, but plums are the most susceptible, especially the variety *Victoria*. The leaves take on a silvery hue and may then turn brown. There is a progressive die-back of shoots and small purple, brown or white fungi appear on the dead wood.

What to do

Cut back all dead growth to at least 15cm (6in) past the affected point. As the fungus enters through open wounds, prune during the growing season when cuts heal quickly. As soon as the symptoms are seen, insert pellets of the parasitic fungus Trichoderma viride into 5cm (2in) holes drilled in the trunk.

Plum rust

This fungus disease causes yellow spots to appear on the upper surface of leaves and brown or orange pustules on the lower surface of the leaves.

What to do

The disease occurs only in weak plants so feed those affected with blood, fish, and bone meal at the rate of two handfuls per square metre/yard and mulch with well-rotted compost or manure. Hand water the area if the soil around the tree becomes dry.

HARD TREE FRUIT

These fruits, which include apples and pears, are prone to attack by many pests and diseases, but organic methods and good husbandry will generally reduce problems to a minimum.

Codling moth

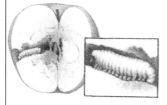

Females lay eggs on developing apples and the grubs enter the fruit. The first sign is often a maggot in the apple.

What to do
Hang pheromone traps in the trees. These triangular plastic boxes contain a sheet of sticky paper, in the centre of which is a capsule containing the pheromone, the substance the female moth excretes at mating time. The male moths fly into the trap, stick to the paper and the female's eggs remain unfertilized.

Apple sawfly

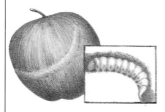

Before burrowing into the fruit, the larvae feed on the surface, causing a ribbon-like scar. Apples that have been attacked fail to ripen and fall in summer.

What to do
Pick and destroy infected fruits when you see any scarring. Spray the tree with derris or rotenone a week after blossom fall.

Bitter pit

Small, sunken areas appear in the fruit, with brown flesh below, usually during storage but sometimes while fruit is on tree. Caused by calcium deficiency and imbalance of potassium or magnesium in soil.

What to do
No effective treatment, but watering during dry periods and mulching with manure will help.

Brown rot

A fungus that turns fruit brown and makes the flesh decay. The fruit becomes covered with white fungus spores and finally shrivels up. Attacks stored fruit.

What to do
No totally effective control. Remove infected fruit and keep soil clean.

Apple aphids

The rosy apple aphid and the rosy leaf-curling aphid feed on shoots and leaves, which turn yellow or red and distort. The green apple aphid sucks sap, stunting growth.

What to do
Spray with insecticidal soap, derris or rotenone and quassia at leaf cluster stage and again when aphids seen. Grow plants that attract hover-flies (see page 195).

Woolly aphids

These insects suck sap from the shoots. They live in colonies and cover themselves with a white waxy coating.

What to do
Paint small infestations of woolly aphids with methylated spirits, or simply scrape them off. Spray large areas with derris or rotenone after petal fall, using a coarse, high-pressure spray. If this does not work, cut out the infestation.

Pear sucker

These pests live in blossom buds and cover foliage with honey-dew, attracting sooty mould. Attacks generally start in early spring and continue all summer.

What to do
Spray with insecticidal soap or derris, three weeks after petal fall.

Winter moth

The wingless female moths crawl up the tree to lay their eggs between autumn and spring. The caterpillars hatch and feed on the leaves until early summer. They overwinter in the soil.

SOFT FRUIT

What to do
Tie a greaseband around the trunk during egg-laying period.

Apple scab

A fungus that appears as dark spots on leaves and fruit, making large, ugly patches.
What to do
Pick off spotty leaves and burn them; sweep up all fallen leaves.

Fireblight

A bacterial disease that causes shoots to wilt from the top and the leaves to turn brown. It generally enters through cuts or damage on the shoots and can pass from one tree to another.
What to do
In most countries fireblight is a notifiable disease. If trees are infected, you must inform the local Ministry of Agriculture office. There is no cure except to pull out and burn infected trees.

Canker

Starts as sunken, discoloured patches on bark. In summer, white pustules appear on the patches; in winter small red fruiting bodies develop. A shoot encircled by fungus will die.
What to do
Cut out diseased patches, shoots and branches and burn at once.

General garden pests and diseases affect many varieties of soft fruit. Birds are especially fond of them so it is essential to protect ripening fruit with netting.

Raspberry beetle

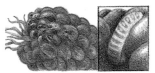

Larvae of this beetle feed on fruit, and cause malformation. They pupate into the soil.
What to do
Hoe to bring pupae to the surface, where birds will eat them. Spraying with derris may also be necessary: raspberries when the first fruits turn pink; hybrid berries immediately after flowering. Spray blackberries when flowers first open, with pyrethrum or quassia in the evenings when the bees are in their hives.

Sawfly

The small, brown, spotted caterpillars of this pest can defoliate a plant within hours.
What to do
Birds, especially robins, will eat sawfly larvae, but cannot control them totally. Spray with quassia or pyrethrum.

Big bud mite

This gall mite attacks buds of blackcurrants causing them to swell. It also carries a virus disease called reversion (*below*). The mites attack buds in early summer, moving on to other buds the following spring.
What to do
Check bushes in late winter and early spring. Burn any big buds.

Reversion

This virus disease is carried by the big bud mite. It is difficult to recognize – mature leaves are narrower, with five pairs of veins on the main lobe. Buds turn bright magenta. Bushes lose vigour and yield is reduced.
What to do
There is no cure for this disease. Dig up and burn affected bushes.

Spur blight

This fungus disease forms silver patches and fruiting bodies on raspberry canes and the briars of hybrid berries. Affected buds die.
What to do
Meticulous pruning of overcrowded canes should prevent infection. If the disease does occur, spray with copper fungicide when the buds first open and again when the flowers are showing white at the tips.

Leaf spot

Brown spots appear on leaves in spring; these spread and the leaf falls off, reducing yield.
What to do
Burn affected leaves. Spray with copper fungicide every ten days.

CHAPTER ELEVEN

ORGANIC WEED CONTROL

There is no such thing as an organic weedkiller, and whatever may be claimed about the safety of chemical weedkillers, there is always danger in their use. It may seem attractive to use a chemical to kill everything in a new garden so that you can start clean and stay on top of the weeds. It is certainly an easier way out, but it is done at the risk of killing the beneficial inhabitants of the soil and even harming yourself. It is also awkward and time-consuming to apply chemical weedkillers between cultivated plants, and the process often takes longer than the traditional organic methods.

Of course, there are some weeds that are very troublesome, such as couch grass (*Agropyron repens*), and ground elder (*Aegopodium podagraria*), but it is always possible to control them, and eventually to eradicate them, without resorting to chemicals, though in some cases it may take quite a long time. Weeds with tap roots, fleshy roots that go straight down into the soil, such as dandelions, can be a problem. There is only one way with these perennials and that is to dig them up and burn them, or put them in the dustbin.

Controlling weeds with gravel
Spreading a layer of coarse gravel, at least 5cm (2in) thick, around ornamental plants provides an effective and attractive barrier against weed growth.

Useful weeds

It is important to be able to recognise weeds that can play a constructive role in an organic garden. Do not grow weeds where they will compete with cultivated plants, but think again before digging up any of the useful weeds shown. Weeds can embellish your garden; attractive ones, like the red campion, will produce flowers to rival any cultivated hybrid.

Geranium robertianum
Herb robert
An attractive annual that colonizes quickly, covering the poorest soil, providing cover for pest predators and, when it dies down, organic matter for the soil. A valuable nectar plant for butterflies and bees, but a nuisance if allowed to seed.

Lychnis dioica
Red campion
Attracts bees, butterflies, and moths – drawn by a perfume released by the plant at night – which attract birds.

Trifolium sp.
Clover
Flower size increases when cultivated. Nitrogen-fixing plant, taking nitrogen from the air and fixing it in the soil for other plants to use.

Papaver rhoeas
Poppy
Butterflies and bees are attracted by the red flowers, and birds are drawn to the seeds. A common sight in corn fields before chemical weedkillers extinguished it.

Medicago lupulina
Black medick
A nitrogen-fixing plant. It attracts butterflies, bees, and hover-flies.

Taraxacum officinale
Dandelion
Rich in minerals, young dandelion leaves blend wonderfully into salads and the roots make a caffeine-free coffee substitute. Also attracts butterflies and bullfinches.

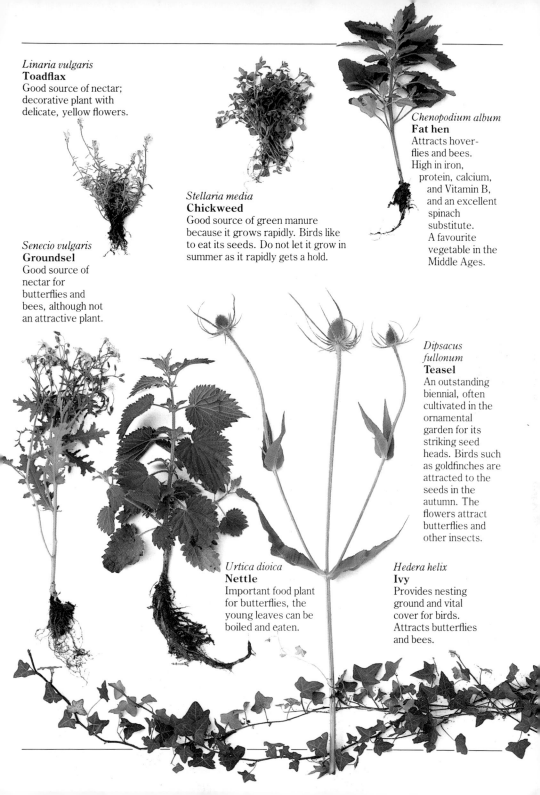

Linaria vulgaris
Toadflax
Good source of nectar;
decorative plant with
delicate, yellow flowers.

Senecio vulgaris
Groundsel
Good source of
nectar for
butterflies and
bees, although not
an attractive plant.

Stellaria media
Chickweed
Good source of green manure
because it grows rapidly. Birds like
to eat its seeds. Do not let it grow in
summer as it rapidly gets a hold.

Chenopodium album
Fat hen
Attracts hover-
flies and bees.
High in iron,
protein, calcium,
and Vitamin B,
and an excellent
spinach
substitute.
A favourite
vegetable in the
Middle Ages.

*Dipsacus
fullonum*
Teasel
An outstanding
biennial, often
cultivated in the
ornamental
garden for its
striking seed
heads. Birds such
as goldfinches are
attracted to the
seeds in the
autumn. The
flowers attract
butterflies and
other insects.

Urtica dioica
Nettle
Important food plant
for butterflies, the
young leaves can be
boiled and eaten.

Hedera helix
Ivy
Provides nesting
ground and vital
cover for birds.
Attracts butterflies
and bees.

Recognizing weeds

Of course, not all weeds are to be despised, and the organic gardener who gets rid of them all is wasting a valuable natural asset. Many weeds will attract insect predators, some also provide food for birds and butterflies and others, like the clovers (*Trifolium* sp.), can be used to fix nitrogen in the soil. So, before making an indiscriminate onslaught on native plants, pause for thought. Indeed, it is a good idea to grow cultivated plants in the ornamental garden that are close to their original wild species because they will attract the same insect life.

However, do not allow nature to take over, as your cultivated "foreigners" will be at the mercy of some pretty tough "locals". Most weeds must be rigorously controlled, but there are a few that should be allowed to stay if you have room for them.

Weeds to remove

The underground creepers should never be allowed to flourish or they will take over in next to no time. Amongst these, be particularly ruthless with ground elder (*Aegopodium podagraria*), bindweed (*Convolvulus arvensis*), couch grass (*Agropyron repens*), creeping thistle (*Cirsium arvense*), rosebay willow-herb (*Epilobium angustifolium*) and Japanese knotweed (*Polygonum cuspidatum*). The surface creepers like creeping buttercup (*Ranunculus repens*), ground ivy (*Glechoma hederacea*) and cinquefoil (*Potentilla* sp.) are slightly easier to control, but be diligent.

Weeds that spread by seed are not difficult to control, provided they are pulled out or cut down before they have a chance to seed. Watch out for spear thistle (*Cirsium vulgare*) and broad-leaved willow-herb (*Epilobium montanum*).

Weeds to remove from the garden

Aegopodium podagraria
Ground elder
The oval leaves have a strong smell if crushed. Spreads very quickly, soon taking over if allowed to remain.

Ranunculus repens
Creeping buttercup
Found on damp soils, with long creeping stems which spread across the soil. It also spreads by seeding.

Epilobium montanum
Broad-leaved willow-herb
Very common weed with pointed oval leaves and small purple flowers with yellow centres. Pull plants out as soon as seen.

Glechoma hederacea
Ground ivy
A vigorous, invasive perennial. Its small, hairy leaves have serrated edges and a distinctive minty smell.

Cirsium arvense
Creeping thistle
The serrated leaves are very prickly and flowers are a pale lilac colour. The flower stalks do not bear thorns like most thistles.

Potentilla sp.
Cinquefoil
A persistent weed with very long, creeping stems. Each leaf is made up of five leaflets.

Anthriscus sylvestris
Cow parsley
The fern-like leaves are pale green. Flower heads are a mass of tiny white flowers.

Cirsium vulgare
Spear thistle
The leaves are sharply pointed and spined. The purple flowers produce numerous seeds.

Plants with tap roots (long, thick, fleshy roots that go straight down into the soil) like docks (*Rumex* sp.) and cow parsley (*Anthriscus sylvestris*) should be dug out.

Storage roots (tubers, corms, bulbs, or rhizomes) often break off in the soil when the plant is pulled up and this can be a means of propagation. The worst of the lot is oxalis, which must be dealt with as soon as it shows even an exploratory leaf! Constant hoeing is the only answer, unless you can leave a sheet of black polythene in place for at least a year.

Beneficial weeds

Having made sure that the real villains are banished forever, try to give room to some of the less invasive plants. As gardeners, our interest lies in the cultivation of plants for beauty and interest, and for the purpose of feeding our families. How far you allow nature to take over is a matter of judgement and will depend largely on the size of your garden, and the range of wild plants you can grow will depend upon the soil, site, and location. For example, the pretty yellow snapdragon flowers of toadflax (*Linaria vulgaris*), and the pure white clusters of white campion (*Lychnis alba*) or red campion (*Lychnis dioica*) are often allowed to remain.

It has been said that if the dandelion (*Taraxacum officinale*) only grew in Tibet, we would be sending plant hunters to collect it and would pay huge sums of money to nurserymen to propagate it. It may be common, but it is an undeniably pretty flower. Do not let it seed, however, or it will outstay its welcome.

Other beneficial weeds that attract insects or birds, or are good sources of green manure, are shown on pages 212–13. Particularly important are the leguminous plants that will fix nitrogen and release it into the soil once they are dug in (*see page 79*). For example, the medicks (*Medicago* sp.) and clovers (*Trifolium* sp.) can be allowed to remain in winter.

Oxalis sp.
Oxalis
Control by hoeing, preferably before the leaves reach the surface, or by covering the ground with black polythene.

Convolvulus arvensis
Bindweed
Although its flowers are attractive, this fast-growing weed quickly smothers any ornamental plants nearby.

Agropyron repens
Couch grass
A very invasive grass. Its roots spread quickly to form a dense underground mat. A tiny piece broken from this can produce a new plant.

Rumex obtusifolius
Broad-leaved dock
Docks have a fleshy tap root and long, broad, dark-green leaves.

Epilobium angustifolium
Rosebay willow-herb
The purple flowers produce many seeds making this a very invasive weed.

Polygonum cuspidatum
Japanese knotweed
This weed has oval leaves and small white flowers. Its roots are difficult to destroy.

Weed control

Whether starting a brand-new garden, taking over a weed-infested one, or incorporating a new area, the first stage in weed control is to make the ground as clean as possible.

Dig over the whole site and remove as much as you possibly can. In an area infested with one of the more pernicious weeds like ground elder (*Aegopodium podagraria*), do not expect to win first time: any tiny piece of root will multiply. Compost annual weeds, provided they have not been allowed to seed. Throw away or burn roots of perennial weeds such as dandelion (*Taraxacum officinale*); composted, they will only be transplanted again.

Planting a cleaning crop

Plant any bare soil the first year with a "cleaning crop". Potatoes have two great virtues for this: their cultivation entails turning over the soil three times in the year – once at planting, once when earthing up, and once at harvest time. Secondly, their dense canopy of leaves excludes light from any weeds bold enough to compete.

Climbers such as bindweed (*Convolvulus arvensis*) will not be crowded out so easily, reaching the sunlight even through a dense canopy of leaves, but on a small scale they are not difficult to overcome.

Hoeing

The hoe is the most effective tool in your armoury and should be used regularly, preferably during dry weather. By pulling it through the top layer of soil you can uproot any weeds that appear.

If waging war against persistent weeds like horsetail (*Equisetum arvense*), never allow them to reach that stage. Hoe before you see any weeds at all on the surface so as to cut off the growing tips while they are still beneath the surface and before they have had a chance to benefit from the sun. Annual weeds are not so much of a problem. Hoe them out when quite

---

PREVENTING WEEDS FROM SPREADING

There are two sources of nuisance – weed seeds flying over the fence and settling on your land, and weeds with creeping roots coming underneath the fence. Ask your neighbours for permission to cut down any weeds before they seed, and install a barrier that runs deep into the soil to discourage permanently roots creeping under the fence.

1 *Close gap between fence bottom and ground by digging out a little soil and nailing a 15×2.5cm (6×1in) board along the fence.*

2 *Dig a trench along the entire length of the fence. The trench must be deep enough to remove up to 15cm (6in) of subsoil.*

3 *Nail one edge of heavy-gauge polythene to the bottom of the wooden board so that the "wall" hangs down to the bottom of the trench.*

small – no larger than about 13mm (½in) – and certainly do not let them flower or seed. Choose a hot, sunny day for hoeing, so weeds will lie on the surface where their roots will soon become dried out and die, returning their organic matter to the soil. If hot days are too infrequent, take off as much of the weed as you can, then use a Dutch hoe to lift the root. Walk backwards to avoid treading on the hoed weeds and effectively transplanting them.

Mulching

An effective way to exclude light and prevent weeds appearing is mulching (covering the soil with a layer of one of several materials). Some mulching materials are not very attractive to look at, especially in the ornamental border, where the most effective and attractive weed control is to provide competition with ground-cover plants forming a canopy over the soil.

Black polythene or paper
Either lay these materials between rows of crops, held down at the edges with stones or piles of soil, or cover the ground completely, burying the edges in a shallow trench, and plant through slits in the material. A wide strip keeps a much bigger area weed free, with no chance of weeds sprouting out between the edges of the sheeting. Areas over 1.2m (4ft) wide must have provision for watering, so lay a length of seep hose on the ground under the polythene. Naturally, polythene is not attractive enough to be used on its own in the borders, but can be covered with gravel or even a thin layer of soil.

THE PRINCIPLES OF WEED CONTROL

- All green plants must have access to sunshine to survive, so limiting or eliminating the light they receive will keep weeds under control. A variety of light-deprivation measures can be used (see this page).
- Constant vigilance is very important: remove weeds as soon as seen. Regular hoeing will deny persistent weeds a foothold.
- Never let weeds flower or seed. Cutting them down and digging out the roots takes a moment; coping with hundreds of their seedlings is a time-consuming job.

Tough brown paper is used in exactly the same way as polythene. After harvesting, dig or rotivate it into the soil, where it will rot down.

Although polythene is not supposed to need to be removed when the crop has been harvested, in fact, it deteriorates into strips which blow about all over the garden. Paper is ideal for deep beds. It can also be used in the ornamental garden without a covering of gravel since it is much less obtrusive than polythene.

Newspaper
A cheaper, but more time-consuming, mulch is newspaper. Lay about six sheets on top of one another, and anchor the edges by burying them. The paper tends to go quite hard and will certainly not rot for quite some time or until dug into the soil after harvesting.

Compost
A layer of compost or manure can be used to improve soil structure and add nutrients, but will not prevent weeds appearing unless it is very thick indeed. The weeds feel as much at home in compost or manure as do other plants.

Bark
Another very effective material in the ornamental garden is either shredded or chopped bark in any grade of coarseness. A thickness of 7cm (3in) should control all annual weeds and many perennials too. Bark is very expensive, although one application will last several years. A cheaper, though time-consuming, alternative is to use a shredder and make your own wood chips.

Grass cuttings
If applied thickly enough straight from the mower box, grass cuttings are effective. They must be at least 15cm (6in) deep, and this can lead to problems. If too thick, no air will reach the bottom and as they rot down (see page 72), they become a smelly, slimy mass. Grass cuttings do not look very attractive, either.

Gravel
In the ornamental garden, a permanent mulch of gravel has excellent water retention and inhibits weed growth. In the right setting, it looks extremely attractive.

INDEX

Figures in italics refer to illustrations

· S ·

sage *29*, 122
salad (spring) onion *33*
salad vegetables *30—1*, 134—5
Salix sachalinensis "Sekka" *12*, 90
sallow (*Salix caprea*) *93*
salsify *40*, 149
Salvia officinalis 29
sand *51*, 64
  choosing suitable plants for 108
Satureia montana 28
savory *28*, 122
saws, pruning 179
sawfly 209
  plum 207
scab 205
  apple 209
  lemon 206
scale insects 201
scarecrows 196
scorzonera (*Scorzonera hispanica*)
  40, 149
seaweed 77, *83*
  calcified 81
secateurs 179
Sedum spectabile "Brilliant" *27*
seed and pod vegetables *34—5*,
  140—2
  pests and diseases 204
seedlings 187
seeds 184—6
Senecia vulgaris 213
serpentine layering 190
setting failure 204
shade 50
shallots *33*, 138
shears 179
"sheet" composting 74
shoot vegetables *32*, 136—7
  pests and diseases 203
shovels 178
shredders 180
shrubs 110
sieves 180
silt *51*, 64
  choosing suitable plants for 108
silver-leaf 207
skimmia (*Skimmia japonica*
  "Rubelia") *13*, 108
slaked lime 81
slopes 50
slugs 198—9
smoke tree *27*
snails 199
snowdrops *13*
soakaways 52
soap
  insecticidal 200
  soft 200
soft fruit *47*, 170—5
soft rot 205
softwood cuttings 188—9

Solanum sp. *36*
Solanum tuberosum 40
soils 62—9
  conditioners 77
  improvement 68—9
  pests and insects 198—9
  pH levels 68
    adjusting 81
    testing 62—3
  profiles 63
  types 51
  see also compost; fertilizers;
    manure
Solomon's seal *20*, 108—9
sooty mould 201
Sorbus "Joseph Rock" *93*
sorrel 124
sowing seeds 184—6
  fluid sowing 130
spades 178
spear thistles *214*
spearmint *28*
spent hops 77
spent mushroom compost 77
spiked water milfoil 97
spinach (*Spinacea oleracea*) *43*, 153
spinach beet *43*, 153
spiraea (*Spiraea bumalda*
  "Goldflame") *16*, 109
Spiraea sp. *18*
spots
  celery leaf 203
  chocolate 204
  fungus leaf 201
  leaf 209
spraing 205
sprayers 179
spring plants 14—19
sprinklers 179
spruce, Colorado *95*
spur blight 209
squash vegetables *38—9*, 146—7
  pests and diseases 203
staking trees 160
stale seed beds 185
Stellaria media 213
stepover trees *159*
steps, wooden 50
sternbergia (*Sternbergia
  clusiana*) *26*
stony soils 62—3
storage rot 203
strawberries *47*, 172
strimmers 180
sulphur 67
  dispersable 200
summer plants 20—5
swedes *41*, 149
sweet basil *28*
sweet peppers *37*
sweet potatoes *40*, 150
sweet-scented rush 97
sweetcorn *34*, 140
Swiss chard *43*, 153

symphyandra (*Symphyandra
  wanneri) 18*
Syringa vulgaris 21

· T ·

Tagetes patula "Royal Crested" *22*
Taraxacum oficinale 212
tarragon, French *29*, 123
Taxus baccata 87
tayberries 173
teasels *213*
terraces 54
Thalictrum dipterocarpum 27
thinning, seedlings 187
  fruit tree crops 160, *161*
thistles
  creeping *214*
  spear *214*
Thuja plicata 87, 95
thyme 123
  lemon (*Thymus citriodorus*) *29*
tickseed *24*
tienturier grape *27*
tip layering 190
toadflax *213*
tomatoes *36*, 144—5
tools 178—80
trace elements 67
Tragopogon porrifolius 40
training
  climbers 116—17
  fruit trees *162*
transplanting 187
Trapa natans 97
trees 90—5
  as garden boundaries 53
  coniferous *92—3*
  deciduous *94—5*
  fruit *44—5*, 158
    cultivation 164—8
    pests and diseases 207—9
triangulation 58
trickle irrigation *101*
Trifolium sp. *212*
trimmers, hedge 180
trowels 178
Tsuga canadensis 94
tulips (*Tulipa* sp.) *17*
  Tulipa tarda 18
tunnel cloches 131
turnips *41*, 150

· U · V ·

Urtica dioica 213
utility areas 57
Vaccinium sp. *47*
vegetables *30—43*, 126—55
  pests and diseases 202—5

ACKNOWLEDGMENTS

Editor: Margaret Crush
Designer: Ruth Prentice
Typesetter: Bournetype, Bournemouth
Reproduction: Colourscan, Singapore

Dorling Kindersley
Managing editor: Jemima Dunne
Managing art editor : Derek Coombes
Editor: Julia Harris-Voss
Designer: Camilla Fox
Production: Helen Creeke

Photography
Andreas Einsiedel: *Still life photography*
Dave King: *Step-by-step and all other photography except:*

pp 6-7 Jaqui Hurst; pp 10-11 Andrew Butler; pp 48-9 Geoff Dann;
p 53 Jaqui Hurst; p 55 (t and b) Geoff Dann; pp 84-5 Geoff Dann;
p 89 Steve Hamilton; pp 104-5 Andrew Butler; pp 118-9 Andrew Butler;
p 124 Jacqui Hurst; pp 126-7 Jacqui Hurst; pp 156-7 Jacqui Hurst;
pp 176-7 Jacqui Hurst; p 195 Geoff Dann.

Illustration
David Ashby, Vanessa Luff,
Andrew Macdonald, Brian Sayers,
John Woodcock